D0054140

B
IBSEN   Zucker, A. E.
         (Adolf Eduard),
         1890-1971.

APR 3 0 1990   Ibsen

              34802 12 02

    $20.50

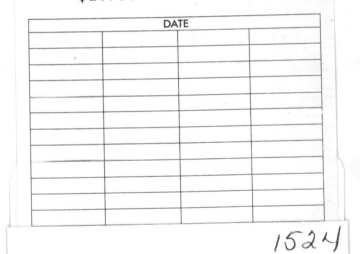

DATE		

1524

San Diego Public Library

© THE BAKER & TAYLOR CO.

IBSEN
THE MASTER BUILDER

HENRIK IBSEN
From a painting by the Norwegian artist Erik Werenskiold.

IBSEN
THE MASTER BUILDER

BY
A. E. ZUCKER

After Shakespeare I unhesitatingly place Ibsen first.

Luigi Pirandello

OCTAGON BOOKS

A DIVISION OF FARRAR, STRAUS AND GIROUX

New York   1973

Copyright 1929 by Holt, Rinehart and Winston, Inc.
Copyright renewed 1957 by A. E. Zucker

Reprinted 1973
by special arrangement with Holt, Rinehart and Winston, Inc.

OCTAGON BOOKS
A DIVISION OF FARRAR, STRAUS & GIROUX, INC.
19 Union Square West
New York, N. Y. 10003

Library of Congress Cataloging in Publication Data

Zucker, Adolf Eduard, 1890-1971.
Ibsen, the master builder.

Reprint of the ed. published by H. Holt, New York.

Bibliography: p.
1. Ibsen, Henrik, 1828-1906.
PT8890.Z8   1973   839.8'2'26   [B]   73-4670
ISBN 0-374-98910-9

Manufactured by Braun-Brumfield, Inc.
Ann Arbor, Michigan

Printed in the United States of America

To

M.C.—E.O.C.—A.E.—O.P.S.

WHO USED TO MEET IN MY ROOM IN COLLEGE
DAYS IN URBANA FOR DISCUSSIONS OF IBSEN
THIS BOOK IS DEDICATED

One day in Oslo Erik Werenskiold met him in the street as he was walking along scanning some new houses very intently.

"Well, you are interested in architecture?"

"Of course, that is my own profession," answered Ibsen.

He regarded his own works as architectural structures.

—Halvdan Koht, "Henrik Ibsen," Vol. II, p. 351.

PREFACE

For about twenty years there has been no biography of Ibsen in English, although there have been many critical appreciations of his plays. During all this time the place of the dramatist in the literature of the world has become more and more prominent, while many of his famous contemporaries have been removed to niches of secondary importance. The distance between them and Ibsen has grown so great that many critics nowadays will probably be inclined to agree with the words of Pirandello quoted on the title page of this volume: "After Shakespeare I unhesitatingly place Ibsen first."

This book attempts to see Ibsen the dramatist a little more *sub specie aeternitatis,* now that almost a quarter of a century has elapsed since his death, but its chief purpose is to present a portrait of the man, painted largely from materials furnished by men and women who actually knew him. My expectation that these people would feel at liberty to speak a bit more freely now than they did twenty years ago about the poet's life, his characteristics, the models for the personages in his dramas, and other details has been, I believe, to some extent justified.

For such a portrait I have tried to gather the traits and anecdotes that are *characteristic,* and to present whatever might serve to reveal the individuality of the great Norwegian, just as he himself felt that the Roman portrait busts, through the play of muscles about the mouth or a wrinkle in the forehead, often afforded a profounder view of the soul-life of the subject than did the more finished and idealized Greek heads. Problems of literary criticism and literary influence do not properly fall within the scope of this volume, and therefore the plays have been discussed only as they throw light on the personality of the dramatist. Likewise, because the formative years serve to explain much of what follows, I have dwelt a bit more fully on the earlier section of his life.

In 1927 I visited the scenes of Ibsen's life. Nowhere but in Norway can one find the contemporary newspapers and magazines, of course. In addition there is much worth the attention of the Ibsen pilgrim, even though the house of his birth in Skien has been burned down. In Bergen—a charming city—the old theater with its museum speaks graphically of Ibsen's dramatic apprenticeship. In Oslo the University Library has the finest collection of Ibseniana in the world, and the museum preserves, among other things, several rooms with the stiff, somewhat philistine furnishings amidst which Ibsen lived. In Skien, too, the museum contains paintings by Ibsen, portraits, photographs, and other memorable objects; while in Grimstad the drugstore has been restored with historical accuracy and serves as an Ibsen House that tells much of the bleak years in the little village on the Skagerrak. In addition to all this there is a certain "atmosphere" in the country, the landscape, and the conversations with Norwegians, that brings one closer to an understanding of Ibsen.

Much more vital, of course, were the contacts with people who had known Ibsen and whose aid I should like to acknowledge gratefully at this point. The man who knows his Ibsen best is Dr. Halvdan Koht, internationally famous professor of history at the University of Oslo and recent biographer of Ibsen. As a native of Skien he knows Ibsen's family and background; he conferred with the poet himself when he edited (with Dr. Julius Elias) his letters, the sketches for his plays, his speeches, newspaper articles, and other miscellanea. In the course of collecting and annotating these

writings Professor Koht corresponded with almost everyone
with whom Ibsen had ever come into contact. He gave cordially and freely of his time during my stay in Oslo, aiding
me in every way possible.

Another literary critic, Dr. Just Bing, told me vividly of
Ibsen's earlier and later years in Christiania. The First Librarian, Herr Sommerfeldt, was gracious enough to put at
my disposal a collection of Ibseniana that he was having compiled for the Ibsen Centenary in 1928. Fröken Daisy Heit-
man found for me a sketch of Aasta Hansteen, as well as a
number of anecdotes concerning this early suffragette. Rektor Stang of Oslo University gave me a lively account of the
attitude of the public toward Ibsen and his works during the
Eighties and Nineties. In Skien Consul Stousland and his
sister, children of Ibsen's sister Hedvig, gave me a Sunday
afternoon, while in Grimstad Herr Knudsen, curator of the
Ibsen House, told me stories of Ibsen's apothecary days.

In Berlin Frau Dr. Julius Elias put at my disposal the
papers of her recently deceased husband, Ibsen's great interpreter in Germany. In Munich the eighty-two year old
editor of *Die Gesellschaft*, Dr. Michael Conrad, told in his
hearty manner of Ibsen's Munich days. In the Tyrol, the
region where Ibsen was in the habit of spending his summers, I saw his German publisher, Herr S. Fischer, and in
Berne Fräulein Emilie Bardach. In Munich I found Fräulein
Helene Raff out of town, but in numerous letters she has told
me a great deal about her friendship with the dramatist.

Mr. Juul Dieserud, of the Library of Congress, told me of
a scene of which he was an eye-witness, Knut Hamsun's lecture described in Chapter XI, and in innumerable instances
he has aided me with his profound knowledge and critical
sense as my manuscript grew chapter by chapter. Two other
Norwegian-Americans have also given me friendly assistance. In Rutherford, New Jersey, there lives Ibsen's nephew,

Captain John Ibsen Stousland, for an account of whose bravery at sea I should like to refer the reader to the *Literary Digest* of July 31, 1920. Another doughty retired sea captain, Nicolai Bie, discussed with me in his Brooklyn home the model for Terje Vigen.

I owe a special debt of gratitude to the pioneer Ibsen scholar in America, Dean Otto Heller of Washington University. He read my manuscript last autumn and offered many fruitful suggestions, all of which I have adopted.

In addition to the above there are many others from whom I have received hints and suggestions in the course of conversations on Ibsen which I have had with them ever since my college days. Even more, of course, do I owe to the authors who have written on Ibsen, but my debt to them I have tried to acknowledge specifically in the Bibliography.

A. E. ZUCKER.

Riverdale, Maryland,
June 24, 1929.

CONTENTS

ILLUSTRATIONS

IBSEN
THE MASTER BUILDER

I

BOYHOOD IN SKIEN

Henrik Ibsen's ancestors were sea captains and merchants, members of the upper middle class. Recent investigations have exploded the paradox advanced in 1888 by Ibsen's biographer, Henrik Jaeger, that this "peculiarly Norse" poet had not a drop of Norse blood in his veins; it has been computed that he was $^{220}/_{256}$ Norwegian, $^{1}/_{256}$ Scotch and $^{8}/_{256}$ German. It seems absurd too to trace to such foreign elements among his forebears the Puritanic or philosophic tendencies in the man, for the Scotchman in Ibsen's family tree (his great grandmother's great grandfather's grandfather! who became a citizen of Bergen in 1504) was not Puritanical, at least in the usual sense of the term, since he lived before the Reformation; nor did the Germans among the ancestors show any philosophic bent. On the other hand, it appears that the few foreign ancestors in Ibsen's line had been thoroughly acclimatized in Norway and that Jaeger's statement, repeated by many other biographers, had its origin in Ibsen's dislike for his countrymen. Thus Henrik Ibsen is "peculiarly Norse" in ancestry as well as in spirit.

He was born in Skien March 20, 1828, in the so-called Stockmann House in the very center of the town. His birth coincided approximately with the death of an older brother; after Henrik were born one sister and three brothers. His father, Knud Ibsen, was a well-to-do merchant, dealing chiefly in lumber, and the relatives of both his parents were the patricians of Skien, judges and delegates elected to represent the town in the Storthing. Wealth and social position were the share of this family living in the atmosphere of gaiety and culture that continued as a heritage from the eighteenth century until in the forties the wave of pietism that swept over Europe as a reaction against frivolous rationalism introduced a more somber atmosphere into Skien. But Ibsen's childhood years were happy.

We get a picture of what a bright Sunday meant for the children of this family from the reminiscences of a character in the first sketch for *Brand*. The scene is probably autobiographical, from the years when the family after 1832 took up their residence in a magnificent house with a garden, higher up in the city than the Stockmann House.

Far yonder, back of those blue crags, beyond the Fjord, believe me, there it is beautiful. From my father's farm you see the hills sinking down gradually to the shady bay in the south. On Sunday mornings it is charming at home, especially, as you'll believe, on summer days. Then we look at the picture Bible, each one wearing his best clothes.

The glass door to the garden stands open; the floor is strewn freshly with elderberry and sand; the flag waves from its post far over the land, and red as fire glow the rose hedges. And there are pigeons which we feed with peas; there is a blue one that is quite tame. This meal we as hosts prepare for these our guests, and the porch stairs serve as banquet hall.

In the hallway stands a sailing brig with a mast and a real smoke stack. What should hinder us from playing with it? And often our Aunt from the city with her children comes out for a visit. An old man drives her in a grand carriage, broad and deep, which can be heard long before we see it. He may ride back who runs to meet it.

We romp in the garden to our heart's content, and eagerly play hide-and-seek. One of my aunt's daughters,—she is saucy! Her name is Agnes, and no one can ever catch her! After the roast at dinner we get cakes, and then we share the room with the grown-ups. Then things are gayest, for our parents and our aunt join in the play.

Late in the evening the carriage draws up again, to the consternation of all of us, for no one is the least bit tired; however, they must go home, for it is a long way to the city. We are permitted

to ride along to the nearest corner. Then we must say good night,
and the wagon rolls away. How quiet it is! A white fog covers
the meadow. On the mountain we hear the partridge drumming.
Then mother calls, "Now quick into your beds!"

The poem describes the day as the child enjoyed it; for
the adults many other pleasures enlivened the days of the
rather exclusive merchant-aristocracy of the town. They
came together at weddings, dinners, balls, and musicals. In
a letter of September 21, 1882, Ibsen writes to Georg
Brandes that his father had been in the habit of dispensing
reckless hospitality and that the life in the house of the "rich
John Gynt" was based on the circumstances and memories
of his own childhood. In another letter—to Peter Hansen,
October 28, 1870—Ibsen states that his mother served as
model "with necessary exaggerations" for Aase, who says to
Peer Gynt:

> How much have we now remaining
> From your grandsire's days of glory?
> Where are now the sacks of coin
> Left behind by Rasmus Gynt?
> Ah, your father lent them wings,—
> Lavished them abroad like sand,
> Buying land in every parish,
> Driving round in gilded chariots.
> Where is all the wealth he wasted
> At the famous winter-banquet,
> When each guest sent glass and bottle
> Shivering 'gainst the wall behind him?

At Christmas time and at fair time the house of Knud
Ibsen was the scene of gay hospitality from morning till night.
Ibsen's father was a daring speculator, and as long as the
boom times lasted, very successful. But when in 1836 the
British market changed suddenly, Knud Ibsen was one of
the first to become bankrupt. He lost all his property except

a little farm a good half hour's distance from the town, to
which the family then removed.   They were separated from
their former social circle through distance; but through the
disgrace of the bankruptcy an even greater gulf was fixed
between the Ibsens and their erstwhile friends, observed most
snobbishly by those who had enjoyed the family's hospitality most.   As Mother Aase puts it:

> Provost, Captain, all the rest,
> Dropped in daily, ate and drank,
> Swilling till they well-nigh burst.
> But 'tis need that tests one's neighbor.
> Lonely here it grew, and silent
> From the day that "Gold-bag Jon"
> Started with his pack, a pedlar.
>   (Dries her eyes with her apron.)

Ibsen's father did not turn pedlar precisely, but he eked out
a very modest income for his family as a jobber who found
buyers for the cargoes that arrived in the harbor of Skien.
He consoled himself to some extent by the aid of brandy and
by his savagely cutting witticisms at the expense of his fellow
citizens, for which he was applauded and feared.

But into the soul of Henrik, then a precocious boy of eight,
this sudden fall into poverty and social ostracism seared life-
long scars.   We do not gather this from the childhood reminiscences Ibsen wrote down at the age of sixty—in fact there
he doesn't mention his poverty at all—but from his lyric
poems, in which he gives a freer rein to his feelings.   One
poem, called *The Tear* (1851) tells how many a time as a
boy he wept bitterly:

> From school the boys come thronging out;
> They run and play, they laugh and shout;
> With joy they seize their sleds.
> With frowning brow pressed 'gainst the glass

I watch them at their pastime gay;
Fast flowing the tears come.
'Tis Christmas eve, the moonlight sheds
Its rays upon the snow. Alas!
My shoes are too worn out for play,
And I must stay at home.

Even more keenly than the deprivations of poverty did Henrik feel the accompanying loss of social standing that cost him his place among the aristocracy of the town of four thousand inhabitants who felt themselves so definitely and securely above "the lower classes." It was this which made it impossible for him to attend either one of the larger and more important schools, the "Latin School" or the "Burgher's School"; he had to go to the despised "Middle Class School," a small institution conducted by two theological candidates. Because he regretted so keenly that no Latin was taught here, —without Latin he could not enter the University or any profession—one of the teachers, Johan Hansen, instructed him in this branch privately; but this work outside of school hours does not seem to have gone further than the reading of Phædrus' *Fables*. The humiliation of having to attend the school for the poor children, trudging two miles in the morning and two back in the evening often along a muddy road, was probably one of the causes for the loathing which Skien inspired in the poet so long as he lived. And there seems no doubt that the boy blamed his father bitterly for it.

Through the family misfortune the quiet boy became all the more retiring. He liked to lock himself away from the other children in a little room opening upon a passage which led to the kitchen of the farmhouse and there occupy himself with such books as had found their way into this store room. He did not enjoy playing with the others; the only out-of-door pleasure he cared for was building. The passage of the letter Ibsen's sister Hedvig wrote on the subject of her brother's youth sounds almost symbolical of the "master builder" who frequently built up a formula in one of his dramas only to knock it down again in the next play—continually dissatisfied with his achievement and continually putting it to the test. "I remember among other things a fort," his sister writes. "It seemed to me then a great work of art, and he and his younger brother had worked at it a long time. But the fort was not destined to stand; as soon as completed it was stormed and demolished."

His sister tells of other traits that seem equally characteristic of the future man. He liked to puzzle and startle the neighbors with performances in magic art—assisted by his little brother who was hidden under the table. He also made and painted puppets with which he gave dramatic performances. Hedvig tells also that one day as he sat painting one of his character puppets he broke out into loud and merry laughter. His mother, thinking that he was doing something nonsensical, told him to draw a nice face for the doll to the best of his ability. Henrik showed her that he had in reality been doing this. He had been laughing only at the thought of what he *might* make of the doll's face. Already at that early stage his imagination was for him as real as actuality.

Through one of Ibsen's school mates an early specimen of his writing has been preserved which gives us a glimpse into the soul-life of the thoughtful boy who, according to his own account, cherished as youthful impressions the solemnity of the church, the cheerlessness of the town jail, the gruesomeness of the pillory, and the terror of the madhouse, all of which institutions were situated within a few steps of the Stockmann House. The Apocalyptic prose of this vision which Henrik wrote when his teacher had assigned the pupils a "free composition" bespeaks the fact that he was an ardent reader of the Bible. When in the school room he read his dream before the entire class a hush fell over the group, and they followed him to the end with breathless attention. So striking was the impression that the teacher accused Ibsen, not yet fourteen, of having taken the material from some book or other, an accusation that the boy denied in an unexpectedly violent manner because he was stung to the quick in his pride as author. Ibsen's school mate sees forecast in this vision, which the dark-haired boy with the piercing eyes read to his fellow pupils in Skien, a great deal of what was to appear in the life-work of the poet.

On a journey through the mountains in the course of which we had lost our way and had become utterly exhausted, we were suddenly overtaken by the darkness of night. Like Jacob of old we lay down to rest, a stone our pillow. My comrades soon sank into slumber; I myself was unable to go to sleep. Finally exhaustion conquered me; then an angel stood before me, saying, "Arise and follow me!" "Whither do you wish to lead me in this darkness?" I asked. "Come," he replied, "I shall permit you to see a vision— human life in its reality and truth." And so I followed him—with a fearful heart. Down we went as though descending enormous stairs until the tops of the mountains seemed to arch above us in mighty vaults and there lay beyond a vast city of the dead with the mysterious marks and traces of death and evanescence on every hand; this whole world one enormous corpse sunk down under the strong hand of Death, a pale, wasted, extinguished glory. Over all lowered a dim dawn—pale like the glow which graveyard walls or whitewashed crosses cast over the burial ground. And in a glow, brighter than natural, the bleached skeletons filled these dark chasms in endless rows.

This vision by the side of the angel inspired me with an icy fear. "Here you see; all is vanity!" Then there came a rushing like the first gusts of an approaching storm, like a thousandfold moaning sigh, until it grew into a howling storm, so that the dead began to move and stretched out their arms toward me; I awoke with a sudden scream, damp from the cold dew of the night.

The future satirist is forecast in another school-boy story of the revenge Henrik took on a red-haired boy who had in-

sulted him by means of some mocking verses. This lad had
gained for himself the nickname "The Astronomer" by his
habit of climbing a tree, looking at the moon through a toy
telescope, and then dropping the sage observation: "I don't
believe that it is inhabited." The morning after he had circulated the insulting doggerel about Ibsen and was still gloat-
ing over his triumph, he suddenly was surprised and infuriated when he noticed that Ibsen was holding up a piece of
paper with a colored picture on it for everyone to see; in fact,
he almost made an attack on Ibsen right there in the school-
room. On the paper was pictured the moon gazer done to the
life, with his red hair and his brown suit, with gaping mouth
looking through his spy-glass at the shining crescent moon,
uttering his thereafter doubly famous scientific observation:
"I don't believe it is inhabited."

When Ibsen was fifteen his family returned to Skien—not
to the aristocratic part of town which they had previously inhabited, but to a humbler section called Snipetorp—and he
was confirmed. In the long course of instruction preceding
this ceremony he showed himself an eager student, spending
hours on end looking up in the Bible the quotations mentioned
in the Lutheran Catechism, determined to compare the doctrine with its basis in Scripture. His first communion, we are
told, made a great impression on the adolescent; the mystery
of the Eucharist demands a great deal of soul-searching for
sins and doubts on the part of the Lutheran believer lest he
appear "unworthy" as one who "eateth and drinketh damna-
tion unto himself, not discerning the Lord's body." Ibsen's
mother was deeply wrapped up in pietism and did all in her
power to instil in Henrik a firm belief in the church dogmas.
Later, when her son's horizon widened, she saw in this only
a symptom of "wicked unbelief"; his life-work was to her
a deviation from "the one thing needful." Hence it became

impossible for him ever to write to her during the years after he left home; he and his pietistic family lived in different worlds. Ibsen explained this to his friend Björnson in a letter of December 9, 1867: "I have taken life very seriously. Do you know that I have entirely separated myself from my own parents, from my whole family, because a position of half-understanding was unendurable to me?"

Ibsen's brothers had nothing in common with him either, and they proved in no way remarkable. Johan, two years his junior, emigrated to America in 1849 and died of the fever in California. The two youngest started a business in Skien, but failed. About 1870 Nicolai also left for America where he died in the humble capacity of a sheep herder on the farm of Charles Coon, Hardin County, Iowa, in the year when his older brother added further glory to his fame as the world's greatest living dramatist by publishing *Rosmersholm* (1886). The story has recently gone through the newspapers of the finding of the tombstone of this quiet man who refused to write to his family about the failure he had made of life: "Honored by strangers—mourned by strangers—Nicolai A. Ibsen." Ole, the youngest, in 1887 asked his famous brother for a letter to Johan Sverdrup, a liberal politician then in power, in support of his application for a position as light-house keeper; Ibsen wrote the letter and his brother received the post which he retained until he was pensioned. Only his sister Hedvig seems to have had some understanding of the poet. She married the sea captain H. J. Stousland in Skien and up to middle age remained a devout member of a revivalistic sect in the church, making repeated efforts to convert her brother. But in the last decades of her life she changed her views and arrived at a keen understanding of her brother's works. Ibsen felt a great affection for this one member of his family with whom he had something in common; in 1869 he wrote on a photograph he sent her: "I think we two have always been close to each other, and thus it will remain between us."

As a young boy Ibsen manifested considerable talent for painting and he was given some instruction in this art by the landscape painter Mandt who was then living in Skien. In the Bergen Museum there hangs a creditable water-color done by Ibsen at the age of fourteen and in the Skien Museum the visitor is shown paintings of wolves and monkeys under whose guise Henrik caricatured some of the people about him. But in the impoverished condition of his family a career as an artist seemed quite out of question and the boy decided to become a physician. However, as there was no money for any education after he had completed his common schooling, it was decided that he should do the next best thing: if he could not become a doctor he might enter a druggist's shop as apprentice. Such a post was found for him in a small town a day's journey by steamer to the south of Skien in Grimstad. The fact that his wealthy relatives, the Paus family, refused to aid this boy who stood head and shoulders above his comrades in school further failed to endear Skien to Ibsen.

Before he was sixteen years of age, Henrik left Skien, to return only once for a short visit six years later. Not one letter did he ever write to his parents, who had both failed to win his affection. His mother was all love, kindness, and devotion to her somewhat difficult son, but the stiff dogma of the church stood in the way of any real human approach between the two. His father irresponsibly sent him out into the world at the age of fifteen; without having given him any particular training or preparation he forced him to make his own way, far from home and without any support from his relatives—among strangers, alone.

II

APOTHECARY IN GRIMSTAD

Shattered was the dream of going to Dresden where lived the famous Norwegian painter J. C. Dahl, or to Rome, the city of inspiration for most young painters of the day. Henrik had to stay in Norway, a country that in 1844 was quite outside the current of European thought, and whose capital, even, was but an overgrown village. And in the then backward country of Norway this lad with artistic leanings and forward-looking thoughts was thrust into Grimstad, of all the towns in Norway perhaps least promising for the development of artistic talent. It lay in the southeastern corner of the country, accessible only by an irregular boat service, nothing but a group of scattered houses between which the cows fed on grass plots where the streets should have been. At night not a single lamp lighted the way for pedestrians, a condition symbolical perhaps of the general lack of enlightenment in the town.

There was but one teacher for all the school-children, more than a hundred in number. Characteristically enough he taught one group every other day; for the burghers felt it necessary to divide their one school and one teacher between the "alms school" on one day and the group that paid tuition on the next. Yet the town was not poor, for the building of sailing vessels brought it great prosperity in these years. In every part of the harbor there were building docks, and as soon as one ship was launched work was begun on another. Everybody speculated in ship-building—clergymen, doctors, book-keepers, seamen, merchants, laborers, even the house-

maids, invested their savings in boats rather than in the banks.
The freight rates were so high that in the course of two or
three years a ship would pay for itself completely and then
earn a handsome profit. Immediately after their confirmation most of the boys went to sea, so that their education did
not advance beyond the elementary branches, even though the
winter afforded them ample leisure.

Small in size and small in character was this community.
There was in it not a breath of largeness of spirit or generous
thought or courageous sincerity. The wealthy shippers or
merchants formed an aristocratic set who shunned no mean or
scurvy trick to preserve for themselves the little difference
in money that caused the unlucky poor to cringe before them.
They and the clergy upheld a rigid orthodoxy in morals and
religion, while in reality the respectability of the pillars of
society was hypocritically maintained by the grace of their
money. It was the community of the compact majority designed to drive a youth of some spirit to drink, to satire, to
revolution, to flight, or to despair.

In this community the fifteen-year-old lad had to find a
footing for himself, for all support from his parents had
definitely come to an end. He came very inconspicuously
and passed for the most part quite unnoticed—this "apothecary boy," small and thin, with a dark complexion and black
hair hanging down over his forehead, and with an unsteady
glance which he generally averted. He had the thoughtful,
strange face of an old man, and an extremely uncommunicative character. In silence he went his own way, and for the
first three years of his stay in Grimstad had not a single
friend, not one confidant for his thoughts. In the old drug
store he was given an attic room with a small window, and
even this he had to share with his employer's young sons.
The description in the first draft of *Brand* of a boy in his teens
is probably Ibsen himself.

> A bairn he was old for his years
> Who did not care with comrades gay
> To romp and tumble on his way;
> Who to himself enough, aloof, appears.

Because the food his employer furnished him was so very scanty he found himself forced to club together with the maid for coffee which they had prepared for them at the house of a neighbor. His pay as apprentice was so meager that he went about in the cold Norwegian winter without an overcoat, without underwear, and at times even without socks. But his constitution was so robust that he bore these hardships without any apparent harm to his health. What he did feel keenly, though, was that his poverty excluded him from association with people above the position of menials. The poem *Memories of a Ball*, written in Grimstad, gives poignant expression to this feeling:

> Either we are guests invited
> To life's feast so gayly lighted,
> Or we stand without the gate,
> Shivering as the cold night wind blows,
> Lonely on the street, and wait
> Looking up at lighted windows.

As the years went on, he kept ever before his mind's eye the ideal of his childhood years—to be a great man. Therefore while he ran errands, prepared drugs, sold candy to the children, or drew brandy from the cask for fishermen who stamped into the drug store in their heavy boots, he was really living in another world. It was the world of the authors whom he read at night. About this time the early death of the poet Wergeland aroused great sympathy, and his tragedies *Sinclair's Death* and *The Infanticide* enjoyed wide popularity. Welhaven published in 1845 his romantic poems, peopling the woods with elves and the streams with musical

sprites called "noecks." There was a loan library at Grimstad where Ibsen could find many standard continental and
English authors in Danish translation; perhaps he read
Goethe, Schiller and Heine in the original, since in his examination at the University in 1850 he received the best mark
in German. Of Scandinavian dramatic literature there were
the comedies of Holberg, Bjerregaard's *Adventure of the
Mountain*, and Wessel's *Love Without Stockings*. The
romantic tragedies of the Danish poet Oehlenschläger, an
imitator of Schiller, were likewise very popular at the time.
In the novels of Mauritz Christopher Hansen, the Norwegian
best-seller of the day, it has been surmised that Ibsen indulged his love for the mysterious and the gruesome; for the
novels of this author deal with crimes committed years before
the action opens, and which, just as in Ibsen's plays, are very
gradually revealed as the action of the story progresses.

At times, too, after his long day's work was done, Henrik
would stroll out into the night to be alone with his thoughts.
His position seemed so hopeless; at best he could look forward to becoming the proprietor of a small apothecary shop,
for his confidence in himself as a great artist, religious leader,
or poet, was shaken. A flash of lightning brightened the dark
clouds for an instant and inspired him with the thought for a
poem; out of his own doubts, despair, and soul-searching
Ibsen at nineteen moulded the poem *Resignation*. He felt
all his struggles to be in vain, his wishes seemed phantoms,
the wings of his soul were flagging, and the fire of his poetry
was growing cold and feeble; he preferred to give it up:

> Lost among the nameless crowd,
> Let me live and disappear.

Allowing his fancy to dwell on death and the grave, he
would stroll on moonlight nights to the churchyard. Filled
with memories of Bürger's *Lenore* or Goethe's *Dance of the*

Dead he imagined a somewhat similar dance of the dead in the witching hour between midnight and one o'clock. On a moonlight ride on the sea Henrik did not dream of love but instead gave himself up to thoughts of death, seeing in the reflection of the stars in the water so many tear-veiled eyes of the dead dancing a mystical dance in which he longed to join:

> The tortures that ever my heart beset,
> These tortures would there be a thing of the past;
> Down there I could find a home at last;
> Down there all is splendor and I could forget.

There was a special tie in Grimstad that bound Ibsen in his imagination to the sea. Some fifty years previously his grandfather, after whom he had been named Henrik Ibsen, had met his death off Hesnaes near Grimstad as the ship which he owned and commanded went down with every man on board. Stories of the sea, which Ibsen heard from old sailors in Grimstad, provided him with the material for the fine epic poem *Terje Vigen* which he wrote many years afterward, in 1861.

There has been much discussion as to whether Terje Vigen ever lived or whether the man whose story every Norwegian child learns in the school reader is a fictitious hero. Whenever Ibsen was asked about this he maintained a mysterious silence. The last lines of the poem speak of Terje Vigen's grave, and to be sure the visitor to Grimstad is now shown a stately monument at the Fjaere Kirke cemetery, inscribed with two lines from the poem:

> Then Terje rowed for wife and child
> 'Cross the sea in an open boat.

But a former Grimstad citizen now living in Brooklyn, Nicolai Bie, has recently given the sources for this poem

which seem to have been rather freely handled by Ibsen.
From his account it appears that no Terje Vigen ever lived,
but that the adventures of Bie's grandfather, a sea captain,
are the basis of the poetic tale.   Captain Bie's ship was seized
by a British man-of-war in 1807 and he was condemned to
two and a half years in prison for attempting to run the
blockade.   In 1810 he returned to Grimstad and married.
In the very bitterest year of the blockade, 1812, he decided
to row his twelve-foot boat over to Denmark in a desperate
effort to procure food for his wife and child.   He accomplished this feat, but when he was again in sight of the Norwegian shore he was stopped by a British ship.   However, as
he told the officer of the plight of his family—here the facts
vary from the fiction—the Englishman took pity on him and
allowed him to proceed with his small cargo.   Bie tells that
Ibsen visited at his grandfather's house and there heard the
story out of which he later made the poem of the brave seaman Terje Vigen, so like Ibsen himself in his stubborn
determination.

It was during the Grimstad years that Henrik began to
grow a seaman's beard.   This enormous, dark-brown full
beard was the most striking thing in Ibsen's appearance to
Christopher Due, the first friend Ibsen made in Grimstad.
Due came to the little town in 1847 as a customs official, and
was attracted by the young drug clerk, whom he describes as
a short young man with rapid movements, of good build,
rather forbidding, unapproachable mien, but with a gleam in
his eye that betrayed the genius.   He tells in his reminiscences of Ibsen that he visited the apothecary shop for the
express purpose of making the acquaintance of the young
clerk—for Henrik had advanced to this stage by virtue of
passing the state examination—but that he did not have the
courage to say more than to ask for a few shillings worth of
adhesive plaster!   But when later the shop was purchased

and moved to more commodious quarters by a certain Nielsen, whom Due knew well, the two young men met and became close friends. A young law student, Ole Schulerud by
name, soon became the third in the circle. These two young
men gradually made something of a social being out of the
hermit.

In the new drug store Ibsen was provided with a cheerful
room immediately behind the shop where he could sleep,
study, and receive his friends in comparative comfort. In
other ways also Ibsen's life became more pleasant; under Mr.
Nielsen's more liberal management his breakfasts and suppers were brought to him, while his dinners he took at the
home of his employer, where the latter's mother kept house
for her unmarried son. She fed the hungry assistant with
motherly care and even tried to do her best to convert him
again to his childhood piety. But the young reader of Vol-
taire and Heine had emancipated himself from orthodoxy,
and with his native wit could puncture the conventional
"proofs" so well that Mrs. Nielsen sighed and gave up the
attempt. However, she surprised the good people of Grimstad by venturing the opinion that the dear infidel who could
so easily best her in an argument would some day become a
great man.

Yet in spite of these improvements Ibsen's situation was
far from being an agreeable one. Practically the whole day
he had to devote himself to the dull drudgery of the apothecary shop, the only one between Arendal and Christiansand,
a distance of about sixty miles. In spite of the rushing business his store was doing, Mr. Nielsen spent a great deal of his
time in shipbuilding enterprises, thus leaving the work in the
shop almost entirely on Ibsen's shoulders. The new shop,
too, was woefully lacking in some of the most necessary
things; there was, for example, nothing in the nature of a
laboratory, and when Henrik wanted to make a decoction he

had to do it on the neighbor woman's kitchen stove between pots in which she was cooking the dinner. Naturally he was able to save but little time for his education or for his poetic interests. Yet in spite of all obstacles Ibsen was determined to follow his ideal. He felt he had to get out of oppressive Grimstad, he had to get into the university at the capital, where a freer spirit reigned. Out of his very meager pay he hired a tutor who coached him in Latin for the university entrance examination; he stole from his sleeping time the hours for study, and out of his study period a little time for poetry. He applied himself firmly, and early in life began to train his will power.

His usual time for study was after midnight when his friends had gone home after a jovial gathering in his room, which soon became a regular institution. Everything under the sun was discussed, with Henrik often laying down very definite opinions on how things ought to be done, as often as not contrary to the customary practices of society. For example, he argued with great fervor for his ideal of marriage; husband and wife should each live in a separate apartment, meet only at meal time, and address each other with the formal pronoun "De"!

Even more revolutionary and startling were Ibsen's ideas on politics, which he developed under the influence of the French revolution of 1848. With glowing enthusiasm he had read in the papers of the mob that stormed the Tuileries on February 24, 1848, forced King Louis Philippe to abdicate, invaded the assembly with shouts of "Down with the Bourbons, old and new! Long live the Republic!" and of the proclamation of the second French Republic three days later on the former site of the Bastille under the leadership of the poet Lamartine, the socialist writer Louis Blanc, and other liberals. With his friends he arranged a "reform banquet" after the French model, where he delivered a fiery speech against all emperors and kings, "these monsters in society," and in favor of republics, the "only possible" form of government! Naturally enough, the "respectable" citizens of Grimstad let Ibsen hear and feel what they thought of such dangerous ideas.

But the subject on which Ibsen felt the most deeply, where his youthful idealism rose to the greatest fervor, and on which he could and did become most eloquent, was the question of Schleswig-Holstein. These two provinces, although inhabited largely by Germans, had for centuries belonged to the King of Denmark. They enjoyed virtual autonomy, however, and were not considered a part of Denmark, any more than Hanover was a part of Great Britain in the last century. But in 1847, just when the growing idea of nationalism was the catchword of the day in Western Europe, the King of Denmark proclaimed that he was going to make these provinces an integral part of the Danish kingdom. This aroused great indignation in Germany along with a desire to take the provinces from Denmark by force; in the Scandinavian countries there arose the feeling that the three nations must firmly unite against the Prussian aggressor.

On this subject Ibsen spoke very eloquently in the meetings with his friends. "The Scandinavians must awake," he would say (if one may so judge from his long poem *Awake, Ye Scandinavians,* written in 1849), "for the thunder of cannon is heard from the region south of the Kattegat and the wild German horde is threatening Denmark. We should arise and unite with the Swedes and Danes, for unless we do that, we shall prove ourselves unworthy of our fathers. It is a delusion if we think that our cliffs are a protection; first let Schleswig, this dam against Germanism, fall, let the Eider become a German river, let the Danish language be expelled from that region, and what will then protect us from the barbarian band? Shall we let Prussia snatch Schleswig from

Denmark, like a child torn from its mother's arms?   No, there is a law that warns us, 'Save your brother'!   Where our ideals are concerned, there is no occasion for empty phrases; deeds are called for.   The Swedes, I feel, love the Danes as much as we do, and they too regard as disgustingly brutal the exultant cries of the Germans.   What is the use of a few volunteers from Sweden and Norway who go to Denmark's aid?   Unless the entire nations go forth, posterity will point the finger of scorn at us, and our grandchildren will feel ashamed of their degenerate ancestors.   I suppose the famous phrase of 'northern faithfulness' has become a *mere* phrase. If we are not going to be faithful to our friend, as we have promised, there will never again be a single great deed reported from Scandinavia!"

In such tirades Henrik would work himself up into a frenzied ardor, which even his friends found difficult to take seriously at times; while some of the older citizens considered it most impertinent that a boy so low in the social scale as an impecunious drug clerk should discuss so positively questions of international scope on which they themselves dared not form opinions.   The King and the ministers surely could be trusted to act wisely without the advice of this young upstart.

Various epithets Henrik earned for himself from the respectable citizens; i.e., those whom he in turn designated as the people "with full pocket and empty brain."   He had a way of caricaturing them in their weakest moments and exposing them to the laughter of their fellows, that caused them to feel Ibsen would never amount to anything unless somebody gave him a good sound thrashing.   In telling of his Grimstad days twenty-five years later Ibsen writes in the introduction to the second edition of *Catiline:* "I found myself on a war-footing with the little society where I lived cramped by conditions and circumstances of life," and in a letter to the Danish literary historian Peter Hansen, October

28, 1870: "*Catiline* was written in a little provincial town, where it was impossible for me to give expression to all that fermented in me except by mad, riotous pranks, which brought down upon me the ill-will of all the respectable citizens who could not enter into that world which I was wrestling with alone."

From Christopher Due's memoirs and from citizens now living in Grimstad one can gather of what nature these pranks were. A certain Martini, for example, grew furious when he found that Ibsen had drawn a striking likeness of him as he one night, a bit befuddled, kissed his horse instead of his beloved. A queer recluse by the name of Ebbell was given such a ghoulish serenade one night just after he had put out his lamp that his hair almost turned white. A local "Beau Brummel" was induced to sing verses composed by Ibsen to the music of the popular operetta of the day, *The Neighbors,* by the Dane, Christian Hostrup, in which the fop unwittingly made sport of his own silly actions. Ibsen even poked fun at citizens who were awarded orders by the state—which is amusing in view of his own actions in this regard in later years—and incited the wrath of the pillars of society by such sketches. With his friends he held card parties in his room, at which they drank some of the druggist's rum out of salve boxes, because these could be quickly slipped into a pocket on the arrival of an unexpected visitor. He also had an illegitimate child by a servant girl for whose support he had to pay for fourteen years. From this Ibsen derived considerable disgust—feeling "befouled and disgraced," as Peer Gynt puts it, after the woman had confronted him with their "brat." He also derived from this incident a great deal of experience concerning the seamy side of small-town morality.

But Ibsen would not have been Ibsen if the dominant motive in his life, even in the adolescent years of poverty and provincialism, had not been an idealistic one. And in the circle of his friends poetry became the one absorbing interest, after the shyness with which they shielded their most sacred feelings had once been overcome. Christopher Due tells how this came about. Like many another young man, he too was in the habit of writing verses. One day he had finished a poem of which he was especially proud, and took it with him in the evening when he went to see Ibsen. With a certain amount of embarrassment he confessed that he wrote verses.

"Do you do that?" said Henrik. "Let me hear something."

Due then read his *Sunset,* one of those sentimental odes in which the young attempt to express their feelings face to face with Nature.

After Henrik had listened to the reading, he remarked quietly, "I write verses too."

"So you do it, too," exclaimed Due, and asked to hear a specimen.

Henrik then read a poem in somewhat similar vein, *In Autumn,* which impressed Due so much that he insisted that it must be printed. But this appeared at first impossible, for Grimstad had no paper of its own, and it seemed too presumptuous to imagine that a paper in the capital could possibly accept it. Yet, after re-reading the poem, Due decided to send it to the *Christiania Post,* for which he was the Grimstad correspondent. A few days later when he received the paper he was rejoiced to find printed on the first page *In Autumn* by Brynjolf Bjarme, the alliterative *nom de plume* which Ibsen had chosen for himself.

The poem in a melancholy mood described the arrival of autumn: the birds cease their singing, the wind sighs through withered trees, a moaning is heard in the stubble fields, and lilies and roses have become a mere memory. Young Ibsen made a regular cult of the solace of memory, as is evident from numerous poems of this time.

When Due triumphantly showed him the paper, Ibsen at
first became quite pale with emotion; he was overwhelmed
by the fact that he had received some recognition. He at
once hoped and feared for his future career. Then his
face brightened up and in a gay mood he invited Due to
a drink which they vowed to the poetic career of Brynjolf
Bjarme! Henrik eagerly listened to Due's praise of the
various points of excellence in his poem, and was readily
persuaded to let his friend see another one, *Memories of
Spring*. This piece, in which spring is not celebrated as a
gay time of gladness, but rather, is wafted through memory
like the echo of an æolian harp, so pleased Due that he
begged to be allowed to copy it. The music-loving friend
took it home and composed a melody to suit the poetic mood
Ibsen's poem had aroused in him.

> The tones are ours,
> And linger long;
> They tell of flowers
> And spring-tide song.

In a poem written a decade later called *Building Plans*
Ibsen tells of this experience that made such a deep impression on him:

> I remember, as clearly as if it were last night,
> The evening my first poem appeared in black and white.
> I sat there in my den with the smoke clouds rolling free,
> Sat smoking and sat dreaming in blest complacency.

He was building a castle in the air—his poetic career. In
the capital they were already reading his verses. If he could
make himself heard on the stage before a great multitude
who would be led to nobler, finer things by his plays,
awakened out of the lethargic slumber of comfort and
cowardice in which his nation was drifting along . . .

He felt himself soiled by some of his acts, but he would win back his self-respect by writing a great drama! There lay his mission; he felt his call to stir Norway to great deeds. He himself must work, work, work! And in this spirit he began his first drama:

> I must! I must! A voice deep in my soul
> Urges me on—and I will heed its call.
> Courage I have and strength for something better,
> Something far better than this present life,
> A series of unbridled dissipations!
> No, no; they do not satisfy the yearning soul.

When Ibsen was reading Cicero in the course of preparation for the entrance examination to the university, his naturally suspicious nature found the smooth flow of words very unconvincing. In fact, he began immediately to sympathize with Catiline, in whom he saw much of himself, and in the downfall of whose revolt he found a parallel to the revolution of 1848 which had failed so signally in Germany, Hungary, and the other states of Western Europe. In his own day the noble young idealists had gone down to defeat and were being condemned as dangers to the nation by pompous statesmen. Very naturally he came to the conclusion that there must have been something great and consequential in a man whom Cicero, the assiduous counsel of the majority, did not find it expedient to engage until affairs had taken such a turn that there was no longer any danger involved in the attack. As he continued to read avidly the story of Catiline in Sallust and Cicero, he gradually merged the characters of the Roman and of himself—revolutionary, dissipated, suspected by the "respectable," but glowing with an enthusiasm to rouse their degenerate and cowardly fellow-countrymen to great deeds worthy of their noble ancestors.

Henrik went to work with a will and a determination to

portray his characters truthfully, penetrating to the very bottom of their souls. He did not take this work lightly, thinking it a simple matter of inspiration; he realized the necessity for hard, heavy work before he penetrated to the truth, hidden—as he put it in a poem, *The Miner,* written at the time—in the very heart of the mountain.

> Beetling rock, with roar and smoke
> Break before my hammer-stroke!
> Deeper I must thrust and lower,
> Till I hear the ring of ore.
>
> Downward then! the depths are best;
> There is immemorial rest:
> Heavy hammer, burst as bidden
> To the heart-nook of the hidden!
>
> Hammer blow on hammer blow,
> Till the lamp of life burns low;
> Not a ray of hope's forewarning,
> Not a glimmer of the morning.

He worked hard, but he was young, living in the company of admiring and uncritical friends, and his first play was very much the effort of a beginner. It has a first act broken up into five scenes, "coincidence" has a great share in moving the action forward, the plot becomes rather obscured in the last act, much seems like direct imitation of Schiller, and the hero opens the play with a monologue revealing in detail his own character for the benefit of the audience. In fact, it is very difficult to take seriously this Catiline who has committed adultery and rape, but is at the same time a loving husband; who has sworn to kill himself, but yet feels that the state needs a man of his caliber badly; who is said to be a man of great purpose and decision, but who follows alternately the advice of the two women he loves, depending on which has spoken to him last. In the very last scene Catiline has a good Christian end, thinly disguised as pagan. For in spite of Henrik's mockery of orthodox Christianity the oppressive teachings in the Skien home, school, and church still held him in thrall to a certain extent. On a stormy night in the winter of 1848 he had written *In Doubt and Hope* in which he regrets that when the thunder is crashing like the trumpet of Judgment Day he cannot pray confidently as when he was a child:

> How oft I mocked with impious vow
> The final Judgment Day;
> But black and wild despair is now
> The scornful mocker's pay.

But it was after all Henrik Ibsen who had written the play, and it bore the marks of his personality on every page. He was not one to make his drama the struggle between two parties, as was indeed suggested by the sources, for example placing opposite Catiline the figure of Cicero; but he made the conflict an inner one between the high ideals and the inadequate strength of the hero. He made love not the central interest, but placed his hero between two women, the fiery Furia and the gentle Aurelia. Under the influence of these women he acts; after listening to the one he says, "Now I am myself." He uses sombre and striking figures that seem prophetic of some of his later work, as when Catiline says in his deep feeling of guilt, "I bend beneath the corpse of Catiline," or "The sun is dead," or, when his hero finds death with the woman who symbolizes his better self,

You have driven the gloom away; peace dwells within my breast.
I shall seek with you the dwelling place of light and rest.

Henrik thought it best to keep his poetic labors a secret from the Grimstad burghers, because they would probably think a youth who wrote verses unfit to fill prescriptions.

But one night he read *Catiline* to the two friends who believed in him, Christopher Due and Ole Schulerud. They felt a like enthusiasm for the Revolution with the author when he read:

> And what became of all my youthful dreams?
> Like flitting summer clouds they disappeared.

They too were partisans of Catiline,

> A man who burns in freedom's holy zeal.

They too suffered in their environment:

> Life here grows stagnant; every hope is quenched;
> The day creeps slowly on in drowsiness,
> And not a single thought is turned to deeds.

They sympathized with the hero—their hero and poet—as he read:

> They scoff and sneer at me—these paltry things:
> They cannot grasp how high my bosom beats
> For right and freedom.

They felt that Henrik Ibsen was right:

> Come let us fly;—lo, to the free-born mind
> The world's wide compass is a fatherland!

They knew a great drama had been written, and that it had but to be offered to the world to be acclaimed a classic and its author a great poet. Practical plans were made with eager enthusiasm. Due, who had a fine handwriting, and, as custom's official, ample leisure, was to make a clear copy of the drama. Schulerud was then to take it to Christiania to have it performed in the theater and printed by a bookseller. This would all be done as a matter of course; the only thing needful was to find the publisher who would make the highest bid. After this play had been published at a handsome profit, Ibsen was to devote himself wholly to the writing of plays— surely he could do two or three a year—while Schulerud was to look after the business end of the venture, the profits being shared equally between them. After a number of years then they could take the trip to the Orient of which they had dreamed.

Schulerud found in Christiania that the theater refused the play politely but firmly, and the highest bidder among the booksellers demanded so and so much for publishing the piece without any fee!

But before the arrival of what Ibsen called *"Catiline's* death sentence," he became deeply involved in his first serious love affair. His friends told him of a young lady by the name of Clara Ebbell who was a great lover of poetry and music, quite superior to the usual type of *Backfisch*. Due and Schulerud both were members of the social set of Grim- stad and tried repeatedly to induce Ibsen to allow them to introduce him at some of the dances. He always refused, until he found that this would be an opportunity to make the acquaintance of so cultured a young lady. Ibsen then really went to a ball, met Clara Ebbell and danced with her —after which a flood of poems poured forth from his soul to "C. E." In the clear Norwegian night after the ball a particular star attracted his attention, and its brightness, beauty, and distance seemed to him to be a fitting symbol for the one who had appeared to him all that was lovely. He decided that Clara Ebbell was his star, his "Stella" as he preferred to call her with memories of Wergeland's poem in mind.

But like most stars Ibsen's Stella was also rather remote. He met her again on some picnics, but his hopes were given very little encouragement. While she enthusiastically adored

poetry and poets in the abstract, this pale, timid youth whose
face was hidden behind an enormous black beard was not
particularly "poetic." His clothing was shabby; in fact, he
was so ill-equipped in this respect that one of his friends referred to his infatuation as "Love Without Stockings," in
allusion to the title of J. H. Wessel's popular comedy. Miss
Ebbell's parents too preferred a wealthy if a bit elderly
suitor to the peculiar and impecunious Ibsen who, besides,
did not enjoy the best reputation.

Meanwhile Henrik went about during the summer thinking
less of Catiline and the revolution than of Welhaven and other
romantic poets. In imitation of their style he wrote many
poems dealing with elves in the woods and "noecks" in the
waterfalls, spirits who inspire the gift of music in certain
individuals, but at the same time make their favorites very
unhappy. In a poem dedicated to "C. E." he appealed to
his "star" to send him "certainty," to relieve his "sick breast"
from the tortures of doubt; but if she could not give a definite
answer at least to allow him the gentle light of hope:

> When the gentle heavenly light
> Sparkles from afar,
> Happy in the quiet night
> I'll gaze at my star.

At other times he pictured himself on a stormy, rainy night
in autumn sitting before his fire reflecting on the faithlessness
of a girl's heart. His worst fears came true: Clara Ebbell
announced her engagement to the middle-aged gentleman,
who—this seemed unspeakable—was her own uncle!

It was a hard blow for Henrik. He read Goethe's *Werther*
and went about in a similar mood of despair. Under the
influence of this emotion he wrote *Memories of a Ball, a Frag-
ment in Poetry and Prose.* The work begins with a prologue
to "Stella" in which he brings her flowers from the bed of

memory, pale asters, blooming over an autumnal grave. A
description of the ball follows in the course of which he
summarizes the whole story of the life of Man in three words:

> Anticipation, hope, and disappointment!

The prose section of this work, entitled *The Last Leaves of
a Diary*, concludes in a mood strongly suggestive of Werther's
suicide:

> The ball is at an end . . . yes, I want to go home. Once more
> live through my life, my love—and then go far out into the dark
> night to dream and . . .

But Henrik was a poet. All was grist to his mill, and his
nature was resilient. On January 5, 1850, he wrote to his
friend Schulerud in Christiania:

> "I have also finished a longer and perhaps somewhat extravagant
> poem entitled *Memories of a Ball*, which owes its existence to my
> imaginary infatuation of last summer."

III

IBSEN FINDS HIS CAREER IN CHRISTIANIA

Catiline's death sentence—as Ibsen called the rejection of the play by the Christiania theater—was such a bitter disappointment to the young author that Schulerud felt extremely sorry for his friend. He took the play from one publisher to another, and when all refused it, he decided that it must at all events be printed, even though he should go hungry to pay the cost.

He did print it at his own expense, and he did go hungry; but at the same time Schulerud had great faith in the ultimate success of Ibsen. He therefore encouraged him to leave the stuffy philistine town of Grimstad and to come to the inspiring atmosphere of the capital. Ibsen had been getting ready for his entrance examination at the university and had by dint of extreme economy saved a little out of his meager pay. He was very impatient to be off, and in March, 1850, he decided that the time had come to change the hated appellation "apothekersvend" (journeyman apothecary) for the much more agreeable "Herr Student Ibsen."

Before going to Christiania, however, he wished to make a visit to his family in Skien, chiefly to see his sister Hedvig. To her he could reveal himself as he was, just as he did in his lyric poems, while for the rest of the world he preserved his sullen, mocking aspect. This attitude of savage sarcasm was largely protective on his part, to guard the privacy of his deeper feelings. He had in his character also a great kindliness and tenderness, as many a child in Grimstad knew from the gifts of chocolate with which the black-bearded drug clerk

33

frequently made them happy. This same tenderness he felt for his younger sister.

As the boat travelled northward between islands covered with somber pines and the rock-bound Norwegian coast, Ibsen had ample leisure to reflect on the changes in himself since he had left Skien six years before. From a boy he had grown into a man with a fair amount of experience in life. Through hard work he had prepared himself for an examination that would—he hoped—ultimately admit him into that superior class of those "who have studied." One thing that Grimstad had given him was his enduring love for the sea. He had furthermore seen his own poems in print repeatedly, and he had written a drama that was about to appear in book form. He had also laid down for himself principles that were the guiding rule of his life. They appeared in some essays which he had ready to submit as part of the examination. Especially the first one, entitled *On the Importance of Knowledge of Oneself,* is full of passages into which Henrik Ibsen put his life philosophy:

> As a means to aid one in judging the characters of others and for a knowledge of mankind in general, it is necessary to have understood one's own character and manner of thinking, because only through conclusions which he draws therefrom is it possible for a man to attain fairly certain results in that direction.

Henrik had made the principle set forth above his daily practice, and in his silent hours of meditation he looked fearlessly into his own motives, no matter how humiliating for himself was the result. He was determined to know himself well in order that he might understand others whom he was describing in the poems, novels and dramas he had projected.

The visit to Skien, with the memories of humiliating poverty and the atmosphere of orthodox religion, was an uncomfortable experience for Henrik. It was on only one occasion when he and Hedvig went for a long walk to the Kapitels Mountain that he felt free from the depression that always overcame him in his native city.   Brother and sister sat on the height lost in the beauty of the view spread before them. Far below them lay the city, the broad Skien River with its two roaring waterfalls, and the island between the falls with the picturesque ruins of an old cloister.   Beautifully wooded hills lay in the background.   It was a scene to stir up child-hood memories of "noecks," nymphs, and wood sprites, and to fill the soul with poetic longing.

He was talking eagerly to Hedvig of his plans.   With a certain amount of shyness he confessed that he was writing poetry and dramas.   He told of what he hoped to find in the University of Christiania.   There he would meet people who were not so smug and self-satisfied as those in Skien, there he would find idealists!   He was going to study medicine, but even at this time he seemed more interested in the literary circles which he hoped to enter.   Hedvig wished to know what his goal in life was, what he really intended to do.

"I wish to attain to the utmost possible clearness of vision and fulness of power."

"And when you shall have attained to it,—what then?"

"Then I wish to die."

His sister kept this saying in her heart, and when forty years afterward her brother had become a famous man, she told it to his biographer.   But in the meantime there was very little about Ibsen that gave promise of future greatness, except his own dreams.   But such dreams of "becoming an immortal man" he cherished continually; this was the sub-ject of the reverie over his pipe in the poem *Building Plans,* and in *Catiline* he says wistfully:

> If but one moment I might shine in splendor,
> Blaze like a falling star upon the night,
> If I might but achieve one noble deed—

Reality, however, looked unpromising and sad. He left for the capital with very little money and very poor preparation for the university entrance examination. After his course in a mediocre grammar school in which no Latin had been taught, he had enjoyed no regular schooling—how was he to compete with the graduates of the "Gymnasium"? He was advised to enter "the student factory."

This was a name popularly given to an irregular school in Christiania whose purpose it was to coach in the shortest possible time candidates for the university entrance examination in branches in which they were deficient. It was conducted by "Old Man" Heltberg, a genius in his way, who seems to have trained in his school all the chief figures in modern Norwegian literature. Arne Garborg says of him: "Tall and proud he stalked about in his long blue frock coat, serious as a senator, but in his keen, grayish-blue eyes there sparkled a roguish look from behind the spectacles." His method of teaching was very original. "Every hour was a feast of reason and wit, of jokes and mockery and unbelievable drolleries. Even grammar in the hands of the 'Old Man' became alive, alive as children's games and fairy tales." For example, he would stand before the class, bend his left arm as though he were holding a violin, while with the right he stroked as with a bow: "amo, amas, amat, amamus, amatis, amant!" he sang to an improvised melody. "Now you sing with me," he would then say, and thus the class learned the conjugations. But he taught more than conjugations; he was an ardent lover of ancient Italy and lectured with enthusiasm on Horace at his banquets with vine leaves in his hair.

Into this school came Ibsen to find there three other youths with literary inclinations, Björnstjerne Björnson, Aasmund Olafson Vinje, and Jonas Lie. In his poem, *Old Heltberg*, Björnson describes Ibsen as he looked on the school bench.

Thin and intense, with the color of gypsum,
And a coal black, preposterous beard, Henrik Ibsen.

The poem goes on to describe the teacher:

But the "boss" who ruled there with his logical rod
"Old Heltberg" himself, was of all the most odd!
In his jacket of dogskin and fur boots stout
He waged a hard war with his asthma and gout.
No fur cap could hide from us his forehead imperious,
His classical features, his eyes' power mysterious.
Now erect in his might and now bowed by his pain,
Strong thoughts he threw out, and he threw not in vain.
If suffering grew keener and again it was faced
By the will of his soul, and his body he braced
Against onset after onset, then his eyes were flaming
And his hands were clenched hard, as if deep were his shaming
That he seemed to have yielded.

"Old Heltberg" had a method of teaching grammar by a
system of short cuts to cram Latin and Greek in the shortest
possible time. For twenty years he talked about publishing
it, and received a grant from the Storthing for this purpose.
But it was always being improved, and therefore never
finished.

Oft the stricken hero scarce his tedious toil could brook,
He wished to go and write, if only just one book,
To show a *little* what he was, and show it to the world;
He loosed his cable daily, though ne'er his sails unfurled.

His "grammar" was not printed! And he passed from mortal ken
To where the laws of thought are not written with a pen.
His "grammar" was not printed! But the life that it had
In ink's prolonging power did not need to be clad.
It lived in his soul, so mighty, so warm
That a thousand books' life seems but poor, empty form.
It lives in a host of independent men,
To whose thought he gave life and who gave it again.

In the school, at the bar, in the church, in Storthing's hall,
In poetry and art—whose deeds and life-work all
Have proved to be the freer and the broader in their might,
Because Heltberg had given their youth higher flight.

Whatever Ibsen learned or failed to learn from Heltberg, the important thing was that in this school and in a students' literary society which he frequented, he met young men who were distinctly his superiors in the breadth of their reading and even more in critical ability. There was Björnson, a pastor's son, four years younger than Ibsen, yet in spite of that very far ahead of him, an enthusiast for the ideas of 1848 and for the poets of the Romantic movement. He was already distinguishing himself as a journalist and theatrical critic. He had told his father, "Do not send me any money. I am able to support myself at the university." But Ibsen was less drawn to this cocksure orator and romantic sentimentalist than to the somewhat older Vinje, a cynical, mocking satyr, who had previously been a shepherd boy, public school teacher, whiskey distiller, seaman, and who was now planning to become a law student. This man did not indiscriminately accept all "ideals," but he was much more Ibsen's sort in the manner in which he could readily detect the seamy side of things. His favorite poets, as well as those of Paul Botten-Hansen, another young student who awed Ibsen with his knowledge, were Heine and Byron. From these two authors, "rusé, rasé, blasé," the conversation of these young men—with the exception of Björnson—took its tone of irony and skepticism.

To give himself the last finishing touches for his examination Ibsen took lessons in Greek (for sixteen specie dollars) from a student of philology, Thore Jensen Lie, a brilliant but erratic youth, a victim of alcoholism. Because he was so poor, Ibsen decided to take the examination as early as August, after just a few months' preparation. He received his best mark in German.   In Norwegian, Latin, French, history, geography, religion and geometry his mark was "good." In Greek and arithmetic he was graded "poor"; and thus he found himself, not failed, but forced to take another examination in these two subjects before he could be admitted to the university as a student.   But he never tried again, because he soon afterward found himself launched in his literary career.   Thus while he quite willingly relinquished his plans for the study of medicine, he adopted the title "Herr Student."   In the spring of 1851 he attended the lectures of the poet Welhaven, dean of the faculty of arts, on the dramatist Holberg and his time.   He conceived a warm affection for this genial writer of eighteenth-century comedies.

He now joined two of his new friends in the publication of a liberal, satirical weekly, first called *The Man*, changed later to *Andhrimmer*, the name of the cook in Walhalla.   The first of these was Botten-Hansen, the son of a teacher who had come to the university in 1847, a great connoisseur of European literature, and four years older than Ibsen; the other, Vinje, Ibsen's fellow student at Heltberg's school, but his senior by ten years, the Heinrich Heine of Norwegian letters, famous and feared for his sarcastic skepticism.   The paper, alas, had to suspend publication after nine months because it was a losing venture, but during this time Ibsen supplied for it some witty articles and clever caricatures.

The particular target of Ibsen's wit in some of his political articles in this paper was a certain member of the Storthing called Stabell.   In a typical example of young Ibsen's satire printed in this paper we read that the statesman reminded him of

"that determined English clergyman, who had firmly resolved to live and die as pastor in his own village.   Under Henry VIII therefore he renounced Catholicism, accepted it again under Mary, renounced it under Elizabeth, and accepted it once more under James,

and thereby attained his goal. Thus also Herr Stabell; his job is
his 'idea'; for it he must fight as a brave man; yes, if necessary,
even become a martyr to the cause. Now the times have changed
(as Pastor Berg says) and Stabell is therefore forced to lay aside
the Old Adam and to assume a new man. That this bath of puri-
fication and regeneration, which Stabell took on the morning of
May 12, caused offense among the uncircumcised in the Storthing,
is readily understood."

An even bitterer attack on this vacillating politician is
found in Ibsen's burlesque, *Norma, or a Politician's Love,*
in which Severus (Stabell) makes love to Adalgisa (the gov-
ernmental party) and to Norma (the opposition), with great
impartiality until the ladies discover his perfidy! Henrik
Ibsen at this time loathed the opportunist and compromiser
just as much as later his Dr. Stockmann did.

When the author of *Catiline* came to Christiania he was
full of ardor for ideas of freedom and enthusiastic to take his
part in action for their accomplishment. When therefore the
government on May 29, 1850, decided to deport a certain
Harro Harring, a man who like Byron had taken part in the
struggle for Greek liberty and who had published a "dangerous" play, *The Testament of America,* Ibsen decided to act
with other students in fighting for freedom of ideas and of
the press. He with Björnson and others signed a protest
against Harring's deportation and marched with the crowd
to the Prime Minister's house to present it. Then they went
to the wharves where their hero already had been placed on
board a steamer by the police. The young men in the procession gave three cheers for Harring, followed by cheers for
the fatherland and for freedom.

Likewise did he become enthusiastic for the labor movement started a short time previous by a certain Marcus
Thrane. A student who lived in the same house with him,

Theodor Fredrik Abildgaard, a devotee of Thrane's, initiated Ibsen into the movement that hoped to carry out the ideas of the February Revolution. The agitation appealed to Ibsen; he went to the secret meetings and wrote for the paper Abildgaard and other revolutionaries were publishing.

Suddenly on July 7, 1851, the police arrested Thrane, Abildgaard and others. The newspaper office was raided. Ibsen too would probably have been arrested, had it not been for the presence of mind of one of the initiated, who destroyed many compromising papers.

Abildgaard was kept in prison for a long period, and in 1855 was condemned to four years at hard labor for his revolutionary propaganda.

The fate of Abildgaard made an enormous impression on Ibsen. In a letter to Botten-Hansen of August 5, 1853, he asks: "What news of Abildgaard?" and again on April 28, 1857: "Abildgaard, how is he really getting on?" Henrik Ibsen never again took part in any political demonstration nor joined any party. He gradually persuaded himself that it was his task to rouse his nation to higher things by means of his dramas.

That he was able to make any progress at all as dramatist was due very largely to the help given him just at the right time by his Grimstad friend Schulerud. On the occasion of the latter's death in 1870 the author of *Brand* and *Peer Gynt* wrote to Mrs. Schulerud:

He was indeed a friend in those times when sacrifice was necessary to prepare for my future; and how rare are those who are with one in such days! Numerous are they who load you with their attentions in their own interest when you have gained your cause, but at the time when he devoted himself to me with all his sincere and faithful heart there were just as many chances against as for me.

Poor as he was, Schulerud had borrowed the money to have *Catiline* printed in an edition of 250 copies. Ibsen's letters show how much the poet's heart had been set on it and how great was his disappointment when the theater and the publishers refused it. Schulerud could not bear to see his friend disappointed; moreover, he had great faith in the play. But the calmness with which the world went on in its customary way after the appearance of the book was difficult for him to understand. Ibsen too was bitterly chagrined. Among young people the play aroused some amount of enthusiasm; there were students who selected some of the idealistic speeches as subjects for declamations. But the critics spoke very harshly of this play by Brynjolf Bjarme.

Still there was one critic who dealt with it sympathetically. Ibsen had the deep pleasure and heartening encouragement of reading in a note by Professor M. J. Monrad in the *Norsk Tidsskrift,* that the main idea of the play was a clear and beautiful one, even though the execution showed infelicities in versification, verbosity, and faults in rhetoric—all signs of an unpracticed pen. "And just for that reason," he continued, "do I find that Brynjolf Bjarme gives great promise— quite in contrast to the poetic mob, especially those who begin to write for the theater, who in general possess some ease and polish of expression and have a certain number of good ideas, but who are not able to seize upon one unified and grand thought. It is better that the development should begin from within, from the thought; where the latter is strongly developed, the form will be found in time."

It was just the proper word addressed to this young author who followed it by taking an infinite amount of pains to achieve form in drama.

Schulerud, in addition to the other kindnesses he had shown his friend, invited Ibsen to live with him and share his meager allowance which was small for one and starvation for two. They were in the habit of eating cold breakfasts and suppers, and for dinner they took a walk in order to give their housemates the impression that they were having this meal out. After about an hour they would return and then, according to Norwegian fashion, have coffee in their room, with which they ate dry bread. Only once, for a short spell, did they have warm dinners, and that was when one day hunger pinched them very severely, and they sold the more than 200 remaining copies of *Catiline* to a huckster for wrapping paper. But this pitiful poverty Ibsen bore with cheerful humor, because there was nothing humiliating connected with it, as had been the case in Skien after his father's bankruptcy. Moreover, he was as he felt on the way toward realizing his "mission" in life.

   That *Catiline* had been rejected by the theater is in no way surprising, because it had been written by a youth of no more than elementary schooling, in a little hole of a provincial city where he never had occasion to visit a theater. But what is surprising is that *The Warrior's Barrow*, which Ibsen had begun in Grimstad as *The Normans* and finished in Christiania during the Whitsuntide holidays two months after his arrival, was accepted by the theater and performed three times during September and October, 1850. Three performances, under the conditions obtaining in Christiania at that time, meant that the young author Brynjolf Bjarme had scored a success. Besides, it earned him a very welcome honorarium and more than a consolation for the failures in Greek and arithmetic in the previous month.

   It may have contributed to Ibsen's success that he followed in the footsteps of the fashionable Danish playwright Adam Oehlenschläger in the subject and the manner of treatment. The old Norse Viking, Audun, stranded on the coast of Normandy, is nursed back to health and converted to Christianity by Blanka, a young princess who has escaped the sword of

the pirates. The princess is then wooed and won by a Norse
hero who turns out to be Audun's son. While she sails to
Norway as his son's bride, the old father remains behind as
a pious hermit after he has buried under a mound his sword
and armor, as an outward symbol of his acceptance of Christianity. While in this story there is much imitation of the
older dramatist, yet Henrik Ibsen followed his own bent in the
contrasting of Christianity and heathenism, and in the realistic treatment of the old Vikings, too rough and vulgar for
the taste of the critics, who found them represented in such a
manner that they "are a credit neither to us nor to our
fathers."

When he met Clara Ebbell again—she had not married her
uncle after all, and was recovering in the capital from her
broken engagement—she told him in her effusive way what a
lucky man he was to have seen his own play on the stage,
portrayed by the best actors in Norway. She wished to hear
all about his triumph and asked whether he had made a
curtain speech!

"No," poor, timid Ibsen had to confess, "it was terrible. I
hid myself in the darkest corner of the theater!"

Miss Ebbell's enthusiasm for poetry, her Grimstad reputation as an interpreter of Beethoven and as an arbiter in all
that was elegant, still awed Henrik. He idealized her as his
guiding star who could lead him to higher things, as Beatrice
did Dante or Frau von Stein Goethe. He therefore looked to
her for sympathy and inspiration. But when he spoke to her
freely of his true feelings, his views of the world in general
and his own aspirations in particular, he found that she was
simply shocked at his godless beliefs. Henrik was very much
disappointed and depressed. In his solitary musings he had
pinned such high hopes to her noble influence that he felt she
would surely understand if she read his best verses, the fruits

of his highest moments. Therefore he sent her about a dozen of his poems neatly copied, with the following letter:

DEAR MISS EBBELL:

In sending you the enclosed copies of my poems, I hope that the mental state in which the verses originated may serve as an excuse for points of view that even you, like many other people, seem to have misunderstood in large part. I beg you to forgive me that I could not omit writing these words, probably the last I shall ever address to you.

By granting Miss Ebbell this look into his restless, eager, embittered, and yet idealistic soul, Ibsen did not gain her sympathy. Among the poems was *The Miner*, which spoke of delving into the depths to find the truth; why, she probably wondered, should he say this when all truth came from Him above?

After all, however, this was not the last time he ever wrote to Clara Ebbell. In the winter of 1851 she appeared at a ball in Grimstad as a troubadour reciting verses. He sent her in memory of that occasion a prettily romantic poem which, however, did not make much of an impression. In these lines, *To a Troubadour*, he gave expression, though not too boldly, to his admiration and devotion. While Clara Ebbell may have liked to be a troubadour at a dance, for life she preferred a steady source of bread and butter. When therefore her uncle renewed his proffers of marriage, she deigned this time to accept him, and she thus became Fru Bie.

IV

APPRENTICESHIP IN BERGEN

1

Norway had come under Danish rule in 1397 and had become independent again in 1814. During this "night of four hundred years" the Danish culture had replaced the Norwegian, just as Christiania (named in honor of a Danish king in 1624) took the place of the old capital Oslo. While the Danes were the ruling class they determined what was elegant and fashionable; and naturally enough the Norwegian tradition and culture was despised. The theater in Christiania, for example, presented almost exclusively Danish plays interpreted by Danish actors.

But during the period of Ibsen's youth Norway began to feel conscious of its own traditions, and to rebel against the dominance of Danish culture. It was at once a new and an old nation. The poet Wergeland put it thus: "The Old and the New Norway are the two halves of a gold ring fitting together perfectly; the Danish period constitutes the solder of base metal which must be removed." Therefore it was very natural for the Norwegians to fall in line with the Romantic Movement of all Europe which was glorifying the Middle Ages, especially since the Middle Ages were Norway's epoch of greatness. Thus there resulted a literary nationalism. Norwegian history and Norwegian medieval literature were made the objects of study. Popular folk tales and popular music were collected. Among the poets there arose a cult of the life of the people, that is to say, chiefly of the peasants as the faithful guardians of the old national traditions.

The glory of their past seemed to vouchsafe to the Norwegians a great national future. The poets felt it their mission to revive in their works past grandeur, as an inspiration to their contemporaries. This idea was shared also by Henrik Ibsen, as he showed in his medieval drama *The Warrior's Barrow,* in his verses re-creating the medieval scenes in the old fortress Akershus at Christiania, and in many other poems of Romantic cast. Along with his cynicism and his critical spirit he nourished this naïve idealism in a very ardent form. In fact, he had put into the mouth of his heroine Blanka, as the last words of his play performed in the Christiania theater, the prophecy that as the medieval Norsemen had swooped down in their ships to fight with the rest of Europe, so now the North was going to rise out of its grave to take part in the battle of the intellects on the sea of thought.

The struggle against the Danish influence in the theater received a great impetus in 1850 when a "national theater" was founded in Bergen. This ancient city with medieval churches, Haakon's banqueting hall dating back to the thirteenth century, and many other historic memories, was much better suited to become the centre of a new national art than the capital, which had lost its very name, and where Danish influence was deeply entrenched. Bergen was the more poetic city, while Christiania had very much the flavor of bureaucracy. It was with enthusiasm therefore that the students in Christiania learned of the Bergen experiment, and they decided to give a festival to raise funds for its support.

A great share of the students' enthusiasm was due to the fact that it was Ole Bull who had founded the Bergen Theater. The great violinist was the idol of all Norway and especially of the students. It was well known that in 1848 he had gone at the head of a number of Norwegians in Paris to the Palais de Justice to present a Norwegian flag to President Lamartine, with an address showing his sympathy for the Revolution. Wergeland had written of him:

> The greatest marvel of all was that he brought Norway home to the Norsemen. Most people knew the folk-songs and dances, but were ashamed to admire them. Lifted by him into their confidence and love, these homely melodies suddenly began to gleam like stars, and the people came to feel that they too had jewels of their own.

Some thirty years later, when in 1880 Björnson spoke at the grave of Ole Bull he recalled the emotions that had animated him and the other young men who had been instrumental in giving Norway the modern national literature of which it is so justly proud:

> But a young generation came, nourished on freedom, without the fear and prudence of their elders, but with more of defiance, more of anger. They lived in the morning of freedom and of honor, and in this dawn came Ole Bull's tones like the first rays of the sun over the mountain tops.

Therefore when "Norse Ole Bull" (this title was given to him by Ibsen's friend Vinje) founded a theater in which he wanted to carry the spirit of Old Norway into the drama as he had already carried it into music, the younger generation was enthusiastically on his side. But the older men in the Storthing refused his petition for government support of the "national theater." He felt somewhat discouraged by this rebuff, but at this point the students came forward with their offer to arrange a great musical festival on the evening of October 15, 1851, for the benefit of the Bergen Theater. This gave Ole Bull a new impulse. He composed a chorus for male voices to be sung after the prologue, while he himself was going to play some of his "Norwegian" numbers in the later part of the program.

Henrik Ibsen had been asked to write the prologue.   On the night of the performance he sat in an obscure corner of the auditorium, which was crowded to the last seat.   If the Storthing had not appreciated Ole Bull's new venture, the students and the citizens of Christiania had turned out in full force to give their approval.   The curtain rose and an actress in old Norse costume began speaking Ibsen's lines. She told of the gray dim past, the glorious time of Norway, when the nation was strong and the minstrel was honored by prince and by people.   The heroes did valiant deeds in battle, and in the festal hall the minstrel's harp in gentle tones called the factions to reconciliation.   But this glorious time passed, and a period of slavery closed over Norway like a long winter sleep.   Now the people had once more broken their chains, but who was to direct their course?   Art—art which is like the sound-board of a lyre whose notes vibrate deep in the soul of the people.   An art rooted in the hearts of the nation will be the force to guide Norway on to a greatness equal to the grandeur of the heroic age.   Like the Jewess by the willows of the waters of Babylon, the artists should sing of the splendor of the past and call up in the memory of the people the glory of their ancestors for the emulation of the young men and women of the present generation.   With a ringing refrain the prologue came to a close:

> For art is like the sound-board of a lyre
> That deepens the vibrations of the strings
> Fixed in the people's soul, till higher,
> Fuller and clearer the sweet music rings.

Stormy applause showed how well Ibsen had struck the note of the hour and expressed in beautiful verse the hope that beat in every young Norwegian heart.   The same note sounded in Ole Bull's melodies of "gamle Norge" that had so long been timidly hidden, but now when played by his magic bow were applauded by mighty rulers; Ole Bull was a festival in the life of the people; he gave self-respect to the Norwegians. Through him they realized that native art also could be great.

After the concert Ole Bull wished to meet the poet of the prologue. He learned that this twenty-three-year-old student and journalist was also the author of several dramas.

Later Ibsen found himself in the presence of Ole Bull, the hero of young Norway, tall and handsome as a Greek god in the royalty of his young manhood, and with a presence that (as Longfellow put it) filled the room with sunshine. The two men conceived a warm affection for each other, and three weeks later Ibsen received from Ole Bull an appointment as theater poet and stage-manager of the Norwegian Theater in Bergen.

After the hunger in Christiania, after the failure in the entrance examination, and after the bankruptcy of the weekly paper, Henrik Ibsen now had a position such as he had never hoped for in his most sanguine dreams in Grimstad. He also had a regular, if rather meager, salary. Best of all, he was associated with the famous Ole Bull in the work of making the people conscious of the greatness of Norway.

2

This beautiful Norway celebrated by the popular violinist appeared vividly to Ibsen on an autumn day in 1851 as his steamer approached Bergen. There is a stern beauty in the coast line whose bare rocks, furrowed and weather-beaten, rise abruptly out of the island-dotted sea. When the ship enters the harbor the wooded heights of the "seven hills" that shut in the old trading city suddenly sweep into view. The steamer lands at the historic Tyskebryggen, the old quay of the Hanseatic traders. The view of this picturesque spot where heroic legends seem to hover dreamily over the wild and rugged hills, a few years later inspired Björnson to write Norway's national air, "Yes, we love this land of ours!"

When Ibsen went ashore he was accosted by a dockhand who offered to carry his baggage, addressing Ibsen as "Min Herre." This touch of politeness, so different from the language used by the roustabouts in Christiania, was an extremely pleasant surprise. He could hardly believe his ears, and he was reminded of Heine's appreciation of the "süsser Ananasduft der Höflichkeit" in Paris in contrast to the German bluntness. He went to the Hotel Sontum where Ole Bull's letter insured a warm and cordial welcome from the motherly Fru Sontum. In later years Ibsen was wont to refer to Bergen as "the city without plebeians."

On November 20, 1851, he read in Bergen's *Stiftstidende* of the arrival of Herr Student Ibsen, who had been engaged as theater-poet and stage-manager for the new national theater; in the course of the season several of his Norwegian dramas would be put on by the local troupe, a fact that would give real significance to the Bergen theater. He felt the importance of his post, for here lay his mission. Could he fulfill it, or would he disappoint these splendid Bergen folk who had shown so much faith in him?

That Ole Bull was deeply interested in the theater was one of its greatest assets. Whenever he appeared to conduct the orchestra he produced a storm of applause. He was then and remained the idol of the public. Many stories circulated about him that served to make him personally popular, quite aside from his qualities as an artist. For example, the police had at first been rather suspicious of the "Norse" theater and had demanded free seats—for all the police officials and their wives! Ole Bull granted them, but over the seats he placed a transparency, "Seats for the Police." The officials and their wives were very angry, but the audience was highly amused. The next day Ole Bull was haled into court and given a heavy fine for "frivolous mockery of the august persons of the police." However, he carried the case to a higher court where it was decided in his favor to the great chagrin of the ridiculed officials.

Next the police arrested him under an obsolete regulation from Hanseatic days that allowed only covered pipes to be smoked on the streets. He was accused of having smoked a cigar on the very market square. The judge, an old friend of the violinist's, dismissed the case, as Ole Bull had smoked *on the market square,* whereas the law forbade cigars *on the streets!* The boisterous air with which he bore himself in this fracas with the police, and the boyish gusto with which he could tell stories, endeared him so much to the heart of Ibsen that he later used him as a model for his great Norwegian national hero, Peer Gynt. However, Ibsen enjoyed Ole Bull's support only for a very short time, as the latter left at the end of 1851 for a six years' tour of America and other countries.

Some other amusing characters Ibsen met were the broker Peter Kieding, known for his witty sayings quoted all over the city, Dahl, the sexton, a somewhat bibulous relative of the great painter, and Parelius, a tailor by trade, but by avocation a thirsty member of the theater orchestra. At times—according to all reports probably very rarely—Ibsen joined them for a few drinks and an exchange of stories.

There were other characters in Bergen much less pleasant to deal with. For example, it was not Ibsen's fault that his days there did not begin with a bloody duel. He sent a challenge to Hermann Laading, a local teacher who had been engaged by the trustees of the theater to cooperate with Ibsen in staging the plays and coaching the actors. This man was older than Ibsen and therefore insisted that his authority be respected; moreover, he told Ibsen that he was a visionary and knew nothing about the practical side of staging a play. Ibsen's nature was always a very irascible one, and after an altercation in which he felt his honor had suffered, he sent off his challenge in the white heat of his wrath. Unfortunately history is silent in regard to the further details. Did it end like the duel between the French doctor and the Welsh priest in *The Merry Wives of Windsor?* At any rate, there was no thought of cooperation between Ibsen and Laading, and the latter's services were soon afterward dispensed with.

Another Bergen pedagogue, Herr Paul Stub, launched a savage attack in a Bergen newspaper on the new theater, on the actors, and especially on the stage-manager. Ibsen found himself accused of "complete ignorance and immaturity." Stub spoke of Ibsen's answer in the paper as "an exercise in Norwegian composition" and claimed that he "had taught the boy to write." As a matter of fact, Ibsen in his Grimstad days had taken a few lessons from Stub when the latter was trying to eke out his meager income by giving correspondence courses. A newspaper controversy ensued in the course of which Stub finally complained that Ibsen seemed to question his competence as a theater critic. "Yes," Ibsen concluded his next and final reply, "that, God knows, is precisely what I am doing!"

But if the truth must be told, Ibsen's ignorance of the practical stage was colossal, and the actors were not slow in noticing it. But as he had defended them in the paper in such a manner as to bring down ridicule on their critics, refrained from foisting advice on them, and in general borne himself with scrupulous politeness, they met him with respect and consideration. One young lady, however, who in the previous season had played the soubrette rôles with a great natural gift for impertinence, but who had since married and retired from the stage, happening to meet the quiet,

mild-mannered youth of twenty-three on the street, decided
to make him feel uncomfortable.

"Well, Herr Student Ibsen," she said with studied malice,
"so *you* are going to teach Jacob Brunn and the others how
to act? Well, God help you and good luck!"

Ibsen looked at the young lady with a helpless smile.
"Yes, my honored lady, it is indeed necessary that God
should help me. The truth is I'm trying to learn something
myself, but don't tell the others about it!"

Ibsen winked at her with a sort of wistful roguishness,
for he was well aware that "the others" knew all about it!

The Board of Trustees saw that Ibsen was learning, and
they were so pleased with his work that in the following spring
they awarded him a stipend to enable him to travel to Copenhagen and Dresden for the purpose of learning more. A
condition was attached to this offer; he had to promise to
remain for five years after his return at a salary of 300 specie
dollars annually, or about $25 a month in American money.
Ibsen did not hesitate, but accepted the offer willingly.

For the first time now Ibsen left his native country to come
in contact with the artistic atmosphere and the thought currents of Europe. In Copenhagen the kindly reception given
him by the playwright and critic J. L. Heiberg and his clever
wife, the greatest Danish actress of the day, was very inspirit-
ing to the still somewhat provincial youth. At an evening
reception in their home, with Mrs. Heiberg just returned
from her triumph in the theater and her sixty-year-old husband gallant to the ladies and sparkling in his witticisms,
Ibsen felt that he was getting a taste of the great world of
letters. Heiberg's wit was famous. Brandes tells how one
day he spoke of Björnson, objecting to the loud ways and
rude manners this "broadshouldered, spoilt child" had shown
on the occasion of a recent visit.

"But you must remember that he is like a powerful young

reindeer bull," remarked one of the guests, "he must knock off his horns."

"That's all very well," replied Heiberg, "only not in my salon. This is not the place where you knock off anything!"

Henrik Ibsen was one to treasure such *bon mots,* but still more he prized the esthetic principles of Heiberg in which were united French *ésprit* and German philosophy as he had absorbed them during his long sojourns in Paris and in Germany. To both the critic and his wife the actress Ibsen bore a life-long gratitude for opening up to him a new world of beauty.

In Dresden on his very first morning Ibsen was at the art gallery to view the paintings whose beauty destined them for eternal life. In the early morning silence he stood before Correggio's *Holy Night* and Raphael's *Sistine Madonna* with a shudder of devotion more profound than even the thrill he had felt at his first communion in the Skien church. But Ibsen also felt this rapture before the truthful portrayal of everyday life in the works of the Dutch realist Jan van Mieris. Not the subjects, but the technique thrilled him; he was ready to worship the mastery that could build so well as to gain for the work eternal value. In the presence of these great masters he felt a like power in himself; he too would train himself with work, work, work, so that his dramas should live forever by the side of these masterpieces. He exclaimed as though he were young Correggio at Bologna before Raphael's *Saint Cecilia:* "Anch' io sono pittore!"

In the Royal Theater Ibsen made the acquaintance of another master who had built for eternity, Shakespeare. Both in Copenhagen and in Dresden he saw performances of *Hamlet,* and here too a new world dawned before his eager eyes. He revelled in the drama of old King Lear driven out on the heath by the selfishness of his own daughters; of Richard III kneeling between two bishops, "two props of virtue for a Christian prince"; and also *Midsummer Night's Dream* with its satirical humor. And when he returned to Bergen he had in his baggage the manuscript of *St. John's Night.*

3

Ibsen as stage-manager was under a board of trustees whom Ole Bull had appointed when he left for a tour in America in 1851. These men were mostly merchants in Bergen, none of them equipped with any special knowledge of the drama or the theater. The actors were all new to the profession, good patriotic Norwegians who had come to the theater without experience in answer to a newspaper advertisement published the previous year by Ole Bull. Thus practically all the work fell on Ibsen's shoulders, while at the same time he had no real authority.

This work Ibsen did very conscientiously. He selected plays and, if they were approved by the board, he prepared for their production. In a volume about ten by fourteen inches, he drew a picture of each scene of the play to be produced. Where Holberg, Scribe, Labiche, or whoever the author might be, had indicated merely "a public place," "a garden," or "a living room" Ibsen drew with pen and water colors each piece of furniture, each tree, each lamp-post, and also each bit of scenery. With dotted lines he sketched the course each actor was to take between his entry and exit. Following this he arranged five columns. In the first one he wrote the number of the act and the scene; in the second, remarks on the scenery; in the third, positions, e.g. "Don Joseph notices the King and takes up position D," or "the King stands between first and second drop," and also the cues for all entries; in the fourth, all necessary properties together with the characters requiring them, as "a letter (Victor)" or

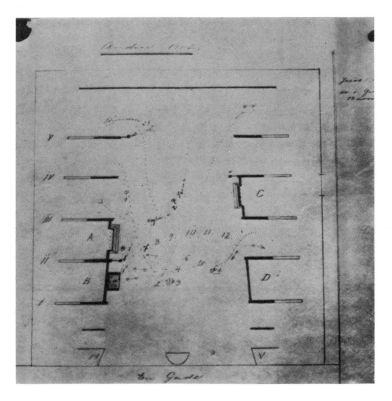

A STREET SCENE FROM AN OBSCURE FARCE

Showing the care Ibsen took in outlining all the plays in his "Regiebog." *A*. House, street-door, and stairs. Window in second story. *B*. House and window in second story. *a*. Kitchen door. *C*. House with door and stairs. Window in second story. *D*. House with windows in both stories. *b, c,* and *d*. Lanterns.

"a corkpuller (Jadom)"; and in the last column remarks such
as "music is heard" or "they clink their glasses."

In this manner Ibsen worked through 145 plays of Holberg, Hertz, Heiberg, Falsen, Hoedt, Hauch, Bogh—all im-
ported from Copenhagen—a few by Shakespeare; more than
half the list were light plays from the French, among them
twenty-one by Scribe. Furthermore Ibsen assigned the rôles,
superintended the rehearsals, and all in all gained thereby a
practical experience of the theater probably equal to that
possessed by Shakespeare or Molière.

In addition to this work his contract called for the writing
of one play annually to be performed on the anniversary of
the founding of the theater. Full of thoughts of his high
mission and great responsibility as a poet of the newly independent Norwegian people, Ibsen went on his way wrapped
in deep thought. To his fellow citizens he appeared as an
extremely modest, silent, unimpressive young man of retiring and timid nature. He was known to have a fluent poetic
vein and he was therefore frequently asked to contribute
poems for weddings or similar festive occasions, but no one
could suspect that behind that pale, scowling face with the
tightly compressed lips there was a brain that occupied itself
with the deepest problems of the human soul and struggled
hard to find the masterful form for their expression.

He went his own way and the people of Bergen practically
forgot about his existence. Yet there was one young girl of
sixteen who found herself fascinated by the enigmatic poet.
One morning as Ibsen sat on the porch of Hotel Sontum
smoking his pipe and drinking his coffee, Henrikke Holst
with flushed face, dark eyes and bright, musical laughter
came running up, tossed him a bouquet of flowers, which all
Bergen people love so much, and asked, "Haven't you any
two-shilling-cake for me, Ibsen?"

"Sit down and try some, you sweet-tooth!" replied Ibsen, filled with the spirit of the sunny day so rare in Bergen and charmed by the informality of this child of nature. She was a different being from Clara Ebbell, that blue-stocking who had after all her romantic dreams finally married her old uncle, thereby spoiling Ibsen's taste for poetry-quoting maidens! And after Henrikke—or Rikke for short—had consumed her fill of sweets, the two went off for a walk up toward one of the seven hills, "Ulrikken," its pine-covered slopes shimmering in brownish grey tints in the sunlight.

Ibsen's poet's heart beat fast in the company of this simple child. In her youth and energy she was to him an incarnation of the figures from the medieval national ballads that at the time filled his mind. She possessed all the naïveté and love of the good things of life that had drawn Goethe to Christiane Vulpius. Like the poet of Weimar he compared her to a plant; Rikke was a wild flower natural and glowing in health, a charming contrast to the tame, formally-tended, hot-house plants so highly valued by "people of taste!" He spoke to her eagerly of his poetic dreams and of his views concerning some of their fellow-citizens; to his sarcastic witticisms she responded with merry laughter, and she did not spoil his poetic flights by forced, painful attempts to follow his Pegasus. Instead she turned her gleaming brown eyes up toward her black-bearded poet in his faultless clothes, which were even adorned with lace cuffs!

After the first walk there followed a glorious picnic in the company of a number of visiting musicians who made the wooded slopes of the Bergen hills echo with their trumpets after they had reached the summit of "Ulrikken." Then Ibsen entertained Rikke, together with his landlady and a few other friends, with a cup of chocolate in his room. Other walks took them out to Nordnes, a wooded peninsula projecting into the fjord. Here they enjoyed the view on distant

islands, on boats floating in the bay, their sails cutting grace-
ful triangles against the horizon, and above all, the seclusion
prized by lovers. Yet all the world might have looked on,
for Ibsen behaved with model chivalry; he always addressed
her with the formal "De" and her exuberant jollity could not
induce him even to hold her hand.

There was but one cloud in this sunny sky and that was
the attitude of the girl's father. Ibsen had asked Rikke to
accept his proposal of marriage, at first through somewhat
veiled poems and then directly, but she had begged him to
wait. She had in mind her father's violent objections to the
poverty-stricken poet and starveling comedian. One day,
just as Rikke had told her lover of her father's terrible threats
of what he was going to do if he ever caught the two together
again, they heard behind them, as it were, "ancestral voices
prophesying war"! On turning around they saw Rikke's
father, his fist raised in an eloquent gesture, and voicing
sentiments anything but fatherly-in-law.

Ibsen ran for dear life, leaving Rikke to meet the irate
parent. The result of this encounter was that she was keenly
disappointed in her lover, and soon afterward married Herr
Tresselt, a solid and respectable merchant of Bergen. Thus
ended the dream of a Bergen summer!

But for Ibsen it meant a great deal. For the first time in
his life he had met a natural, normal, charming young girl,
and he put all that he had found in Rikke into Eline in *Lady
Inger of Oestraat*. As for Lady Inger, the heroine who exclaims, "But woe to whoso is charged with a mighty task!"
she was to a large extent Ibsen himself. Just as she felt
called by God to free Norway from the Danish rule, so Ibsen
felt upon his shoulders the mission of freeing his nation from
the dominance of the Danes in cultural matters, the theater
in particular. And he felt grave doubts as to whether he was

acquitting himself as a dramatic poet any better than he
had as a hero before Herr Holst.

His *St. John's Night* had been performed early in 1853.
In the *Midsummer Night's Dream* atmosphere of this play
a magic potion had given to "poetic" people the power to see
the Mountain King with his gnomes and sprites; with characteristic satire Ibsen had presented a long-haired romantic
poet who was, however, so prosaic that he saw nothing
extraordinary. This mockery of affectation was probably
understood by the spectators as making fun of the romanticism and nationalism that were the slogans of the hour and
the piece was hissed and hooted. Bitter disappointment, so
different from the enthusiasm he had felt in Dresden, made it
impossible for him to write a new piece in the course of the
year; but, as his contract called for one play annually, he
staged in 1854 his *Warrior's Barrow*, already performed in
Christiania in 1850. The result was still worse. The Bergen
papers were silent and did not even cast a bouquet on the
play's grave as they had done in the previous year, when
they said of *St. John's Night*, "The play is a failure, but there
are a few beautiful details."

Henrikke Holst had given Ibsen some inspiration, but none
too much self-confidence. Therefore it was with fear and
trembling that he carried his *Lady Inger of Oestraat* to the
home of Herr Peter Blytt, a member of the board of
trustees, on a September evening in 1854. He drank a bottle
of wine with his host, but showed by his silence and nervous-
ness that there was something oppressing him.

He arose to take his leave, but just before going he said,
"Herr Blytt, in spite of all my best efforts I have been unable
to write a play for the anniversary day this year. The two
failures have been too crushing. I have been in despair what
to do, for here it is September and I have no drama to show,
although it is part of my contract that I furnish one annually.

Now just this morning I received from a friend in Christiania the manuscript of a play. I'd like to leave the book here for you to read and to decide whether this new play might be substituted for one of mine. The author, by the way, wishes to remain anonymous."

"Well, Herr Ibsen," said the merchant, "do *you* think this play worth staging? What is your opinion?"

Ibsen averted his face, and then answered hesitantly, "I don't know, but of course I have shown by my two failures how little I know of what is effective on the stage. Then too, I'm a friend of the author. I should rather leave the matter entirely in your hands, but I will say that it would be a great relief to me if this play could be accepted."

"There is nothing to worry about, Herr Studiosus," said the merchant in his reassuring manner. "No one is going to prescribe to you the day and hour for you to deliver so and so many pounds of poetry. Just let the muse inspire you at your own sweet time. But as regards this manuscript I shall be glad to read it."

Ibsen drew his well-worn overcoat about his shoulders and went out into the night. Herr Blytt sat down by the fire and read the play to the end that very night. He became quite enthusiastic over it, because it seemed to him precisely the thing they had wished to get for their theater, and it was easy for him to persuade his colleagues on the board that this play from Norwegian history by a Norwegian author ought to be staged on the anniversary day. The rehearsals were begun, but the actors were told that this year no new play by the stage-manager would be given.

Christmas was already past and the last rehearsals of the play intended for January second were being held. In the half-dark and icy cold theater—they had to be saving and could heat the hall only at the performances—there was present but one spectator, Herr Peter Blytt. Ibsen had "ar-

ranged" the piece as usual, but had given very few directions
as to how the lines were to be spoken. The actors knew very
well how extremely difficult it was for the shy manager to
address a word of correction to an actor and especially to
an actress! As usual he was slinking about in his gray
overcoat, avoiding whenever possible a direct meeting with
anyone behind the scenes, to all appearances lost to the reality about him.

Suddenly the actors were petrified at seeing Ibsen rush on
the stage, snatch the manuscript from the prompter, and,
turning to the actor Prom who was playing Nils Lykke, ex-
claim, "This is the way you ought to say it!" And then in
a weak voice, but one trembling with emotion, Ibsen read the
passage Prom had been rendering in beautiful but formal
declamation:

As you have dwelt here at Oestraat, alone with your changeful
thoughts, how often have you felt your bosom stifling; how often
have the roof and walls seemed to shrink together till they crushed
your very soul. Then have your longings taken wing with you,
then have you yearned to fly far from here, you knew not whither.—
How often have you not wandered alone by the fjord; far out a
ship has sailed in fair array, with knights and ladies on her deck,
with song and music of stringed instruments;—a faint, far-off
rumor of great events has reached your ears;—and you have felt
a longing in your breast, an unconquerable longing to know all that
lies beyond the sea.

They all stared at him. Could this be Herr Student Ibsen?

Then Ibsen realized that all eyes were fastened on him, and
that an almost audible silence followed his eloquent speech.
He was himself again immediately and shrank together as
though he felt ashamed for having shown so much emotion in
public.

He quickly returned the book to the prompter, and, without looking at the actor, he said, "Yes, Herr Prom, you under-

stand, something like that, you know. In this way the *replique* will perhaps be a little more effective. But—of course—if you think differently, then—to be sure, you are the one who is to act it—yes." And he disappeared into the wings.

Suddenly Ibsen felt an arm in his; Herr Peter Blytt was quietly leading him upstairs to the bar of the theater. He had observed that while "reading" the lines Ibsen had not so much as glanced at the book.

"I had my suspicions in the first place concerning the anonymous friend in Christiania," he said, filling two glasses from a bottle of "the best." "Let us clink to the author of *Lady Inger of Oestraat*—Henrik Ibsen!"

On the night of the performance there were enthusiastic calls for the author and Henrik Ibsen bowed to the applauding auditorium.

Yet the play did not seem to grip the people and there was little call for a repetition of the performance. For a long time, too, Ibsen looked in vain for a criticism of his work. At last in an anonymous article in *Bergensposten* of July 12, 1855, he saw a review that began with the excuse "better late than never." Neither the heroine nor her fate could possibly grip the spectator, it went on to say, and considered, mildly speaking, the choice rather unfortunate.

We look upon it as highly meritorious in a dramatic author to produce from our history half or entirely forgotten memories of a time that is past, and place them before the people in such a light that they can derive therefrom inspiration; but if he can only raise pillars of shame, then let them rest, the pale shadows. They do not harm us when they are forgotten, but they harm us when they are recalled. . . . We have proceeded from the point of view that the author owes us gratitude even when we find fault. . . ."

Ibsen's road to fame as an author was an extremely laborious one, so unlike the triumphant rise of the younger Björnson. A few years after *Lady Inger* their respective positions

were such that Björnson could write to the Danish critic
Clemens Petersen on March 5, 1859: "As soon as Ibsen
recognizes that he is a minor writer (literally that he is
small), he will at once become a charming poet."

4

THE NORSE THEATER
January 2, 1856
(The Theater's Anniversary Day)
The Feast at Solhoug
Play in three acts by
HENRIK IBSEN
Music by Herr Schediwy
Performance begins at 4.30 o'clock and ends at 6.30

The above advertisement in *Bergens Adressecontoirs
Efterretninger* of January 1, 1856, announced Ibsen's first
popular success. The play was written in the current romantic fashion with the minstrel of medieval times, with
songs in the manner of the recently revived ballads, with
castles, knights, fair ladies, honor, poison, and passion, with
vice punished and virtue rewarded in the end, as the hero
marries the good sister and the wicked one retires to a nun-
nery. The charm of poetry, music, and romance combined
to give the people of Bergen an entertainment full of the
mood of medieval glory.

The play was received with great enthusiasm, the author
was called out repeatedly, and after the performance the
orchestra and a large part of the audience serenaded Ibsen,
while he answered with a speech from his window. He went
to sleep amidst dreams of greater works in the future and
he felt extremely happy. Here was balm in Gilead—support for Ibsen's hopes and refutation of his gnawing doubts
concerning his mission as a dramatist.

The play was performed six times during the course of
the winter and spring.   The people of Bergen applauded the
beautiful lyrics and the romantic mood; however, some of the
most characteristic notes of Ibsen passed without notice, for
example, the individualism and social anarchism of Margit,
married to a wealthy but worthless man.   She says to the
minstrel, with whom she had been secretly in love seven
years before:

<blockquote>

Teach me, I pray
How to interpret the ancient lay
They sing of the church in the valley there:
A gentle knight and a lady fair,
They loved each other well.
That very day on her bier she lay;
He on his sword-point fell.
They buried her by the northward spire,
And him by the south kirk wall;
And theretofore grew nor bush nor briar
In the hallowed ground at all.
But next spring from their coffins twain
Two lilies fair upgrew—
And by and by, o'er the roof-tree high
They twined and they bloomed the whole year through.

How read you the riddle?

(The minstrel looks searchingly at her)

I scarce can say.

(Margit)

You may doubtless read it in many a way;
But its truest meaning, methinks, is clear;
The church cannot sever two that hold each other dear.
</blockquote>

It was a royal year for Ibsen when he tasted for the first
time the sweetness of enthusiastic applause and a royal year

for Bergen, because the city enjoyed two visits from royalty
during the summer.   First came the Swedish-Norwegian
crown prince, who later became King Charles XV.   On July
22, 1856, the Norse Theater gave an entertainment in his
honor consisting of a vocal selection, a greeting composed by
Henrik Ibsen and spoken by the actress Madame Brunn, an
orchestral number, and a vaudeville in one act.   Next was
announced the visit of Prince Napoleon, son of King Jerome
and cousin of Napoleon III, but week after week passed with
no sign of him.   Suddenly at noon on Saturday, August 23,
there came a thundering salute from the harbor announcing
the arrival of Napoleon on the warship "La Reine Hortense."

Herr Peter Blytt tells in his memoirs the droll story of how
Ibsen acceded to Napoleon's wish for a theatrical performance.   The request came as a complete surprise to the
trustees, late on a Saturday evening.   They called Ibsen out
of bed to make the plans for the performance on Sunday, but
he protested that it was too late to arrange it, since the actors
were out of town on their vacation, the orchestra had been
engaged for a boat excursion, and the theater cateress also
had left the city.   Herr Blytt then suggested that it was too
bad for Ibsen's sake since the committee had been planning
to present *The Feast at Solhoug*.   This put an entirely different aspect on the matter for Ibsen; he sent for the actors and
held a rehearsal on Sunday morning; he persuaded the orchestra to play for the performance, while the ladies of Bergen consented to serve a supper in the theater buffet.   Between acts Ibsen was introduced to Napoleon and presented
him with a leatherbound manuscript copy of the play, which
the prince promised to have translated for the theater at St.
Cloud.   In the account which the Frenchmen wrote of their
journey this performance in Bergen was spoken of with great
admiration.   Another thing they set down in their record was
that in Bergen, where a highly Puritanical atmosphere ob-

tained, the annual prize awarded to an actress was given on
the basis both of declamation in the theater and of exemplary
conduct in private life!

To the triumph of the performance before Napoleon was
added the fact, very gratifying to Ibsen, that in the capital
The Feast at Solhoug was acted six times in 1856, the play
being especially honored by being selected for performance
on May 17, the national holiday. Björnson by means of three
enthusiastic articles in the *Christiania Morgenblad* contributed not a little to the popularity of the piece.

But then came the crash. The Danish critics and those
with Danish sympathies in Christiania pounced on Ibsen like
a pack of wolves. They accused him of plagiarism and in
general acted as though a young author who dared to write a
play was a villain and a scoundrel. It was a scathing attack
that embittered Ibsen, turning all the pleasure in his first
success into gall and wormwood. There was no discussion of
the merits of the play at all—they all condemned it on the
ground that it was a villainous imitation of Henrik Hertz'
Svend Dyrings House.

Björnson, the dear, blundering fellow, of course meant
very well. Still what he wrote did not altogether please
Ibsen: "In the author of *The Feast at Solhoug* we have before
us not a dramatist; a purely lyric poet comes on the stage and
charms us with his songs. He has no other purpose. . . .
Who then would ask about character development or action?"

This, after Ibsen in the last eight years had written six
plays, and outside of his dramatic work had done practically
nothing!

5

In *Lady Inger of Oestraat* Ibsen wrote the words: "A
woman is the mightiest power in the world, and in her hand it
lies to guide a man whither God Almighty would have him

go." Such was his high ideal of woman when at the age of twenty-eight Ibsen found his life companion in the daughter of Dean Thoresen of the Cross Church in Bergen. And their long life together during which Ibsen slowly climbed to the heights of fame proved that his view of woman's power was quite justified.

He came into the hospitable home through the pastor's wife, who later was to become the well-known novelist Magdalene Thoresen. She was writing plays at the time—anonymously—and Ibsen staged one of them, *Mr. Money*, in the Bergen Theater. She was a very striking, stately woman, with dark hair, dark eyes, and beautiful olive complexion, at the time thirty-seven years old and the mother of four children. In her movements there was something extremely vivacious that made her appear almost Italian.

She was the daughter of a Danish fisherman, and before her marriage had been the governess of the widowed pastor's children. Magdalene Thoresen seemed to stand in a peculiar relation to the sea and all that belonged to it. That is to say, the open sea; she was in the habit of saying that the water in the fjords was sickly. Every day from early spring till late fall she swam far out into the sea; she was absolutely fearless. Her daughter, Susannah, who adored Mrs. Thoresen though the latter was really her step-mother, said to her one day: "Mother, do not swim so far out into the sea; I'm afraid some day we'll find you washed ashore like a dead mermaid!"

Her husband treated her with great love and consideration, wishing her to develop her literary talent, of which he was very proud. For this reason he encouraged her to visit Copenhagen, the literary center of Scandinavia. She was worshipped in the same way by her two step-daughters, though she took but little notice of this remarkably contrasting pair of sisters. Marie was always gentle, mild, and even willing to be imposed upon; Susannah on the other hand had a very decided and definite character. No one could take advantage of her if she did not wish it. This difference was particularly noticeable when as young children they played at theatricals. Marie, the gentle and womanly soul, always impersonated the victims; Susannah, manly, proud, and aristocratic in her bearing, liked to play masculine rôles. One day they were playing *The Robbers*, a home-made continuation of Schiller's drama, and in the course of a battle real blood flowed. Their father heard terrible shrieks and came running to the nursery. Here he found some of the boys in tears, but he heard Susannah—who also was wounded—say, "Since I have been worthy of wearing a beard, I shall not cry!" She bit her teeth together, took off her cotton beard and pasteboard armor, and did not shed a single tear!

When Ibsen, on January 7, 1856, for the first time came to the Thoresen home, he found that Susannah possessed a great familiarity with Norse sagas in which at the time he too was particularly interested. She had seen both his *Lady Inger* and *The Feast at Solhoug;* the former tragedy, which Ibsen considered his best work and in which he took real pride, this girl of independent judgment appreciated much more than the romantic *Feast at Solhoug,* whose happy ending everybody was praising. In the cool gray eyes of this young lady Ibsen saw more than mere youthful charm, and following a momentary impulse he said to her: "Now you are Eline, but soon you will be Lady Inger."

She continued to appear to Ibsen as the spiritual kinswoman of the strong and noble Lady Inger; such were the words he inscribed for her twenty years later in a copy of the German edition of the play which he gave her as a Christmas gift in 1876:

> Til denne bog har Du ejendomsretten,
> Du, som andeligt stammer fra Ostrat-aetten.

A few weeks after his first meeting with the young lady there was a ball at the Bergen Philharmonic Society, and Ibsen went there knowing he would meet Susannah Thoresen. To him she stood out among all the light-hearted, frivolous, empty galaxy of Bergen beauties. In her eyes he read a deeper meaning; she was for him "the only one."

That very night he wrote her a poetic proposal:

> Ah yes; there is one, one only,
> Among so many but one.
> Her eyes have a secret sadness,
> I read in them sorrow begun—
> I read in them dreaming fancies
> That rise and sink without cease—
> A heart that longs and throbs upward,
> And finds in this world no peace.
>
> Dared I but rede thee, thou riddle
> Of youth and deep dreamings wrought,
> Dared I but choose thee boldly
> To be the bride of my thought;
> Dared I but plunge my spirit
> Deep in thy spirit's tide,
> Dared I but gaze on the visions
> In thy innocent soul that hide;
>
> Ah, then what fair songs upspringing
> Should soar from my breast on high;
> Ah, how free then I'd go sailing
> Like a bird toward the coasts of the sky!
> Ah, then should my scattered visions
> To one single harmony throng;
> For all of life's fairest visions
> Would mirror themselves in my song.
>
> Dared I but rede thee, thou riddle
> Of youth and deep dreamings wrought;
> Dared I but choose thee boldly
> To be the bride of my thought.

.   .   .   .

Of course, Ibsen had to call personally to receive his answer, and came dressed in his finest and most formal clothes. At the parsonage he was shown into a room where he was to await Susannah. But no Susannah came. Ibsen walked up and down in the room, sat down, and rose again in a state of feverish excitement, absolutely at a loss what to do. At last, in a despondent mood, he was about to make for the door, when he suddenly heard a merry peal of girlish laughter, and from under the sofa peered a curly head! Then Ibsen received his answer!

Shortly afterward their engagement was celebrated in the family circle "without any violent display of emotion" as Fru Thoresen wrote to a friend. And with Susannah Thoresen as confidante Ibsen began to work seriously on the tragedy, *The Vikings at Helgeland.*

In a description of Ibsen dating from this very time Magdalene Thoresen says: "Ibsen is a remarkably reserved man with whom no one is going to take any liberties. He never tells anything about himself and keeps all curious and familiar persons 'drei Schritt vom Leibe.' Even in vivid conversation he stands on guard over his own personality, lest he betray his real feelings. His clear, firm glance, however, shows that he is a man who knows his goal and is going to get there. Still it is a bit hard not to smile once in a while at a man who takes himself so seriously."

V

THE FIGHT FOR A NATIONAL NORWEGIAN DRAMA

1

Encouraged by the success of Ole Bull's "Norwegian" Theater in Bergen, the enthusiasts for national poetry in Christiania also had founded a "Norwegian" playhouse in competition with the "Christiania Theater" which was then still under Danish influence. Its fortunes were at times quite encouraging, at times it faced crises that threatened total ruin. Such a crisis occurred in 1857, and the trustees debated as to whether they had best give up their idealistic enterprise or whether they should reorganize for a renewed, more vigorous effort. The latter policy prevailed; and it was decided that the best guarantee of favorable results would be to secure as stage-manager the poet Henrik Ibsen, who had done such successful work with the stage in Bergen. Accordingly the trustees offered him twice the salary he was getting in Bergen; he was to receive $7\frac{1}{2}$ percent of the theater's net income, with a guarantee of at least 600 specie dollars annually. Ibsen, having finished the five years stipulated in his contract, eagerly accepted this offer which would bring him to the national capital.

From his twenty-fourth into his thirtieth year Ibsen had been director of a popular playhouse in Bergen, presenting each year one of his own plays and directing the production of scores of works by other authors. One would think that the departure of a man in such a position would create quite a stir, but there was no trace of a torch-light procession, a banquet, nor even of an article in the newspaper! Not one syllable did the press devote to Ibsen when he left Bergen.

He had entered the city quite unnoticed; he had lived almost exclusively to himself; and now his departure did not cause a ripple.

In the summer of 1857 he quietly boarded a steamer for Christiania, where he finished *The Vikings at Helgeland*. How different, how much more vigorous and how infinitely better constructed was this drama written after years of association with the theater, from *The Warrior's Barrow*, the play he had staged in Christiania at the time of his former sojourn there! And also how different the womanly ideal that now filled his thoughts from the "Stella" of Grimstad for whom he sighed in 1851! There was nothing of the simpering parlor-poetess about Susannah, his fiancée. When in his mind's eye he saw her and used her as a model for his heroine Hjoerdis, he pictured his future life-partner as one of the Valkyries, who says to her hero:

I will follow thee and fire thee to strife and manly deeds, so that thy name shall be heard over every land. In the sword-game will I stand by thy side; I will fare forth among thy warriors in the storm and on the viking-raid; and when thy death-song is sung it shall tell of Sigurd and Hjoerdis in one!

Instead of his having to plead for an understanding of his ideals, as he had done with Clara Ebbell, his model for Hjoerdis, he felt, was heart and soul with him in deep understanding of his life's purpose:

It is the Norn's will that we two shall hold together; it cannot be altered. Plainly now do I see my task in life; to make thee famous over all the world.

While his heroic Susannah was there with him in spirit, his work progressed rapidly, and in September he offered the play to the Christiania Theater, because he believed that the larger playhouse was better equipped than the somewhat primitive Norwegian Theater for the staging of this ambitious play. For now he was free to do with his plays as he wished, and could draw royalties upon them; it was not part of his contract that he furnish them to the theater free as had been the case in Bergen, where he did not receive one penny for the five plays he wrote and staged during his managership. The director of the Christiania Theater, a Dane by the name of Borgaard, accepted the play and promised to stage it in the course of the season. At about the same time Ibsen entered upon his own duties as stage-manager of the Norwegian Theater, confident that now at last he was approaching the recognition that was his due.

But he had to meet, as usual, the disappointments of a man who is years ahead of his generation. There was considerable prejudice against the "New Norwegian" art at the Christiania Theater where the director and most of the actors were Danes, and consequently nothing was done about Ibsen's play. When he called on Herr Borgaard in January, he was told that the play would be staged in March. When March came, the play was returned to him with the excuse that the financial condition of the theater did not permit the payment of royalties for original plays!

Henrik Ibsen boiled with rage! He knew that the theater had made payments to other authors, that they had but recently increased the salaries of the Danish actors, in short, that it was nothing but prejudice against the new national literature on the part of Herr Borgaard. In a scorching article in the *Aftenblad* dated March 9, 1858, Ibsen pointed out that the real reason was not a financial one; they might well have asked him to wait a bit for the payment of his royalties, only they were afraid that he might accept the condition! Of the artistic director he said:

Either he agrees with his trustees that original plays must be eschewed in the Christiania Theater, in which case he stands condemned by his own words. Or he does not agree with them—and in this case what does he intend to do? I don't know. But this much I know, a man of honor would have resigned.

This answer to the gratuitous insult offered the young nationalist poets, was the beginning of a hot controversy between Ibsen and Björnson with their followers on the one hand, and the adherents of Danish influence in the theater on the other. It required years to do it, but finally the enthusiastic young men succeeded in carrying the day, and Herr Borgaard was forced to resign in 1863, while *The Vikings at Helgeland* became one of the ornaments of the Christiania theater.

The season at the Norwegian Theater had been a fairly successful one, and in June Ibsen felt that he might now bring his bride from Bergen. When he reached the city, however, it was quite like Ibsen's usual somber fate that he should enter a house of mourning. At the very time of his arrival there appeared in the *Bergens Adressecontoirs Efterretninger* the following:

DEATH NOTICE

It is my hard fate to announce to my near and dear friends and acquaintances that my noble husband, Hans Conrad Thoresen, Parish Priest in Holy Cross Church, at the age of 56, has gone to his rest in God, leaving behind him 9 children and a beloved memory among the congregation whose shepherd he was for 14 years under heavy bodily suffering.

Bergen, June 14, 1858.

ANNA MAGDALENA THORESEN, NEE KRAGH.

Owing to the death of the bride's father, the marriage of Henrik Ibsen, age 30, to Susannah Thoresen, age 22, was solemnized very quietly on June 18, 1858.

When the steamer touched at Grimstad on the journey to Christiania the newly married couple were met by Ibsen's old friend Christopher Due. The latter noticed with a sly satisfaction that Ibsen did not address his wife with the formal "De" and that the two did not occupy separate apartments!

2

The long rivalry between Ibsen and Björnson began with friendship. They had both been pupils in Old Heltberg's school, and when after 1851 they were separated by the entire breadth of Norway, their friendship deepened through their pursuit of the common ideal of national Norwegian poetry. Björnson in Christiania wrote in enthusiastic support of *The Feast at Solhoug* and later from Bergen he defended *The Vikings*. Returned to Christiania in 1859, he and Ibsen founded the "Norwegian Society" to combat the Danish influence in the Christiania Theater—the boot-licking attitude among "society" in Norway that would cause a gentleman to thank a Danish lady for visiting his country and for affording him an opportunity of hearing a civilized language spoken! Björnson was elected president and Ibsen vice-president of the society for furthering the Norwegian language, drama and native culture in general. Ibsen spent the rest of his life living down this one lapse into society-founding!

When on December 23, 1859, a son was born to the Ibsens, Björnson, as a close friend of the family, became his godfather. The boy was christened Sigurd after the nobly impetuous hero of the drama written during the engagement of Henrik and Susannah Ibsen. And when less successful days came to the Norwegian Theater and Ibsen received only a fraction of the stipulated salary Björnson made every effort to borrow or beg money for his friends when the wolf was at their door. For hard days did descend on Ibsen, so that the debts with which he had come to Christiania from Bergen steadily increased as the affairs of the Norwegian Theater went from bad to worse and the expenses for his family mounted.

But in Susannah Ibsen the poet found a firm supporter. Throughout all the hardships not one complaint escaped her lips, and she bore her difficult position with dignity. The Hjoerdis of Ibsen's drama was determined to lead her hero to the greatest heights. It was due to her influence that he gave up dilettante painting and concentrated on the drama. She permitted him to go his own way, because she wished to do everything in her power to allow him to realize the genius that she believed he held in his soul. Like Hjoerdis too, she had an almost violent antipathy to all petty considerations; she did not have the well-meaning altruism which Sigurd in *The Vikings* showed for his friend Gunnar by yielding to him the woman he loved. She was one with her husband in the knowledge that alas! too often, the people who mean well are the real causes of catastrophes. She discussed her husband's works with him, displaying a real poetic insight, but also an uncompromising frankness where she felt that he was not at his best. Like the Valkyrie she was hard; and her harshness led to many sharp discussions in the earlier years of their married life. For both of them much bitterness lay in the coming years before the heights were scaled—especially in the Christiania years.

In one other circle beside his home Ibsen found an escape from the black despair in which the unrecognized genius often was thrust by the pettiness of his surroundings. This was in the rooms of his old friend Paul Botten-Hansen, one of the three editors of the *Andhrimmer* of a decade before. Since 1851 he had started an illustrated weekly of his own which was quite successful, and in which he had printed a number of Ibsen's works. He was a connoisseur and collector of Norse and Danish literature. His two large rooms on the third floor of Raadhusgaden 28 were filled to the ceiling with book-shelves in every possible place, even around his bed, so that it looked as though he were sleeping in an alcove. Vinje, the mocking radical, Asbjoernsen, the humorous collector of fairy-tales, at times even Welhaven, the poet,—in fact, all of the finest and most progressive spirits of the new movement in literature, met here almost daily for brilliant discussions of all that was new in various fields. They called themselves "The Hollanders" in allusion to a quotation from the patron saint of the society, Holberg: "Plague take the Hollander, he has his spies out everywhere." Ibsen, because among these friends he was often the center of the witty discussion, received the nickname Gert Westphaler, the talkative barber in a Holberg play. For despite his usual taciturnity Ibsen could talk very eloquently indeed, especially when he was angry or stimulated by alcohol.

There were gay evenings among "The Hollanders." Not least one day when Botten-Hansen perpetrated a joke worthy of a Holberg comedy. His landlord was a green-grocer by the name of Haslund. He feared that the large library accumulated by his roomer might cause the house to sink, and therefore he forbade him to bring in any more books. This made it necessary for Botten-Hansen to hide all his new purchases under his coat as he introduced them, but in the long run this proved to be very inconvenient. Therefore one day he congratulated old Haslund on being a fifty-year-citizen of the capital. The old man, none too certain of his dates, but agreeably surprised by the honor, asked how Botten-Hansen came to know it. The latter then showed him a huge tome as the source of the information. After that the landlord had more respect for books and allowed his roomer to introduce any number of them, in which after all there had never been one word about Herr Haslund!

But one of the younger literary men preferred to avoid "The Hollanders," and this was Björnson. The Heine-like wit bandied back and forth in the meetings chilled his enthusiasm and his confidence in his ability to make the world over. He felt that much of the ironic laughter of these young men was aimed at him, and he would have liked to thrash them when he met them on the street, for he felt they were grinning at his best efforts. He called them a "band of theorists and mockers without any productivity whatever." And of Ibsen he wrote to the Danish critic Clemens Petersen, "In appearance Ibsen is a very short, crazy fellow, without loins or chest; therefore he feels clearly that just because he has no talent for oratory he must slash away so terribly whenever he wants to say anything." One reads between the lines that Björnson knew *he* had loins, chest, and a talent for oratory!

But Ibsen who was scoring a failure and a rebuff for each success and honor garnered by his younger rival, Björnson, was quite in his element in the cynical, critical atmosphere of "The Hollanders," where the current ideals were not held to be sacrosanct. He came regularly and generally as the first one to their meetings at Botten-Hansen's rooms or at the Café L'Orsa where the host reserved a little back room for the group. Here he could talk at times, with his glass of beer before him, savagely, sarcastically, and in startling paradoxes about literature, political events, gruesome criminal cases, or whatever happened to be under discussion. His friends enjoyed his talk, and he was a favorite in the circle; but when it came to his poetic ideals he found very little understanding. Such was the case, for example, when he read them his poem, *On the Heights.*

The only one to understand the first work after his marriage was his wife. It was a symbolical poem picturing Ibsen's soul life under the guise of a hunter who climbs to the heights. He leaves behind him his mother and his beloved with the intention of returning to them soon. Up in the mountains however he meets another hunter, a gruesome uncanny fellow, who teaches him to tear out of his heart the longings for home, maid and mother which at the moment were strengthened by the sound of the Christmas bells ringing through the wintry air. So he learns to live in the heights and loses his softer emotions to such an extent that he can view the burning of his mother's house or the bridal procession of his beloved as an esthetic spectacle, his hands hollowed like field-glasses to procure a better view.

The meaning of the poem is, of course, that the man who wishes to devote himself to art must give up the usual pleasures of life. He must become dead to human emotions and must view life apart, see in it only models for his work. This ideal of single-minded concentration on his one chosen task as a dramatist ripened in Ibsen at the very lowest, most hopeless period of his life. This singleness of purpose finally after many years enabled him to outstrip his rival Björnson—but only after long and determined struggles. He gave up painting, and it was probably at this period, as Georg Brandes put it, that in the battle of life a lyrical Pegasus was shot down under Ibsen. Perhaps the mother and the beloved symbolized these two art forms which Ibsen abandoned to become a master in his one field.

But meanwhile reality was very sad. The otherwise ever conscientious, hard-working Ibsen now neglected his work as stage-manager of the Norwegian Theater; the only way in which the trustees could get him to come to a meeting was by holding this meeting in the café where Ibsen would regularly sit for hours every day staring savagely at the other guests. One day a trustee, the high school teacher Knudsen, scolded Ibsen publicly "like a schoolboy"; but the latter replied not a word. From *The Vikings* in 1857 he published no drama until *Love's Comedy* in 1862; the toil in the theater, even though he slighted it, and the continual call on him for occasional poems, were equivalent to a daily fœticide of what should have been his real poetic creations. He read in the paper, "Herr Ibsen as a dramatic author is a complete nonentity." When *Love's Comedy* was reviewed by the influential Danish critic Clemens Petersen in a Copenhagen paper in anything but favorable terms, Ibsen humbly thanked him: "I have a deep personal feeling that you have done me a good service by not putting my book aside in silence." Björnson and Vinje had received government stipends for travel, as Welhaven and Munch had in previous years, and had gone abroad in 1860, while a member of the ministry said in regard to Ibsen's application, "The author of *Love's Comedy* ought to receive a sound thrashing rather than a stipend." The theater that employed him went into bankruptcy, and Ibsen had to swallow his pride in accepting charitable financial aid from friends. These friends were even thinking seriously of securing for him a subordinate position in the custom-house, where he might have rotted away spiritually while for long hours each day he weighed bags of sugar and coffee! He who was so fastidious in his dress was now compelled by poverty to go about in shabby clothes. People generally spoke of him as a conceited, misdirected genius gone to seed. And at times students returning to their rooms late at night saw a black-bearded man lying drunk in the gutter; it was Henrik Ibsen.

Like Lieutenant Alving Ibsen was a victim of that "half-grown town which had no joys to offer—only dissipations."

3

But Henrik Ibsen had the strength to rise even out of the deepest slough of despond. At the very time when all seemed most tragic he published *Love's Comedy*, perhaps the wittiest and drollest work Ibsen ever penned. He showed

grimly that he himself was not going to be deflécted from his
mission, for he made the special target of his wit Lind, an
idealist who allows himself to be persuaded by a number of
elderly ladies to renounce his plan of becoming a missionary;
he gives up "this warfare for the faith," his "most cherished
dream," at the very moment when others have persuaded his
fiancée on her part to make the sacrifice of going with him
to Africa!   So much for people who turn back after they
have set out on a certain course, but as for the hero of the
play and Ibsen, they defy opposition and shout lustily:

> And what if I shattered my roaming bark,
> It was passing sweet to be roaming!

The play was not accepted by the Christiania Theater and
was published only through the kindness of one of Ibsen's
friends, Jonas Lie, then editor of a paper in Christiania in
which he printed the play.   Ibsen found that the reviews were
very unfavorable; for example, the same professor Monrad
who had a dozen years before written so kindly about *Catiline* called the play "senseless, immoral, and unpoetic."   The
startling paradox that the first condition of a happy marriage
is the absence of love and the first condition of an enduring
love is avoidance of marriage, was called a sentiment to be
expected of a "philistine uncle or aunt, but one that would
never occur to a poet."   They missed entirely the ethical seriousness of the struggle in the hero's heart between his art and
his happiness—met without any thought of compromise.
From the fact that the current conception of love and marriage was pitilessly ridiculed in this play, gossips arrived
at certain conclusions in regard to Ibsen's own marriage, and
many unpleasant things were whispered.   Because Ibsen
dared to make sport of a clergyman with twelve children and
hope for more in the near future, he made many enemies

among "right-thinking" people. In general, the play did anything but raise the already dubious repute of the poet. But Susannah Ibsen, the model for Svanhild in this play, a young woman with a mind of her own, and a willingness to sacrifice for the sake of her lover's career, was the only one to approve of *Love's Comedy*. This shows how truly this union was a real marriage, and how profoundly mistaken were the gossips who looked for the cause of Ibsen's satire in his own disappointment in marriage.

But even though Ibsen aimed many keen shafts at cherished institutions in contemporary Norway, still the play did not arouse so much of a storm as he had hoped for; it harmed his chances for winning a stipend, but after all, it was read by comparatively few. One day he was sitting in the Café L'Orsa with two "Hollanders," when one of them, Carl Lie, who had a passion for telling people home-truths in such a manner that they hurt most keenly, said, "Say, Ibsen, you probably wished that your comedy would cause a great uproar, but it doesn't look as though anyone would bother about it at all—not a soul is breathing a word about it—that must be most exasperating." Ibsen did not answer a word, became pale as a corpse, beat with his fist on the table till it rattled, arose from his seat and left the café.

In the narrow confines of Christiania Ibsen felt himself attacked by misunderstanding and jealousy from all sides. Nor was this a figment of his imagination, for it was just the way in which he was seen by other people, among them the cartoonist of the humorous weekly *Vikingen*. In the number for March 7, 1863, Ibsen found himself pictured as a very sad-eyed, long-haired, long-bearded man in evening clothes in his characteristic attitude, with his hands behind his back, while arrows pierce him from all sides. Two copies of Botten-Hansen's *Illustreret Nyhedsblad* flutter at his sides,

but they afford very ineffectual protection. The caricature is
labeled: "Friendship's Comedy," and under it appears a
typical specimen of Christiania criticism:

> Here you see, gentlemen, how Botten-Hansen protects Ibsen from
> attacks directed against him. This touching and beautiful relation-
> ship is reminiscent of that which existed between Hertz and J. L.
> Heiberg. To the latter Botten-Hansen has great similarity, espe-
> cially in his conceit; it would now only be necessary that he achieve
> some likeness to him in good taste and judgment, and then he could
> be called the Norwegian Heiberg. . . .

Little wonder that Ibsen thought of himself as "God's step-
child on earth" especially in contrast to Björnson, who at
this very time had been given by the government an annual
award of 400 dollars to enable him to devote himself exclusively to his poetic endeavors. All that Ibsen had received so
far were two travelling grants in the summers of 1862 and
1863 of 110 and 100 specie-dollars respectively, to collect
folk-songs in the mountain regions to the north. During the
first summer he collected energetically, but the publisher
who had contracted to bring out the book failed in business.
When on Ibsen's plea the stipend was given to him the second
time, his financial situation was so desperate that he took
the money but never made the journey for which it had been
awarded. A letter addressed by him to the King, March 10,
1863, gives in Ibsen's own words an account of his position.
Misery and despair cry out eloquently between the lines of
the matter-of-fact statement. It is a petition for a yearly
salary of 400 dollars from the exchequer to enable him to
continue his literary activity. It reads in part:

> I resigned my appointment at the Bergen Theater in 1857 and at
> once accepted that of "artistic director" of the Norwegian Theater
> here in Christiania, which I held until last summer when the theater
> was given up and its affairs came into the bankruptcy court. Since

January 1st of the present year I have held a temporary appointment as advisor in artistic matters to the Christiania Theater. In 1858 I married a daughter of the late Dean Thoresen of Bergen, and I have one child by this marriage. My salary at the Bergen Theater was only 300 dollars per annum, and I had to leave the town in debt. My appointment at the Norwegian Theater in Christiania brought me in, on the average, 600 dollars per annum, but the failure of that theater meant a loss to me of over 150 dollars and the loss of steady employment. At the Christiania Theater my nominal salary is 25 dollars monthly; but the payment of the full amount is contingent upon the theater's making larger profits than it has done this year. It is an impossibility to live entirely, or even chiefly, on literary work in this country. My best paid work, *The Vikings at Helgeland,* which occupied my whole time for nearly a year, brought me in all 227 dollars. Owing to this condition of things I have contracted debts amounting to nearly 500 dollars and being unable so far to see any prospect of improving my position in this country, I have been obliged to make preparations for emigrating to Denmark this spring.

One small mark of recognition came to Ibsen at this very time. He was invited to be a guest at the fifth great "Festival of Song" held at Bergen in June. This visit to the beautiful "city without plebeians" acted on him, as he afterward wrote in a pitifully cordial letter to his host, "like an inspiring church-service, and I hope and believe that the feeling produced will not be a mere passing one. They were all so good to me in Bergen. It is not so here, where there are many who seek every opportunity to pain and wound me." He met again the trustee of the theater, Peter Blytt, and also the friend of his Grimstad days, Christopher Due. The latter remarked that the once so lively and talkative drug clerk had changed into a silent, uncommunicative personality—the Ibsen later known to fame. Due felt that Life had seared scars into his friend's soul. One day he was sitting with Ibsen and several other acquaintances, when the poet was asked to explain some parts of *Love's Comedy,* copies of which had recently reached Bergen. Ibsen replied, "Read the book again," and when the questioner insisted, the sphinx-like Ibsen said only: "Read the book once more."

In Bergen, too, he met Björnson again, recently signally honored by the Norwegian government as the author of the new national air; Björnson, the mere mention of whose name in a meeting, as Georg Brandes later said, was equivalent to hoisting the flag. He had just returned from a two-year sojourn abroad on a government stipend, full of the "free" atmosphere outside stuffy Christiania. He was a poet, proclaimed as such by everyone and not in the least assailed by doubts as to his own ability, as was poor Ibsen. On the contrary; when at the age of 24 he had visited Sweden with a party of students and had seen the museums, cathedrals, and other ornaments of Sweden's great past, he felt an "historical jealousy" of the country, and determined to make his nation conscious of its great past through works of poetry. He was so full of these plans that when at the time of departure a little girl handed him a laurel wreath he felt this was his consecration as a poet. He placed it on his head with the calm and self-assurance of a Napoleon crowning himself emperor. And on his return to Christiania he wrote in a fortnight his historical play *Between the Battles*, while within the year he had completed a novel and another drama, all of which made him indeed Norway's greatest poet of the day.

Something of this spirit descended on Ibsen, for on his return from the "Festival of Song" he finished in two months a new play, *The Pretenders*. It was a drama which bore most definitely the stamp of Ibsen's own thought and personality, instead of being a play in the spirit of Schiller, Shakespeare, or Scribe, as had been his previous works for the most part. In Haakon he pictured the self-assured, confident claimant to the crown, in Skule the man with gnawing doubts in his heart. Thus to some extent the rivalry between himself and Björnson was symbolized; but Skule is only part of Ibsen. For beside the doubter there was in Ibsen also the man confident that he had a mission to perform and that he would by his dramas set himself a monument *œre perennius*. And as to his suffering, he was strong enough to say with his singer Jatgeir: "The gift of sorrow came to me and I was a skald.—I needed sorrow; others there may be who need faith, or joy—or doubt."

Just as Ibsen was a doubter and a believer at the same time, so he was also a cloud-soaring idealist in addition to being the keenest-visioned critic of his time. In *Love's Comedy* he had lampooned "love" such as it was among philistines; but at the same time he had caused two lovers to part lest their love be sullied by everyday life, as the aroma of the finest China tea is lost through long transport. The critics said, no doubt correctly, that no true lovers had ever parted because they feared their love might not last; but Ibsen cherished the impossible ideal of a perfect love, which for the sake of its perfection had best live only in memory. Likewise in the political field Ibsen had his ideals in which he naïvely believed. As in his Grimstad days he had called on the Scandinavians to unite for the protection of Denmark, so now he really believed that the Norwegians and Swedes would do as they had promised, and help the Danes defend Schleswig-Holstein against the Prussians and Austrians. Therefore he placed his play in the thirteenth century, when the union of Scandinavia was the question of the day, and under the symbolism of the historic scene he portrayed the burning question of the hour. He glowed in his enthusiasm for a patriotic Scandinavian rising but when it seemed that prudent statesmen were going to remain neutral and the students were not going to do what they had pledged with champagne glasses lifted in solemn token of their enthusiasm to sacrifice life and blood in Denmark's cause, it was the bitterest disillusionment of Ibsen's whole life. In writing *The*

Pretenders at a time when the final decision had not yet been made, Ibsen pictured the power for evil in Bishop Nicholas, one of the most striking characters in all literature, a villain "who could send the murd'rous Machiavel to school" in his diabolically conceived plottings to keep alive the disunion in Norway. A phantom monk from hell, "an envoy from the oldest Pretender in the world," says that the spirit of Bishop Nicholas is abroad

> While to their life-work Norsemen set out
> Will-lessly wavering, daunted with doubt,
> While hearts are shrunken, minds helplessly shivering,
> Weak as a willow-wand wind-swept and quivering.

This play, dealing with Norway's heroes of the past, was intended by Ibsen as an inspiration for the Norwegians of his day face to face with a crisis. It was filled with allusions to names and places the mere mention of which makes every Norseman's heart grow bigger. When it appeared in August, 1863, it met with a very favorable reception both by the critics and by the Christiania Theater where it was performed seven times during the season 1863-64. Now at last, it appeared, Ibsen's affairs had very definitely taken a turn for the better. On September 23, 1863, the government awarded Ibsen a stipend of 400 dollars from the funds for enabling scientists and artists to travel abroad, for a journey that would bring him in contact with the fresh currents of thought in the larger nations of Europe.

Because he had, by virtue of the government subsidy, been recognized more or less officially as one of the "skalds" of his nation, Ibsen felt it doubly his duty to arouse the Norwegian people to idealistic thinking. He wished to make them rise above mere business interests—what Ibsen called "Americanism." There was still time for Norway to come to Denmark's aid; so he worked desperately to encourage their helping *The Brother in Peril,* as he called a poem published December 13 in Botten-Hansen's paper.   He scornfully recalled the solemn pledge:

> 'Twas but a lie, then nothing worth
> A Judas kiss of hate,
> That proudly Norway's sons sent forth
> Down by the Sound of late.

These were the thoughts uppermost in his mind while he was making preparation for his departure in the coming spring— an event that he came to look upon as a voluntary exile because of his disgust with his people.

Early in 1864 Paul Botten-Hansen was appointed university librarian, also with a travelling stipend, and therefore "The Hollanders" held several farewell gatherings to honor their departing friends.   On one of these evenings they heard a speech at the Students' Club which was to leave its mark upon Ibsen's next work.   A young theological student by the name of Christopher Brunn was addressing a gathering on the question of Norway's attitude in the Danish-Prussian War.   He had just accompanied his mother, sister, and a sick brother to Rome, and had then returned to enter the Danish army as a volunteer, a private in the infantry. On the eve of his departure for the field of battle he spoke the following words of Norway's oft-repeated promise to come to Denmark's aid:

> If now, where the opportunity for *action* has arrived, we offer only *words,* will not all those triumph who find a cynical pleasure in dragging into the dust ideas and a belief in ideas?   They will always quote this when they wish to brand as folly any devotion to an idea or any willingness to make sacrifices in the service of an idea.   You see, thus a man dies a spiritual death when he says good-bye to his ideal, and the people will lose its faith and sink into moral dissolution. . . . I am not speaking for Scandinavianism,

for me *that* is not the burning question—I speak for *truth;* not for Denmark, but for Norway, for the victory of truth in my fatherland. . . . I call upon every manly student to show to the pettiness and cowardice about us what is meant by grandeur of soul and firmness; above all else should he witness to the fact that idealism, truth, and right are not there for the purpose of furnishing subjects for fine speeches, but they are there for us to live for, to fight for, and—if need be—to die for.

With these words ringing in his ears Ibsen left Norway. His destination was Rome, though he visited several cities in Germany en route. But what a spectacle awaited him in Berlin! The Prussians were celebrating the victory they had meanwhile won over Denmark with a triumphant parade in which 118 captured Danish cannon were exhibited. In their own delightful way some of the patriots expressed their feelings by spitting into the mouths of the cannon. Ibsen writhed and sweated in a Berserker rage as he watched this insult to the Scandinavians—and, as he later said, it seemed to him that these Prussians were spitting straight into the eye of Norway, the country without a sense of honor.

But as one of Norway's poets he felt that the guilt for this disgrace rested more on him than on others. He should have been one to teach his nation "high thinking" instead of a smug policy of neutrality by means of which they could save their own skins.

VI

NATIONAL FAME THROUGH BRAND

1

After a night spent in a wild carousal the Norwegian poet Wergeland had, in 1833, delivered an inspiring oration (on May 17, the Norwegian Independence Day) before a loudly cheering mob of thousands of Christiania citizens. The tall, blond, broad-shouldered "skald" was applauded to the echo as he leaned for support on a monument and spoke of the free Norwegian nation who had in their veins the blood of King Haakon, yes, even of the God of Thunder! The intoxicated orator intoxicated the mob with his glorification of the "small but firm nation, firm as the cliffs of Norway's coast" and "hurrahs" and trumpets joined in the wild patriotic orgy!

As Ibsen travelled southward from Berlin he thought of this scene, but also of another of which he had read in the Christiania *Morgenblad:*

Last Friday at Gadermoen a 24-year-old soldier from Hadeland, for fear of having to go to war, conceived the idea of mutilating himself in order to escape service in war. According to his own confession he cut off the first and half of the second joint of the index finger of his right hand; but the physician judged it impossible that he could cut off the finger with his left hand, thinking that he had perhaps chopped it off with an axe. . . .

The blood of this timid Norwegian youth, brave enough to mutilate himself by reason of his cowardice, seemed to Ibsen scarcely the blood of King Haakon! In directing his anger toward his nation he also searched his own heart and reins, or as he expressed it in a letter to Björnson, "I can assure you

91

that in my quiet moments I sound and probe and dissect my own inward parts—and where it hurts most too!" He recalled with blushes how some years ago in Bergen there had been a May 17th celebration with Ole Bull present when he, Henrik Ibsen, dressed as a miner, had come out of a grotto erected on the speaker's stand in the market place and had delivered a warm, poetic, patriotic address to the youth of this nation with a glorious past—that now alas! had so ingloriously saved their skins through disgraceful neutrality. He had written plays about King Haakon and other Norwegian heroes—the thought nauseated him as he recalled the triumphal entry of the Prussians into Berlin. As a result he decided that there had been enough such romantic dramas from his pen; he gave up all plans for a play on the sixteenth century free-booter Magnus Hejnessön, on which theme he had been taking notes during his last months in Christiania. What his nation now needed was satire of the present, and the venom for such a book was steadily accumulating in him.

When his train carried him through the tunnel under the Alps and he came out into the Italian sunshine where all was resplendent as white marble, it seemed to him symbolical of his life in the last years. He had now escaped from the dark cramping tunnel of Norwegian life where all was cold and bare, where all emotions and passions seemed frozen up, and where all moved in the spirit of miserable everyday routine. In Italy there was sunshine, life and action. It was the time when Garibaldi was the national hero and mothers were taking their fourteen-year-old boys out of school to send them with the great leader on his adventurous, patriotic expeditions. How many of the self-proclaimed patriots of the Storthing would do the same? Hadn't some of his countrymen placed their sons in the Norwegian army to prevent effectually their volunteering for the Danish cause?

Through the contrast of the luxuriant Italian landscape

with its temperamental inhabitants the bleakness of his own country became vividly visible to his mind's eye, especially as he had seen it on his journey through the northern mountain regions in the summer of 1862. At the Sognefjeld he had been forced to make the rather dangerous descent to the Fortundal while a terrible storm was raging. This was the region in which had lived the great King Bele, whose glory Ibsen noted cynically was quite ample for his descendants to live on, while the Italians were becoming heroes in their own right.

Other memories of his summer wanderings came back to him with vivid force. Near Hellesylt, amidst high mountains, he had seen the ruins of a parsonage crushed by an avalanche. The pastor with his wife and children were living with a peasant whose hut was built directly against the mountain side. When Ibsen asked the pastor's wife whether she was not afraid to continue living there, she pointed out to him that their abode was so close to the mountain that any avalanche would pass over it without touching the house. He had also seen the type of people produced by such a harsh and destructive environment. Near Lom he had seen an aristocratic peasant woman about whom it was told that she had fallen in love with and married a beggarly peasant boy; but so harsh was her disposition that when after years of unhappy married life the man died, she dressed the corpse in the rags which he had worn on coming to her father's estate and which she had preserved in her box throughout the years. "As you came to me, so shall you go from me!" had been her words. And when he heard of his own nationals in Rome, and even Danish men and women, sitting in the chapel of the Prussian Embassy amidst the Germans and listening quietly while the preacher implored God's aid for the Prussian army in their "just cause," the war against Denmark,— then Ibsen flew into a terrible rage and told those people what he thought of their lukewarm spirits, their utter lack of pride, temperament, or courage! No longer did he feel any fear such as had gripped him when he had always sensed grinning and sneering faces behind his back. Now he no longer felt "like Samson after the harlot had shorn his locks"; now he was himself. What he had lived through he was going to put into a new work in which he was planning to call his nation to account for its continual compromising.

As a contrast to this attitude he remembered a preacher who had come to Skien while Ibsen was at Grimstad. This man, Pastor Lammers, had become impatient with the luke-warm Christianity of the state church and had electrified his congregation with a clear-cut demand: "Either—or!" The empty ceremonies and formalities were cast aside, paintings (many of them by Lammers himself), and other vanities were discarded, and even the church was deserted for the mountain top where Lammers delivered his fiery sermons under the open sky. The whole town was stirred out of its smug con-tentment by this voice calling in the wilderness to bring the people to true repentance. Here was something that was genuine, not a mere matter of phrases. Ibsen's mother and sister wrote letters to him pleading with him for the sake of his eternal salvation to lead a truly Christian life in humility of spirit and to trust in his Saviour. While he could not accept this simple faith, yet Ibsen followed with a certain admiration the career of the revolutionary who was defying the established church, because in the ardor and the genuine emotion of Lammers he felt a spirit kindred to his own.

To be sure, the historical Lammers came to a rather in-glorious end. After he had boldly defied the state church for years, he became humble and penitent when the conse-quences of his revolt brought him face to face with hunger and starvation. Then, in 1860, he sent out a public con-fession of his wrong-doing, apologized for his false doctrine in regard to the sacraments, gave up his post as head of a "free congregation" and even joined the state church for the sake of a pension. And he who had raged against the vanity of paintings in the House of God ended his days as a painter of altar pictures!

But it was Ibsen's method as a poet to select only certain external features from his models and to supply most of the inner life from his own personal experience. Therefore he decided that his next hero should be a preacher by the name of Brand, a word that has in Norwegian as in English the two meanings, fire and sword.

2

On the evening of Sunday, June 19, 1864, Henrik Ibsen and Lorentz Dietrichson, a Norwegian student of art, sat in the arbor of an inn on the banks of the Tiber, drinking Roman wine. After a hot day spent in visiting St. Peter's, the Forum, and other notable places of the Eternal City, these two happy young men were enjoying the cool breeze, the brilliant sunset, the gradual lighting of the lamps in the garden and across the river in the Palazzo Farnese, the city mirrored in the flood, and the music of a mandolin in the distance. Dietrichson was a native of Bergen, a childhood friend of Mrs. Ibsen's, and Ibsen had made it a point to seek out this genial companion of Christiania days immediately on his arrival in Rome. In his society and in these inspiring surroundings Ibsen could forget the smallness of his enemies in Christiania, he could laugh at the nasty gossip that had followed like a nightmare on the publication of *Love's Comedy,* and he could, for the time being, overlook Norway's desertion of the "brother in need" during the recent unhappy war. Now he could rejoice in the seven full houses that had applauded his *Pretenders,* and look forward to a period of freedom with leisure to devote all his energies to his art far from the envious gossips in Christiania.

But the utter desertion of ideals on the part of his nationals kept gnawing at Ibsen's heart, and out of the abundance of the heart the mouth speaketh. A few evenings later the Scandinavians in Rome were holding a picnic on the Esquiline Hill. After the frugal supper had been eaten, Ibsen, as the latest arrival, was asked for news from the North. He began to tell of the disheartening, humiliating impressions of his journey in Copenhagen and in Berlin. Gradually his conversation took on the character of an improvised speech in which his warm love for his native land and all his raging anger at recent happenings came to the fore. As darkness gradually settled down only Ibsen's glowing eyes were visible and his voice ringing with emotion sounded, as Dietrichson put it, like the Marseillaise of the North. The impression Ibsen made on his little audience was enormous; his speech was followed to the end with breathless attention, and in thoughtful silence the guests then scattered into the Roman night. Dietrichson tells that never in his life had he been so moved by the power of the spoken word. Ibsen, when roused to anger, could be a very telling orator.

Just as a dozen years before the art treasures of Dresden had made an overwhelming impression on Ibsen, so now he revelled in the works of the great masters. Characteristically, Michelangelo and Bernini attracted him more than the works of antiquity where he missed the individual and personal expression. In fact, the grandeur of Rome distracted him to such an extent that he found himself unable to settle down to the work he had planned. Therefore he joined Lorentz Dietrichson in leaving the city for the village of Genzano, where a number of Norwegians were spending the summer, among them the mother, brother, and sister of Christopher Brunn, the gallant volunteer in the Danish war.

Here the hot months were spent in a most agreeable manner. The mornings were devoted to work; Ibsen was struggling with a narrative poem, the epic *Brand*. But he rarely discussed any of his works until they were completed; in fact his friend Dietrichson thought that he was busy with a drama on Julian the Apostate, because Ibsen manifested great interest in Ammianus Marcellinus' account of the life of this emperor. At noon the friends all met in a wine cellar; the afternoons were passed in reading or in conversation under some shady trees; and in the evening they strolled across the hills, frequently meeting processions singing their religious chants as they marched from one shrine to another in the warm summer night.

One day it was announced that Pope Pius IX was coming to his summer residence in the neighboring Castel Gandolfo, and, as Ibsen had never seen the Pope, he and Dietrichson decided to view his entry. With some misgivings Ibsen consented to ride over to the town on a donkey. All went well at first, and he began to feel quite at home on the back of the animal. On approaching the village they noticed that thousands of devout Italians were lined up along the one street of the town, and the only thing to do was to ride in past the merry populace awaiting impatiently the arrival of the papal cortege. Therefore the Norwegian poet—at the time somewhat Bohemian in his dress, wearing the huge hat with sky-blue lining nicknamed by his friends "The Blue Grotto"— boldly guided his mount down the street at a slow walk, rather uncomfortably feeling himself stared at by everyone. After they had thus for a short distance run the gauntlet of the populace, who were laughing and bandying none too complimentary remarks about the two "matti inglesi" the donkeys suddenly began to gallop, amidst whoops of joy from all sides. Ibsen hung on for dear life, when, just as suddenly, the donkeys stopped and lay down on their stomachs, and the riders found themselves standing over the prostrate animals. Great cheers greeted this feat, when suddenly the papal procession arrived. Willing hands dragged the hee-hawing and kicking donkeys out of the street, and Pio Nono approached extending his blessing on the people, which Ibsen felt none needed more than he.

When fall came the friends returned to Rome and Ibsen met some other Scandinavians, among them the law-student Klubien and the Swedish poet Count Snoilsky, four sculptors, a few painters, and also the theological student Christopher Brunn. With the latter Ibsen had many long conversations about the recent disgraceful action of his countrymen in failing to live up to the pledge to come to the aid of Denmark. The bluff young man, after listening at length to Ibsen's sentimentalizing about the brave cannon at Dybböl—"The cannon that received no help and yet went on shooting until they burst"—asked the very natural question, "Why in the world then didn't you go to war?" Ibsen was very much embarrassed by this query; he lowered his eyes and replied, "We poets have other duties to fulfill."

He did not need to have the inconsistency of his position pointed out to him; for he knew full well that he was equally guilty with the rest. But this conversation made a deep impression on him who was wont to consider the writing of poetry as "sitting in judgment over oneself." For another thing, it steeled his determination to fulfill in the highest possible measure his mission as a poet who was to lead his people to "high thinking."

Ibsen had a rare faculty for turning the conversation to some matter that would afford him material for the particular play on which he happened to be working. In these days in Rome while he was building up the character of Brand with his demand "All or Nothing," he would frequently raise the question, "whether one ought to swallow the latchkey?"

This was in allusion to the English poet Thomas Chatterton, the attic-poet *par excellence,* who after starving for days, according to one version, had committed suicide by swallowing his latchkey rather than abandon his ideals of devoting his life to poetry.   Many good citizens replied that even the idealist must make some compromises in this world of relative values.   Ibsen would reply in most paradoxical fashion, leading his opponent in the debate on to make further reasonable but quite philistine replies, and thus he gathered material for the speeches of the time-serving pastor, the opportunistic mayor, and the vacillating schoolmaster in *Brand.*   In this way many people sat as models for Ibsen without having any inkling of what was going on.   And if he met at times a man strong enough in argument to prove that sometimes one must make compromises in order to realize one's purpose in the end, just as clearly as two and two make four—then Ibsen would answer, "Are you sure that two and two always do make four, for example on the planet Jupiter?"

As a matter of fact, in these debates Ibsen did defend what was to a considerable extent his own position.   He felt very strongly that he had a mission as a poet, and to compromise with this by splitting his energies in doing journalistic work or writing anything to meet the popular taste—that was something *Ibsen* would *never* do.   Instead, humiliating as it was to him, he accepted sums of money which Björnson solicited for him from some men of means in Christiania who were interested in the progress of the Norwegian drama.   In the spring he had not the funds to bring his family with him, and Susannah Ibsen with Sigurd had remained in Copenhagen. On September 16, 1864, we find him writing to Björnson:

My wife and my little boy are to join me here in the autumn. I hope that you will approve of this arrangement. Leaving more directly personal motives out of the question, I shall only remark that it will be cheaper for us to live together than for me, as hitherto, to keep up a separate household in Copenhagen. . . . Four hundred specie dollars ($400) will cover my expenses in Rome for a year. My brother-in-law in Christiania will provide my wife's travelling expenses out of what remains of my travelling grant. We expect them to be moderate, as she is coming with a lady from Copenhagen who has been here before and is experienced in travelling economically.

By the beginning of October I shall be in need of money, as I see by your letter you are prepared to hear. Will you kindly manage to have some sent me by that time?

On the day Ibsen's wife arrived in Rome Dietrichson was with him. Ibsen hardly ever could give free expression to his deepest emotions; on this day it seemed he was all the time on the point of speaking of her, but he never did. When she did arrive with little Sigurd, Ibsen indulged in no conventional phrases, he simply gave her a kiss—long, tender and heartfelt. In speaking of this meeting afterward, Dietrichson remarked, "I have never seen a heartier reception, and this I felt sure of; these two individualistic and seemingly so different persons have an inner something that unites them, and she is precisely the wife suited to him."

It was a period of great poverty for the Ibsen family, but how much easier it was to bear it in Rome than in Christiania! With the Dietrichsons and other friends they went on long walks among the historic ruins or the environs of the Eternal City which every Northern European yearns so ardently to see. One enthusiastic member of these family excursions was little Sigurd, dressed in the Zouave uniform sent him by his god-father Björnson. And when his five-year-old legs tired, one of the men would let him ride on his shoulders and he enjoyed such rides—as he once remarked, —quite as much as those on four-legged donkeys.

More often, however, Ibsen would wander through the streets of Rome alone, wrapped in a dense silence, his hands plunged into the pockets of his faded velveteen "artist's" jacket, he would lie for hours in the sunshine that he loved so much among the tombs of the Via Latina, or he would loiter along the Via Appia not recognizing friends who met him. He writes to Björnson that he did not believe he was wasting his time when he was loafing in this manner; we know that he certainly was not, for in these months he conceived the plan of the drama, at once so lofty and so original, as well as so far in advance of what he or any of his countrymen had done before, that it established overnight his position as the greatest poet of his country.

3

Dietrichson, who was a student of art, and the long list of books translated into many European languages which he later on came to write attest his great ability in matters esthetic, gives to Ibsen a very striking testimonial as a guide in art appreciation. He himself had no particular liking for the portrait busts of the Romans but preferred Greek works, such as the bust of Sophocles or the head of Pericles in which the artist did not have recourse to the portrayal of external, accidental traits. One afternoon in the Vatican he and Ibsen had a violent argument on this subject. Ibsen pointing to the Roman heads insisted that just exactly by these means should character be portrayed; the play of muscles around the subject's mouth or a wrinkle in his forehead could afford a deeper view of the life of his soul than an ever so nobly idealized representation of the larger features of his countenance. Writing thirty years later Dietrichson says he realizes how right Ibsen had been, and that he had often longed for more opportunities to wander through museums at the side of his country's greatest artist.

Life in Rome, however, proved once more too distracting for Ibsen, so in the spring of 1865 he with his wife and son left the city to settle down to quiet work in Ariccia, a little town in the Alban hills surrounded by wooded heights and with a view toward the sea in the west. Perhaps economic reasons also played their part, for here they could live very frugally, without even the simple social intercourse they had enjoyed in Rome. To a large extent they lived on money borrowed from the Danish consul, and Sigurd told years afterward that at times there was not even bread in the house. Yet Ariccia is of the most vital importance in Ibsen's life, for through the work he did here the course of his whole life was changed as by a magic stroke from defeat into victory with ever increasing fame and fortune.

In addition to his desperate economic situation, Ibsen's work also caused him intense despair. He was writing in the form of a narrative poem the life of his hero Koll (later changed to Brand), from childhood to manhood, prefaced by a powerful indictment of his countrymen as "fellows in guilt." But in spite of the ringing quality of the verse, the striking metaphors, and the soul-stirring story, Ibsen could not feel satisfied with the work; indeed the words of the hero probably came from the bottom of the poet's soul:

> As gray in gray each thing is like the other,
> Today as yesterday provides but care,
> In the old frame the same old picture,
> No matter how far back we stare.

Then one day he went to Rome on some errands and also found time to visit St. Peter's. Under the dome built by Michelangelo, an artist after the heart of Ibsen, he had a revelation. What passed there must have been very like what is told in *Brand:*

> And yet in uttermost despair,
> In shuddering sorrow's deepest deep
> .   .   .   .

What felt I if it was not prayer?
Whence came that trance, that ecstasy,
That rushing music, like a blast,
That sang afar and hurried past,
Bore me aloft and set me free?
Was it the ecstasy of prayer?
Did I with God hold converse there?

For suddenly Ibsen saw in strong and clear outlines the form of what was to be his message to his nation.

Then he did an extremely courageous thing. The poem on which he had spent a full year's labor he threw to the winds, as he wrote to Björnson, and in the middle of July he began something new, which progressed as nothing had ever progressed with him before. In Ariccia there were no distracting visitors, and his only reading was the Bible. At four o'clock in the morning he arose and, before the heat of day arrived, strolled about in the woods or in the Chigi Park. As the sun rose higher he sat down at his desk and wrote, practically without interruption, until the day came to a close.

Before him on his desk he had a glass with a scorpion in it. "From time to time," he wrote to P. Hansen, "the little animal was ill. Then I used to give it a piece of soft fruit, upon which it fell furiously and emptied its poison into it—after which it was well again. Does not something of the same kind happen with us poets?"

In the evening he liked to sit on the grand staircase before the church enjoying the coolness after dusk. Like "the hand that rounded Peter's dome" Ibsen's pen too seemed inspired; as early as fall he could send off the completed manuscript of the colossal drama *Brand*.

Brand, like a fiery Zarathustra (two decades before Nietzsche, however), comes down from the mountain to rouse a sluggard generation. He is not one to look at events in the world with his hands hollowed like a field-glass as did the hero of *On the Heights;* recent events had turned Ibsen's interest from the esthetic to the ethical.   He calls for ennobled, superior men, and condemns the leveling influence of the mob, for when a nation becomes democratic it has inadvertently gone a good way toward becoming plebeian.   It is a ringing call for character and the courage to be oneself— regardless of the conventional moral values.   Rather than a vacillating compromiser or a passively good person, he says

> Be passion's slave, be pleasure's thrall,
> But be it utterly, all in all.

Apathy was the quality this prophet hated with a holy anger. "Be what you are with all your heart."   His rule for life was: "Be yourself"—a rule to be followed "by living it and not by preaching."

There was nothing particularly new in these ideas; even some of Ibsen's friends considered this a blemish, as for example his mother-in-law, Fru Thoresen, who remarked that he really ought to be more than a mere co-worker of Kierkegaard.   This keen Danish critic of the church had written a work entitled *Either—or,* of which Ibsen's "all or nothing" was really but another form, while Kierkegaard's "Others complain that the times are wicked, I complain that they are contemptible" might serve as a motto for the play.   But time was to prove more and more how Ibsen had given life to Kierkegaard's abstract ideas in the creation of the figure of Brand, modeled on Pastor Lammers and to some extent also on the theological student Christopher Brunn, a man who had the courage to give, if need be, his life, for the sake of his convictions.   And as a deadly satire the portrait of the time-serving Dean, who thinks of religion as a government institution to keep the people in check had even more of a sting in it than Pastor Strawman of *Love's Comedy.*

In every way this drama was an enormous advance over

the plays written in Norway, a fact to be attributed largely to the inspiring influence of his Italian environment.   Ibsen wrote to Björnson on January 28, 1865, that the statue in the Vatican called "The Tragic Muse" had taught him the real spirit of Greek tragedy.   His Brand was closely related to the hero of the classical stage as Aristotle describes him: a man of considerable position and noble nature who has in his character some flaw for which he suffers doom at the hands of inexorable Fate.   Brand certainly wins our sympathy through his idealism and his courage, but his lack of humanity or love leads him to share the fate of many another reformer.   The mob's cries of "Hosanna" were soon followed by "Crucify, crucify him!"; and as the only disciple with Christ at the time of his death was the Thief, so the Dean proposed as an epitaph for Brand, deserted by all but the half-witted Gerd:

> Here lieth Brand; his tale's a sad one,
> One soul he saved—and that a mad one!

Like the modern poet he is, Ibsen shows how Brand's harsh fanaticism is the product of his heredity and environment, and thereby brings him much nearer to the reader's understanding, not to say sympathy.   Brought up by a mother who had slapped her husband as he lay in his coffin, gathering all his early impressions from the harsh, somber mountains— what else would one expect him to be?   These inhuman qualities of the hero have their foil in Agnes, a creature wholly made up of love and heroic devotion.   She leaves her feeble fiancé for Brand, and she abides by her bargain faithful and devoted to the end.   The model for this figure was the sister of Christopher Brunn, who faithfully nursed one of her brothers when he fell a victim to tuberculosis and then died quite young of the same disease.   Her great charm, felt by all who met the young lady, moved Ibsen to write these lines, perhaps the most wistfully poetic among all his verse:

Hers was a rest here,
Like one brief dawn;
She was a guest here;
Now she is gone.

Through the kindness of Björnson Ibsen found a new publisher, Hegel, in Copenhagen, who published his works in
editions worthy of the poet, paid him royalties that forever
banned the specter of poverty for Ibsen, and became his life-
long devoted friend.   To Ibsen's great disappointment the
publisher thought it best to wait until March to publish Brand,
because he considered it too stirring a book for the Christmas season.   When the book did appear Ibsen could surely
not complain of its attracting no attention; there were reviews
and reviews of reviews, imitations and continuations, and all
manner of stupidity as well as sensible criticism.   After two
months the first edition was exhausted, and then followed in
that very year four editions, with many more later, making it,
as Halvorsen put it, "The most stirring event in Norway's literary history of the nineteenth century."   One of life's little
ironies, received with mixed feelings by Ibsen, brought it
about that many well-meaning souls considered this a devotional book, a fitting confirmation present!

On May 10, 1866, the Storthing, almost unanimously,
granted Ibsen a life-long "poet's pension" of 400 specie dollars ($400) annually.   Ibsen had advanced to a position
side by side with Björnson as a recognized national poet.

VII

"PEER GYNT" AND THE BEGINNINGS OF INTERNATIONAL FAME

1

Just before the dawn of Ibsen's fame there certainly came his darkest hour. When the publication of *Brand* was delayed, Ibsen had six long months to wait for the appearance of the book he had written, as the phrase goes, with his own life-blood; there was the humiliation of having to borrow money from the consul for the barest necessities of his family; then he had humbly to petition the King of Norway and also the Scientific Society of Trondhjem for stipends in order merely to exist. All this meant very exasperating waiting, waiting, waiting. In the midst of these difficulties he was attacked by malarial fever and in his delirium almost committed suicide. Though hampered on every hand by their poverty, Mrs. Ibsen nursed him through his disease and bore all in uncomplaining, stoical faithfulness. She believed in her hero.

In addition to this, Ibsen suffered unnecessary rudenesses such as are likely to be inflicted on those who happen to be poor. Björnson was regularly supplying him with funds, and at one time when Ibsen was pressed to pay his debts to the consul he drew a draft on Björnson. Owing to some misunderstanding this draft was not honored and was returned to Ibsen with an insulting remark on the part of a certain intermediary: "This sort of thing won't do here." In writing to Björnson about it Ibsen called this expression: "words one might use if one caught a swindler in the act of doing some rascally trick which one could prevent. But such

107

words must not be written about me. The man who said them to me, I would kill on the spot." Shortly after this one of his Christiania creditors, without any warning to Ibsen, seized his household possessions stored in the Norwegian Theater and sold them at public auction. It cut so deeply into Ibsen's heart to have his wife's heirlooms and his private papers handled by rough strangers, that he did not tell her of this new humiliation, but attempted to have his friends buy back the most highly prized articles. In the letter to Björnson quoted above Ibsen writes, if ever man did, *de profundis.*

In consequence of your silence on the subject I have not sent in any application to the Storthing or the Government; I knew that it would only have meant fruitless humiliation. . . .

My book will appear in a day or two, I expect. . . . About my present position,—waiting, worn out with anxiety and suspense— looking forward to the appearance of the book and to the possibility of its producing strife and attacks of all sorts—unable in such circumstances to begin something new, which, nevertheless, is already fully developed within me—about all this I will say no more.

Dear Björnson, it seems to me as if I were separated from both God and men by a great, an infinite void.

Last summer when I was writing my drama, I was, in spite of all that harassed and perplexed me, indescribably happy. I felt the exaltation of a Crusader, and I don't know anything I should have lacked the courage to face; but there is nothing so enervating and exhausting as this hopeless waiting. . . .

If it had not been that Susannah Ibsen was at his side in these days Ibsen's career would probably have come to an untimely end, as did that of the promising young Danish lawyer, Ludvig David, an intimate friend of Georg Brandes. Plagued by fever and the sirocco, this member of the Scandinavian circle at Rome who always kept very much to himself, one night shortly after having chatted gaily with Ibsen at the Club, stripped, and leaped from the window of his third-story room to the pavement, in all probability under the delusion that he was diving into the cool waters of the sea at Sorrento. When an Italian and a German doctor in the presence of the police performed a post mortem examination Ibsen characteristically was present, as always observing life and death with open eyes.

But instead of being snuffed out Ibsen's career now took its upward flight. Almost simultaneously with the spring of 1866 came his life annuity as a poet, the stipend from Trondhjem, edition after edition of *Brand*, publication by Hegel of *The Pretenders*, and a translation into German of the same play. Although the drama had not really been written for the stage, there was a repeated demand for the performance of the fourth act of *Brand*. There was no longer any thought of procuring for Ibsen a post as amanuensis in the Christiania Library (one more humble hope that like so many others had failed Ibsen in the dark days); now he paid his debts and even wrote to his publisher to save his royalties for him in Copenhagen, to contribute to a fund for the widow of a courageous liberal editor, and to invest for him a modest sum in the state lottery, because he enjoyed the excitement of this game of chance. To the King he sent an elegantly bound copy of *Brand* "as a small expression of my most submissive gratitude."

Filled with new courage Ibsen moved with his family to Frascati for the summer to wrestle with a new subject for a play. He reports to his friend Botten-Hansen that he is living "most comfortably and cheaply" in rooms in the old Palazzo Gratiosi, near the ancient Tusculum where Cicero had his villa. Two thousand feet above the sea, the palace afforded a view of the Mediterranean, the Campagna, and Rome. From the windows of his study he could see in the extreme distance Mons Soracte rising, isolated and beautiful, from the level of the immense plain. Small wonder that the

play conceived in this environment became what some critics
have called "the most cheerful or rather the least gloomy of
Ibsen's plays."

The failure of his countrymen, himself included, to follow
the ideal in 1864 still filled his mind to the exclusion of
everything else, but he was able to see it in a less stern mood
than that pervading *Brand*. With humorous rather than bitter
satire he chose for his hero Peer Gynt, a great hunter from
Norse fairy tales who meets with Sæter girls, monsters such
as the Boyg, trolls, and is "such an out-and-out tale-maker
and yarn-spinner, you couldn't have helped laughing at him.
He always made out that he himself had been mixed up in all
the stories that people said had happened in the olden times."
Thus he read in Asbjörnsen's fairy tales and he saw in this
boaster the image of the romantic Norwegians who revelled so
much in the great deeds of their heroic ancestors, but did very
little on their own account.

Very closely associated with this was another romantic
illusion of his people, as Ibsen saw it, namely the "poetic"
presentation of the peasant. Wherever he saw any lie, cant,
delusion, or other falsehood, Ibsen throughout his life felt
the urge to lay it bare. Now the chief sinner in this respect
was Björnson with his extremely popular novels of peasant
life, in which the hero lies in the fields dreaming of fairy
tales, drinks and fights with his fellows at weddings, or is
made a noble character through the love of a pure, simple,
devoted girl. Ibsen chose just such situations for his hero,
only he pictured him in a realistic rather than a poetic color-
ing. The really quite unesthetic Norse fairy of the woods,
the Huldre with her cow-tail, was also stripped of some of her
romantic tinsel by Ibsen; while at the same time he made fun
of the ecstatic nationalism that venerated everything so long
as it was "home-made."

The true story of Arne, one of Björnson's idealized

peasants, Ibsen told one day in his facetious manner over a glass of wine. Arne announced to the priest that he wished to marry Eli. "But she is a widow, seventy years of age!" cried the priest in horror. "She owns a cow." "Nevertheless, think it over well. Of course, if you wish it I'll have to publish the banns; that costs two dollars. But think it over well!" A week later Arne came back: "I have thought it over —there will not be any wedding." "That is right; I had hoped that your better self would gain the upper hand." Arne answered: "Her cow is dead. Can I now get my two dollars back?"—"The two dollars have already gone into the church treasury."—"Into the church treasury! Well, in that case I believe I'd rather marry the widow after all." (Nothing could better illustrate the temperamental incompatibility of the two Norwegian poets than Björnson's tenderminded and Ibsen's tough-minded view of the peasant.)

In the political realm too Ibsen had a few compliments to pay. The Swedes were forever bragging of their glory under Charles XII, while in the present they appeared despicable to Ibsen; to symbolize this he put into the play an Egyptian fellah carrying a corpse on his back. In the same scene, located in an insane asylum in Cairo, he presents an idiot who believes that he is a pen, representing the Swedish foreign minister Manderström who through his diplomatic notes in 1864 believed that he was achieving marvellous things while in reality he played rather an ignominious rôle. In the course of the winter Ibsen had a characteristic experience in regard to Manderström with the latter's nephew, the dashing poet Count Snoilsky. This young man discovered one day in a bound volume of a Scandinavian newspaper a picture of his uncle desecrated by having a noose drawn in pencil about his neck. He demanded indignantly of the librarian, Dietrichson, who it was that had hanged his uncle in effigy. Accordingly at the next meeting of the Club the librarian re-

quested that the assassin give his name and explain his conduct to Count Snoilsky. Ibsen immediately announced that
he had done it with two strokes of the pencil, and in a private
conference with Snoilsky he explained why Manderström dis-
gusted him. Many years afterward Ibsen met Snoilsky again
and mentioned that he had since modified his opinion in regard to the statesman, whereupon the nephew replied that
alas, once more he could not agree with Ibsen, for he had
meanwhile read the documents in question and now thought
that his uncle had really deserved the hanging Ibsen had
inflicted!

With the general lines of the play gradually developing
in his mind, Ibsen worked on his new drama the summer of
1866 at Frascati and during the winter in Rome, finishing it
the following summer on the island of Ischia and at Sorrento. In many respects Ole Bull was the model; he was a
handsome fellow attractive to the ladies, he was filled with
the Norse fairy-tale lore, he won a fabulous fortune in America, he wished to found a colony in Pennsylvania called
Oleana (Gyntiana) which however suffered shipwreck, and
in general he was swayed by many purposes in turn.

At Ischia the Norwegian novelist Bergsöe happened to be
summering at the same time. He relates that one morning a
man greeted him cordially, introducing himself as Henrik
Ibsen. Never in his life would he have imagined the author
of *Brand* to look like that; a short, stocky figure, with black
hair, big black whiskers, and a pair of sharp, piercing eyes,
wearing a seaman's jacket and an embroidered Roman scarf
—anyone would have taken him for a rough seaman rather
than the poet of a quasi-religious drama.

As Bergsöe stared at him Ibsen said gaily, "Yes, I am the
one, I am; and that is you too, isn't it? I have read your
new novel and have seen that it is based on reality; that is

what we are forced to do now—the time for the romantic hero
of the novel is past."

"Then you have read Clemens Petersen's criticism?" asked
Bergsöe. "It is not especially friendly, and I fear it will
ruin my novel."

"No, never!" said Ibsen with unexpected violence. "When
someone writes so long and so fierce a criticism it arouses
opposition and awakens attention.—But what inn do you
frequent?"

"I am still so weak that I stay at the hotel and drink tea
with Collin."

"Fie on such rustic innocence!" Ibsen exploded. "That
will never do; in that way you will become a regular mis-
anthrope. Come down in the evening to the 'Buffalo,' and
after one or two 'Foglietti' Petersen's criticism will no longer
bother you. I don't know him, but since he is now blowing
Björnson's horn, it is clear that he will play another piece
for us. But the time will come when we can turn tables on
Clemens Petersen."

With these words Ibsen saluted and went off. After this,
doctor or no doctor, Bergsöe drank wine every evening at
the "Buffalo." Every day the two artists went for a walk
together. At the time of the writing of *Brand* Ibsen had
read only the Bible, but as he composed *Peer Gynt* he lived
in the witty atmosphere of Holberg. To Bergsöe he gave the
nickname Jacob Skomager, after the innkeeper in Holberg's
Jeppe of the Hill.

"Now I shall work," he said one day. "I feel like a young
stallion." And work Ibsen did, in spite of the sweltering
heat, keeping regular office hours, so to speak, with the day
divided so that he was like a clock that showed the hours of
the day. He arose early, took a walk, then his morning
coffee, and then began the work. At this time Mrs. Ibsen
went down to the shore with Sigurd, allowing the poet to be

undisturbed during his creative hours. At two came a siesta, then, according to the Norwegian fashion, dinner, and in the afternoon Ibsen copied in his calligraphic hand what he had composed in the forenoon. But if the day was devoted to work, the evening would be dedicated to Bacchus. As soon as the darkness lowered over the sea, Bergsöe would regularly hear Ibsen calling, "Hi, Jacob Skomager! Come on out and have a snifter!" And then they walked along the acacia avenues where the fireflies gleamed like dancing stars, down to the little inn on the Piazza. Here Ibsen would bubble over with amusing stories, usually turning about life's little ironies.

At times too Bergsöe visited at the home of the Ibsens, where he gained great respect for Mrs. Ibsen's independence of thought. One evening she objected to her husband's round condemnation of the Swedes, by pointing out Gustavus Adolphus and Charles XII. In the heat of the argument Ibsen called this all humbug and pounded on the table so that the glasses rattled. Then little Sigurd observed, "Yes, Father can't stand the Swedes and I know what I'd like to do to them!"

Bergsöe inquired what that might be.

"I'd like to scratch their eyes out!"

Thereupon Mrs. Ibsen quietly took the boy off to bed. Bergsöe says that he felt pity for the seven-year-old boy, who was leading a rather lonely life, far away from home, far from any play-fellows, and hearing only the talk of his elders.

At this time Ibsen was haunted by the fear that something might happen to him to cut him off from the possibility of attaining the goal he had set for himself. For that reason he undertook nothing that seemed in the least dangerous. He refused absolutely to ride on a donkey, to climb mountains, and even to go over to Capri, because he said in case of a storm the Italian boatmen would not act like sturdy Norse sailors, but would kneel down in the bottom of the boat and call to the Virgin for help. Likewise he had a great fear that someone would steal his manuscript, and his suspicions at times must have been trying to those who were living with him.

One morning very early he came to Bergsöe, not shouting "Jacob Skomager," but asking his friend to come down because *she* was sick.

"What she?" inquired Bergsöe.

"Why, my wife, of course. She has cholera and I don't know what to do."

"Well, fetch the doctor."

"No, I'll not go down," said Ibsen. "I might catch it. Then what would become of us—and Sigurd?"

Bergsöe then fetched a doctor, who diagnosed it not as cholera, but as a harmless disease from which she recovered in four days.—Susannah Ibsen had to put up with many strange actions of this sort, for Ibsen had his full share of "artistic temperament."

One evening the two men set out to see the Garibaldi house and returned when it was quite dark. Suddenly a big dog stood in their way. Ibsen refused to go past, but finally, after a good deal of argument, during which the dog glared at the two Scandinavians suspiciously, he declared that he was not afraid of the dog and walked past on the far side. Bergsöe told him to act as if he did not fear the dog in the least; but just as Ibsen was passing the dog he made a movement as though he was going to run, whereupon the dog snapped at his hand. A well-aimed blow from Bergsöe's cane drove the beast away, but Ibsen shouted, perhaps none too logically, "The dog was mad; you must shoot him, otherwise I too shall go mad." Nothing could calm Ibsen and it required days before he got over his terror.

Ibsen, who had absorbed a good deal of the soul of his *Brand*, felt very conscious of his mission in the world, and on one of their long walks told Bergsöe that he was writing not for Time but for Eternity. In his calm way Bergsöe argued that this was very difficult to foresee, that in the course of millenniums even the greatest spirits would be forgotten—upon which Ibsen flared up and answered, "Spare me your metaphysics! If you rob me of Eternity, you rob me of everything!"

Bergsöe said no more, but, looking at the little man in his rather Bohemian attire, he thought it very unlikely that this fellow would ever be very famous.

2

"Peer, you lie!"

This opening note of Ibsen's new drama was, of course, in the first place addressed to the Norwegian people whose patriotism and heroism, as expressed by their "Skalds," had turned out to be vain boasting. The writers of stories about idealized peasants might consider it also a little message delivered at their address. Furthermore, there are satirical passages in the play on the super-nationalists and the language-reformers, as well as many other topical allusions. But in the main it is the biography of a very human character, so human that probably every reader can find more of himself in Peer Gynt than he would like to acknowledge even to his closest friend.

Peer is not a bad fellow at all. He is lazy, to be sure, but who wouldn't be after he had been brought up the son of a rich father and the spoilt favorite of a weak mother? Yet he is too idealistic to marry a girl simply for her property, although his mother urges him to do so in order to improve their really very miserable lot. He is not vulgar, for he is attracted by Solveig, the incarnation of maidenly modesty. Nor is he a coward, for it required a great deal of dash and courage to carry off the bride at the rich peasant's home. He certainly does not lack charm, nor kindness, nor wit. He is not without a sense of delicacy, for when confronted by the results of his wild oats, he feels himself soiled and cannot face Solveig again, happy as he had been to have found and won his "king's daughter." Nor is he an unsuccessful man, for when he makes the effort he amasses a huge fortune in America and later becomes a venerated prophet with the same ease with which he had carried off the bride.

But he is not a great man, one who would boldly cross the Rubicon. He prefers never to commit himself to such an extent that he cannot draw back. Hence he has no core to his life, only smatterings of this and that; he is like the onion that underneath all its many layers contains no kernel. He is never willing to "be himself" in the sense of devoting his all to one cause; he is not one who would save his life by losing it. He finds it unpleasant to look fate squarely in the eye; he prefers to change the subject when unpleasant things face him. He deludes himself by taking credit to himself for whatever circumstances do for him, and by blaming circumstances for his failures. He believes that he remains the master of the situation just because he refuses to burn his bridges behind him. He always "goes around" his difficulties instead of overcoming them or dying in the attempt. The result of his calculating selfishness is that his character shrinks and shrinks more and more the older he grows. His life is a desolate field of missed opportunities and his morality as egoistic as that of the superman without the latter's greatness.

Les personnes faibles ne peuvent être sincères said La Rochefoucauld, and by this token Ibsen was an exceedingly strong man, because he dared bare in all sincerity and with-

out any glozing the innermost springs of human action. Just
as Ibsen to some extent was Brand he was also in a certain
measure the model of Peer Gynt. From the days of his
childhood onward he had felt an enormous ambition, while
his reality seemed as ragged as Peer Gynt's exterior. He
had felt the herd laughing at him as they leered behind Peer
Gynt's back at the wedding. When it was "a terrible thing
to look fate in the eyes" he too had taken recourse to "brandy
and lies." On a number of occasions he had even felt that
he lacked physical courage; he had talked of Norway's duty
in the war, but unlike Christopher Brunn he had felt that a
poet has other duties than to join the army:

> Ay, think of it—wish it done—will it to boot—
> But *do* it—! No that's past my understanding!

If this word spoken of the youth who chopped off a finger to
escape service in the army applies in a sense to Ibsen, then
the word from the same man's funeral sermon applies even
more:

> No patriot was he. Both for church and state
> A fruitless tree. But there on the upland ridge
> In that small circle where he saw his calling,
> There was he great, because he was himself!

This was certainly *true* poetry, with the accent equally on
poetry. When a mass of commentators read one meaning
after the other into *Peer Gynt* Ibsen was bewildered. He
wrote, "Why not read the book as a poem?"

Why not, indeed? Where can nobler poetry be found than
in Peer Gynt's story of the reindeer ride, in Aase's death
scene, in the figure of the Button-Moulder with his profound
conception of immortality, or in Solveig's devotion? What
a deeply moving, profoundly ironic scene as the white-haired
vagabond Peer returns to find Solveig, now old and almost

blind, exclaiming: "Thou hast made all my life as a beautiful song!" How many idols, seen through eyes as sharp
as Ibsen's, are not as hollow as Peer Gynt, and how much
devotion is not as undeserved as was Solveig's toward her
beloved? The play ends with a Pietà as noble in its way as
Michelangelo's, as Solveig's song symbolizes Death. What
man can say that Life has not often treated him better than
he deserved?

Besides this, the play bubbles over with wit, perhaps its
most obvious quality. Björnson guffawed loudly as he read
Peer Gynt, although it would seem that much of the humor
is of a profoundly sly type, to make one smile rather than
roar. But above all, Ibsen created a character in Peer Gynt
who, as Georg Brandes remarked in a review, deserves to
rank with the greatest in literature, very near to the immortal
Don Quixote.

3

> Now that, you see, came of the
>   devil's stupidity
> In not taking the measure of his
>   public first.
> *Peer Gynt,* Act V, Scene 4

The above moral is appended to a tale Peer Gynt tells his
fellow-townsman about the devil as an entertainer. He promised the crowd a perfect imitation of the grunt of a pig.
Stepping before the well-filled house in a long cloak—under
which he had secretly concealed a real pig—he gave forth a
series of pig squeals and grunts, induced by cunningly pinch-
ing the unfortunate porker. When the performance was
ended the critics expressed their opinions; some said the
voice had been too thin, others called it too carefully studied;
but all were agreed that this grunting was grossly exaggerated.

But even though Ibsen knew full well what to expect of the critics, yet the things written about *Peer Gynt* drove him into desperate anger. He was beside himself when he read that Clemens Petersen classed the play as polemical journalism, asserted that it was "full of riddles which are insoluble, because there is nothing in them at all," and also that "it is not poetry, because in the transmutation of reality into art it falls halfway short of the demands both of art and of reality." Petersen said the play lacked the Ideal, "the uplifting element," as Ibsen had expected from this man who was "blowing Björnson's horn."

Björnson, who had said of *Brand,* "Your book is not poetry," in his review of *Peer Gynt* also said nothing of its wonderful poetic content. He too saw mostly the satire "upon Norwegian egoism, narrowness, and self-sufficiency, so executed as to have made me not only again and again laugh till I was sore, but again and again give thanks to the author in my heart—as I here do publicly."

This sounds generous enough, but to Ibsen, who had been "writing for Eternity" and who had hoped that amidst all the fool critics these two men at least would have some insight, the failure of Petersen and Björnson to recognize the great poetic values of *Peer Gynt* was maddening.

Immediately after he had read Clemens Petersen's review Ibsen wrote in fiery rage to Björnson on December 9, 1867:

If I were in Copenhagen, and someone there was as good a friend of mine as Clemens Petersen is of yours, I would have thrashed the life out of him before I would have permitted him to commit such an intentional crime against truth and justice. There is a lie involved in Clemens Petersen's article—not in what he says, but in what he refrains from saying. And he intentionally refrains from saying a great deal. You are quite at liberty to show him this letter. . . .

My book *is* poetry; and if it is not, then it will be. The con-

—From Koht, "Björnson's Letters."

BJÖRNSTJERNE AND KAROLINA BJÖRNSON (1858)

ception of poetry in our country, in Norway, shall be made to conform to the book. . . .

And tell me now, is Peer Gynt himself not a personality, complete and individual? I know that he is. And the mother—is she not? . . .

However, I am glad of the injustice that has been done me. There has been something of the God-send, of the providential dispensation in it; for I feel that this anger is invigorating all my powers. If it is to be war, then let it be war! If I am no poet, then I have nothing to lose. I shall try my luck as a photographer. My contemporaries in the North I shall take in hand, one after the other, as I have already taken the nationalist language reformers. . . .

Dear Bjornson, you are a good, warm-hearted soul; you have given me more of what is great and fine than I can ever repay you; but there is something in your nature that may easily cause your good fortune—yes, that more than anything else—to be a curse to you. . . .

I will not follow good advice. But one thing I will do, even though the powers without and the powers within drive me to pull the roof down upon my head—I will always, so help me God, continue to be—Your faithfully and sincerely devoted

HENRIK IBSEN.

This letter shows how deeply Ibsen was hurt at not finding among the few men he admired the recognition which every artist craves. They had called him a journalist while he knew himself to be a poet, and they had failed to recognize the creations of his genius, Peer Gynt and Aase. Perhaps both men began to sense that Björnson was going to become even more definitely than in *Peer Gynt* the target of Ibsen's satire, —of his "photography."

Yet Ibsen knew that he owed Björnson a great debt of gratitude—Björnson, the model for King Haakon, who had given to Ibsen the courage to believe in himself. From Björnson's *Sigurd Slembe* he had learned a great deal, even if he had outstripped his rival when he wrote *The Pretenders*. Furthermore, when Ibsen was about to go abroad, Björnson had induced some of his friends to make up a purse of 700 specie dollars for him, much more than the stipend granted by the state. And when *Brand* appeared Björnson spoke, wrote, and visited politicians in Ibsen's interest until finally the government granted him a poet's pension. These were truly touching proofs of friendship.

But while he thus helped Ibsen he felt at the same time that he ought to give him good advice; he tried to influence Ibsen, the man whose very religion it was to "be himself!" He wrote to Ibsen that the poet ought to avoid the particular, the special case, and deal only with the general, "express feelings and thoughts that can find an echo in the hearts of millions." Such advice must have infuriated the individualistic and undemocratic Ibsen; yet gratitude forbade him to speak his mind freely, though he probably *thought* his full share! It is for this reason that there appears to be something strained, almost hysterical in the assurances of gratitude and friendship sent by Ibsen to his slightly meddlesome benefactor.

There were other causes too that made a deep friendship like that between Goethe and Schiller impossible with the two great Scandinavian poets. Björnson was full of the milk of human kindness, but a bit indiscreet in his manner of searching for the hidden sentiments and emotions in the hearts of his friends; Ibsen, on the contrary, was like the skald in the *Pretenders,* he did not care to bare his innermost feelings. He was frequently drawn toward the darker sides of life, while to Björnson much that Ibsen wrote appeared extremely morbid. The lusty Björnson felt that Brand was in every way his opposite, while Ibsen had much of the ascetic about him. Therefore it seems natural that the two men should have drifted apart when there was no longer the Norse "cause" to hold them together.

A somewhat amusing incident fills the last letters they were to exchange for many years to come. Since Ibsen had marched shoulder to shoulder with his friend in the movement for getting rid of the Danish literary influence in Norway, Björnson wished to win his assistance for another cause. He had learned that the King was planning to bestow an order on both of the poets, and since he considered orders undemocratic and childish he planned to refuse the honor. He wrote to Ibsen asking that he join him in making a "demonstration," which he felt sure would have a wholesome effect on their fellow citizens.

But in this he quite misjudged his friend. Ibsen's heart leaped up when he heard that perhaps the King would decorate him; for he had in his soul a goodly share of philistine vanity that prompted him always to bow low before aristocracy and royalty. He answered immediately with many eloquent arguments to prove that there is no harm in accepting orders. This letter of December 28, 1867, shows how Ibsen's heart was fluttering in anticipation of the star and riband! His only concern was lest Björnson should spoil the affair. "If the finery comes my way," he wrote, "why then, no ado about it!"

Of course, it is a question as to which is more snobbish, to accept a decoration from the King or to make people talk about you by refusing it. At any rate, when the time came, Björnson had to do his "demonstrating" all by himself.

VIII

IBSEN SETTLES DOWN TO HIS LIFE WORK IN GERMANY

1

"In Ischia the earthquake fright, cholera in Naples, brigands at Sorrento, and now war with the Garibaldians here, and wrecked railways in the Papal States!" This is the report Ibsen gives of conditions in Italy toward the end of 1867 and, although Bergsöe considered that he was more alarmed than was necessary, we find him leaving Italy in the spring of the following year. What had delighted him in Rome he described as "the idyllic peacefulness, the association with carefree artists, an existence that can be compared only with the mood in Shakespeare's *As You Like It.*" This mood, the bright Italian sunshine and the inspiration coming from Michelangelo and other "characteristic" artists had given Ibsen that halcyon ease of production which enabled him to publish in successive years the two vast poems *Brand* and *Peer Gynt.* But when this peace was threatened Ibsen left, because he was forever intent on his ideal of realizing himself.

He considered going back to Norway, but after some reflection he found it impossible to return to Christiania, the city that had branded its mark on his soul. He compared his feelings toward Norway with those of a bear who had been taught to dance by being placed in a brewer's kettle under which a fire was lighted. No, he preferred to remain at a distance; and therefore after visits to Florence, Berchtesgaden, and Munich he settled in Dresden—"a community well ordered even to weariness."

As he walked about on the shores of the Königssee among the placid, snow-covered mountains of the Bavarian Alps he thought a great deal of the political situation in Norway. There was absolutely not one bit of idealism in the political life of the country; what his fatherland needed, he felt, was a national disaster. In the struggle between the conservatives and the liberals he could see only the quarrel between those who possessed power and those who would like to. And Björnson was in the midst of the political battles, wasting his time in speaking tours from one end of Norway to the other, while, as Ibsen thought, he should have been increasing his talent ten-fold. There was something peculiarly exasperating to Ibsen in the thought of this tall, broad-shouldered, enthusiastic orator standing on the platform towering above thousands of Norwegian peasants and in mighty tones, with sincere conviction, expressing in religious language the thought that the liberals must oust the conservatives because God was on their side—a sentiment that would be greeted by a storm of jubilant homage the moment his sonorous voice ceased. Ibsen could see no principle involved in these campaigns of Björnson's, and his intolerant condemnation of the opposing side seemed to him to betray a lack of humor. Of course, much worse than Björnson was the host of followers aping the leader.

For years Björnson had attempted in his cordial, manly way to make out of Ibsen an ally in his campaigns. It was impossible for Ibsen to follow such advice, for he could see but one goal: the realization of his powers as a poet. But with a certain grim humor he thought of Björnson's advice to write a comedy—here for once he could follow a suggestion on the part of his friend! And if he should lose his friend—well, the artist's calling demanded all or nothing, and friends were a luxury that must be sacrificed.

With great attention to form and to truth Ibsen began to

write the drama in Dresden. In the play he found an opportunity of paying a delicate tribute to his beloved master
Holberg, by the allusion "How long was Jeppe in Paradise?",
just as Shakespeare celebrates his friend Marlowe by quoting
one of his lines in *As You Like It*. He studied the work of
the realist Freytag whom he far surpassed in the realistic
quality of the dialogue, and especially in the creation of living rather than theatrical characters. He also advanced beyond the French authors whose works he had frequently
staged, by avoiding all monologues and asides. Ibsen must
have enjoyed a very pleasant time with the characters of
the *League of Youth*, to which he wanted at first to give the
sub-title *The Almighty and Co.*, for he writes in his roguish
manner to his publisher Hegel, that he is employed on a very
peaceable drama. In this same spirit of sober facetiousness
he had previously written that *Peer Gynt* was not intended as
satire, "But if the Norwegians of the present time recognize
themselves, as it would appear they do, in the character of
Peer Gynt, that is the good people's own affair."

On October 18, 1869, this first prose comedy of any importance in Norwegian literature was given its première at
the Christiania Theater before a crowded house. The actor
Reimers, playing the rôle of Stensgaard, made himself up to
resemble Björnson and spoke his lines in the warm, unctuous
manner of this popular poet. The conservatives were delighted and the liberals bitterly angered when they heard in
perfect mimicry of the spirit and the manner of Björnson:

Be faithful and true! I shall be the same.—Oh, isn't it an unspeakable joy to carry all that multitude away and along with you?
How can you help becoming good from mere thankfulness? And
how it makes you love all your fellow-creatures! I feel as if I
could clasp them all in one embrace, and weep, and beg their forgiveness because God has been so partial as to give me more than
them.

Or a little later toward the end of the first act:

(Shouts and cheers from the tent.)   There—listen!   They are drinking my health.   An idea that can take such hold upon people —by God, it *must* have truth in it!

There was merry applause from those who enjoyed seeing "the youth" lampooned, but savage hissing and whistling from Björnson's friends.   The actors were frequently interrupted before the final curtain was lowered.   For the next performance the liberals prepared in advance, providing themselves with whistles and tin-horns to kill Ibsen's play. The very opening words, Lundstadt's Independence Day speech, were met with a din of whistling that provoked a counter-demonstration from the conservatives in the audience. Hand-clapping and whistling continued until the curtain was lowered and the manager stepped forward, asking the audience if they desired the play to go on.   For some time then the infernal racket stopped until the line "The people, they who possess nothing and are nothing" again aroused a storm that raged intermittently until the fall of the curtain upon the closing act.   Then it broke out anew threatening to turn into a free-for-all fight, when the gas was turned off, and the rioters went out into the street to hiss Ibsen some more.   For the third performance the house was so closely packed that seats were placed in the space reserved for the orchestra; this time again there was what the Norwegians call a "whistling concert," but from the fourth performance onward the disturbances ceased.

The papers treated the play as a partisan document; the conservatives grinned and the liberals shrieked.   Not one writer saw that Ibsen did not attack liberalism, but merely demagoguery, not any principles but merely the methods of windy politicians.   Much less did anyone appreciate the play as a work of art; the labor that Ibsen had expended on

the composition and on the dialogue, on the creation of characters—among them the sarcastic bankrupt, Daniel Heire,
modelled on Ibsen's father—went quite unnoticed. Björnson
felt that he had been stabbed in the back:

> If poesy's sacred grove be made
> The assassin's hiding place, if this
> The new poetic fashion is,
> Then I for one renounce its shade.

Ibsen was at Port Said when the news of the reception of
his play reached him. He felt, just as he had on the occasion
of the criticism of *Peer Gynt*, that his work of art was treated
as a political pamphlet. "The poem-mirror polished for
male prostitutes" as he phrased his disapproval of politicians
more emphatically than elegantly, had been soiled by this
reception of hisses. But, with the composure he gradually
developed in the face of the receptions of his plays he added,
"Thank Heaven, my country is still the same old place!"
He realized that he always was about a decade before his
time and that the critics had to "acclimatize" themselves.
Ibsen could wait patiently now, because he now no longer
doubted his powers.

2

In the fall of 1869 Dietrichson, then professor of art in
Stockholm, received a letter in a handwriting wholly unknown
to him. He opened it eagerly and discovered it was from
Ibsen. He found that the poet had utterly changed his
former scraggly, rather untidy writing into a vertical, firm,
and most impressive hand. Even greater was his surprise
when he read, "Herewith I am sending you my mug" and
found that the Ibsen whom he had known as a man with a
full-beard, whose chin he had never seen, and whose dress
had been in his Roman days carelessly Bohemian, had been

metamorphosed into a personage wearing an elegant velvet frock-coat, white vest, stiff shirt and white bow-tie, with a carefully barbered beard that left free a very sensitive mouth and an enormously firm chin. The outward and visible symbol of the change in Ibsen during the last four years!

This was the Ibsen who was selected by the Norwegian government to represent his country at a convention in Stockholm in July 1869, the purpose of which was to arrive at a more unified orthography for the three Scandinavian countries. The poet's appearance in the Swedish capital caused great surprise; for his Swedish readers had expected to find in the author of *Brand* an old, serious, stern ascetic, while now he proved to be an elegant young man in a velvet coat, refined, charming, full of wit, and glad to drink a good glass of wine. Some expressed to him their surprise, even disappointment; but Ibsen conquered them all, especially the ladies. Everywhere the now famous poet was received with great admiration, and his stay of several months in Stockholm proved to be, as he put it, "one continuous festival." Especially at the country home of the Limnells, where Fru Limnell was the center of a literary salon, did Ibsen spend many pleasant summer evenings. The manager and the actors of the Royal Theater gave a dinner in honor of Ibsen and Dietrichson, at which a free translation in Swedish of Falk's toast from *Love's Comedy* was recited. One evening in the theater King Charles XV invited Ibsen to sit with him in the royal box and afterward in the palace presented him with the order of Gustav Wasa. And long past midnight this very human king drank with Ibsen a glass of champagne to their eternal friendship, which meant also that they thenceforth were to address each other with the familiar pronoun "du."

At the same time another honor was bestowed on the poet: he was selected to represent Norway at the dedication of the

Suez Canal. Thus Ibsen came to see the Sphinx where Peer Gynt had talked with Professor Begriffenfeld and also Cairo where this hero had found his empire in the insane asylum. On October 9, 1869, he sailed from Marseilles with a very international group of 86 dignitaries. In Egypt they were entertained on a 23 day tour up the Nile as far as the Nubian Desert, carefully planned by the French Egyptologist Mariette. In the middle of November the party returned to Cairo and Port Said, witnessed the dedication of the Canal, and then returned to Europe. Ibsen further took advantage of the occasion by making a visit to Paris to study its art treasures. Then he returned to his family in Dresden. A result of the trip was another order, a Turkish one: The Commander Star of the Order of the Medjidie, "a beautiful thing," as Ibsen called it in a letter to his publisher Hegel.

As a mark of his gratitude for the hospitality shown him in Sweden Ibsen sent to Fru Limnell a whimsical rhymed letter describing the journey through Egypt; this "Balloon Letter to a Swedish Lady" was published in the volume of Ibsen's poems which made its appearance a short time after this. In characteristic manner Ibsen saw the various travellers as animals: Norse bears, Spanish stallions, "Lutetia cocks," German boars, or Swiss chamois. As might have been expected, an anonymous writer in the journal *Das neue Reich* felt his nation insulted by this poem and also by some others written at the time of the Danish War by an author "who was enjoying German hospitality in Dresden." Ibsen was somewhat annoyed, but he answered in a dignified, gentle fashion, quoting a German poet who had said that each poet ought to go with his king and asking very cleverly whether any unprejudiced German could respect a Scandinavian who had at the time of the war flattered the Prussians? This letter served to silence Ibsen's super-patriotic critics.

Among Ibsen's friends in Rome there had been a certain

lawyer, Herr Klubien, who in 1870 was holding a post at the Supreme Court in Copenhagen. Ibsen wrote him September 9th of that year, while he was on a visit to Denmark, mentioning the fact that numerous other Norwegian poets had been honored with the Danebrog Order and asking whether he had done anything to offend the persons in authority. Ibsen adds: "And I must tell you, that I am actually greedy for every recognition coming to me from Denmark. You have no conception of the effect of such a thing in Norway. But from your own Parisian diplomatic period you know just as well as I that one must drop a hint; and that is what I am doing herewith. You know the ministers who, as I believe, are quite favorably inclined toward me. Interest yourself in the matter. A distinction conferred by Denmark would mean a mighty support for my position in Norway. I need not ask you to employ the necessary diplomatic caution. . . ."

Yet this affair was at bottom contrary to Ibsen's finer sensibilities, as a letter from Dresden, dated January 8, 1871, shows:

MY DEAR KLUBIEN!

I cannot do otherwise; I must write you while there is still time.

Last summer when I was in Copenhagen, so near to my own country, it seemed to me to be more than all else desirable to return home under certain circumstances which I deemed necessary and I expressed a wish that I should have repressed if calmer reflexion had been possible.

It is clear to me now that I did not succeed in presenting the matter to you in such a light that I can be considered other than a quite ordinary vain person. And at the same time you were unable to create any other conception of me among the others concerned in the matter.

This affair has since tortured me very much; I have had a feeling as though I had gone out without washing my face.

I cannot bear that; I must raise myself again in my own estimation. And therefore, I beg of you, let the whole matter drop and see to it that I rise again in the estimation of these men, since I

cannot do without that. By the side of this consideration everything else is immaterial.

You see, now I feel at ease once more. Receive me back into
your memory again as your old Roman carissimo and devoted
friend

Henrik Ibsen.

But scarcely had Ibsen decided to renounce nobly and
honorably when he was notified by the Danish government
that he had been appointed a Knight of the Order of Danebrog! He sent letters to all who had aided him, inquired of
Klubien what formalities were to be fulfilled, and closed:
"Once more many thanks! The bestowal of this honor is a
great thing for me, greater than I can tell you at the moment!" To Hegel he wrote: "I cannot thank sufficiently the
men who have brought this about. Now my countrymen will
think twice as much of my collected *Poems!*" This is the
only case in which Ibsen refers to orders in a lighter vein.
He took them very seriously and before long he could and
did appear in public resplendent as a Christmas tree.

If Ibsen was worried about decorations that were to win
him recognition in the country where he had been so deeply
despised, he actually longed for some critic who would
understand him. But it must be said: Ibsen did not want
adulation, he wanted the truth, no matter how sharply expressed. At the time when *Peer Gynt* appeared the young
Danish critic, Georg Brandes, wrote a review in which he
stated that the play was neither beautiful nor true; but he was
able to see "almost everywhere a wealth of poetry and a
depth of thought." Brandes spoke his mind frankly and
Ibsen accepted his criticisms gladly, because he realized that
here was a man who brought to his work sympathy and understanding, one who saw eye to eye with him in matters of the
art of the future. Moreover, it seemed this meant for Ibsen
the fulfillment of Brand's ardent wish:

> Oh, for one heart with faith in me!
> How quiet, strong, and rich I'd be!

Denmark's leading critic, Clemens Petersen, because of a scandal in which he was involved in a girls' school where he had been lecturing, was forced to leave early in 1869, between days, for the United States, where he then devoted himself to religious journalism among the Scandinavian-Americans. Immediately after this Björnson, who had previously attacked Brandes because of his anti-religious attitude, invited the latter to join him in a summer journey to Finmark: "I have such a strong feeling that you must be standing at the parting of the ways, that, by continuing your path further, you will go astray, that I want to talk to you, and consequently am speaking to you from my heart now." Brandes declined with thanks; he was not in the least drawn to the "tender-minded" Björnson; the "tough-minded" Ibsen with his demand for "a revolution of the spirit of man" attracted him much more. He wrote Ibsen a poem in which he expresses a hope that the two might fight side by side.

The Hospital in Rome—the Night of January 9, 1871.

> Brother, at last I've found thee!
> Be thou the captain of our high endeavor,
> And I the armor-bearer; ever
> The tie of kindred souls hath bound me.

Soon after this Brandes visited Ibsen in Dresden. He mentions that there are many examples of Ibsen's gruffness —the manner in which he would drive away annoying visitors with a demand for "Arbeitsruhe!" is famous—but that he recalls also many instances of the poet's cordiality and nobility. The essay is dated 1906:

I learned these things a long, long time ago in the course of long walks in Dresden and vicinity, when Ibsen explained to me the

German character, as he believed to have come to understand it after years of residence in the country, or when he criticised Schiller's dramas, the rhetorical flights of which annoyed him; likewise Runeberg's poems, which he disliked because they were written in hexameters. He was always on guard against all that was academic, traditional, or removed from life; in the end even verse as such such went against his grain. We would enter a restaurant; the waiters noted the rosette of some barbarian order in the buttonhole of this stranger, and hastened to bring whatever he ordered. Until late in the evening Ibsen could sit thus at a little table, his keen glance peering out from behind his glasses, presenting his views, questioning, at times, praising—this latter always in one set formula: "What you have just told me affects me quite like a poem."

In the early seventies Ibsen frequently visited the Dresden Literary Society. He showed great interest in the lectures, which as a rule were good and informative. Toward the modest, very little known Saxon authors he conducted himself as a colleague; he respected their knowledge and their solid, unprejudiced literary culture.

Henrik Ibsen's appearance indicates the same qualities that mark his poetry. The but rarely altered stern or sarcastic seriousness of his physiognomy serves to hide a spiritual gentleness. Ibsen is stout, well-built; he dresses tastefully and elegantly and looks very impressive. His gait is slow, his bearing noble, and he moves with dignity. His head is large, interesting, surrounded by a full mane of slightly gray hair that he wears rather long. The forehead that dominates his face is steep, high, and broad, yet well-formed, unusual through its stamp of greatness and wealth of thought. When he is silent his mouth appears pinched shut, as though without lips, and betrays uncommunicativeness and silence. In the presence of several persons Ibsen frequently sits quite silently, as the mute, at times almost gruff guardian of the sanctuary of his spirit. . . .

I know two expressions in his face. One, when a smile, his kind, delicate smile breaks through and makes mobile the mask of his face, when the cordial kindliness that rests at the bottom of his soul comes out to meet one. Ibsen to a certain extent is ill at ease in company, as very serious natures frequently are. But he has a beautiful smile, and by means of his smile, glance, and hand-clasp he says much that he cannot or does not wish to put into words. Furthermore he has a little trick of interjecting in a quietly smiling (schmunzelnd, as the Germans say) manner, with an expression of good-natured roguishness, brief asides into the conversation, which are anything but good-natured, by means of which he reveals the most charming side of his nature.   The smile serves to conciliate one with the harshness of his outbursts.

But I know another expression that impatience, anger, or biting mockery can give to his face, an expression of almost cruel severity, that reminds one of the words in his beautiful old poem of *Terje Vigen:*

> Yet at times in his eye a hard light blazed,—
> Most when the sea ran high,—
> And then folk fancied the man was crazed,
> And there were few that unfearing gazed
> In Terje Vigen's eye.

It is the expression that his poet's soul has most frequently assumed face to face with the world.

The delicate kindliness of Ibsen's character is shown in his attitude toward those members of his family who were dear to him.   In 1869 he sent his sister Hedvig one of his photographs with an affectionate dedication.   She had written him the news of their mother's death in a letter filled with pleadings that he should mend his ways and come to his Saviour.   Ibsen did not write to his father; it was months before he could bring himself to answer his sister's letter— the chasm between them was too great.   He stated simply that a chasm was dividing him from the family in Skien; asked Hedvig gently to make no efforts at converting him, but to write him often.   He added some news about himself, about Sigurd, and also, "I wish you knew my wife; she is the very wife for me."   In closing he states that he cannot write any-thing concerning what Hedvig wished most to hear about— i.e., the state of his soul.   Yet it is in this letter that he gives in a nut-shell his whole biography: "I look into myself; there

is where I fight my battles, now conquering, now suffering
defeat."

While Ibsen recognized that Susannah was the very wife
for him and frequently expressed his love, admiration and
indebtedness to her in heartfelt manner, there lay for him
also a distinct attraction in the type that was the direct opposite of Lady Inger or Hjördis; this was the type of Eline or
Dagny, the gentle, self-sacrificing, comparatively insignificant
woman who serves as a foil for the heroine. For the contrasting sisters so often found in Ibsen's plays he had the
opportunity of observing models at close range in his Dresden years when Marie Thoresen, a sister of Mrs. Ibsen, came
to live with them.

Susannah Ibsen was a distinct personality who frequently
defended her opinions in heated arguments with her head-
strong husband; if Ibsen insisted excitedly that what he called
his academic training gave him better judgment in political
or literary questions, then Mrs. Ibsen, playing quietly with
her fan, replied that a woman's instinct was a much surer
guide in such matters than all the acquired knowledge of a
man. Very frequently guests present on such occasions,
feeling sure that any difference of opinion between married
people is a certain sign of conjugal unhappiness, jumped to
the conclusion that Ibsen was most unfortunately married,
while in reality he was very fortunate in having the corrective
guide his wife's judgment afforded. Ibsen himself certainly
recognized what a wife who did not docilely swear by all
his opinions meant for his own development.

But in Marie's mildness and harmony there was a charm
that Ibsen found very pleasing. In the chivalrous manner
he always showed toward ladies he tried to make her stay in
Dresden as pleasant as possible. He showed her the sights
of Saxony's beautiful capital and introduced her to modern
German literature by presenting her with the works of con-

temporary authors, especially Paul Heyse. The presence of
the cheerful young lady shed brightness over the whole house
and an idyllic happiness invaded Ibsen's home. One day
he presented Marie with a bouquet of water lilies and a poem,
in which he gave expression to his appreciation of her gentle,
profound character. Marie read the verses and preserved
them as a treasure, as well she might, for *With a Water Lily*
is one of the most melodious and delicate lyrics Ibsen ever
wrote. Grieg set it to music, enhancing thereby the haunting
charm of the verses. Marie died young; a few years after her
visit in Dresden she met her death in Copenhagen after a
lingering illness, faithfully attended by Mrs. Ibsen. The
memory of this beautiful character remained with Ibsen for
the rest of his days:

> See, O sweet love, what I bring thee,
> Flower with white-winged petals gleamy,
> Bright upon the clear, calm water
> It hath floated, spring's fair daughter.
>
> .   .   .   .   .   .
>
> Child, thy bosom is a stream!
> Danger, danger, there to dream!
> Though above the lilies peep
> And the sprite pretends to sleep.

As Ibsen became more and more famous in his own country, Norwegians travelling in Germany frequently made it a
point to pay their respects to the poet living in self-imposed
exile. One of these visitors was a physician from Christiania,
Dr. August Koren, who happened to be in Dresden in 1874.
He looked up Ibsen's address in the city directory and found
his way to a small three-story house, with one family living
on each floor. On the first and on the second floor he inquired in vain for an author by the name of Ibsen; the people had never heard of him. When on the third floor he found

Ibsen's name on the door, he felt a pang of sorrow that the most famous poet of his country should dwell so unknown in Germany, that the very people in his own house failed to know his name.

The door was opened to him by thirteen-year-old Sigurd, who expressed regret that his parents were not at home. Dr. Koren then invited the lad to go to the opera with him, but Sigurd declined because he had to do his school work; he was required to memorize sixty lines of Greek, a voluntary task assumed by some of the leading students in the class. Dr. Koren suggested that if it was a voluntary task Sigurd might drop it to enjoy the opera, only to be told that such a task when once assumed was counted as work to be accomplished and failure in it would bring him a punishment, confinement in the school prison, according to the stern customs of German schools of that day. The visitor found that this lad of thirteen had already learned more Greek than was required in Norway for a *Magister Artium*. Ibsen, conscious of what he had missed in his youth, was sending his son to the best schools available.

On the following day Dr. Koren received a letter inviting him to spend an evening with the Ibsens. He found that Mrs. Ibsen took a dominating part in the highly interesting conversation, so much so that Ibsen said to her jokingly: "Would you be kind enough to be silent for a moment while I tell one little story; after I have finished with it you shall have the floor again as long as you wish." And then he told of their stay on an island near Naples during the cholera epidemic, where the mistress of their inn had assured them that they need not fear cholera on their island because they had a saint who was quite potent against cholera. "Over there on that other island," she had added, "they never have typhoid, for there they have a saint who is good against typhoid fever." This naïve faith had been of the highest interest to Ibsen.

In the course of the conversation Dr. Koren returned to his thought that it was a pity to find Norway's great poet so unknown in foreign lands and he asked Ibsen why he did not do something to have his plays translated into German; *The Pretenders*, he thought, would at once make him famous throughout Germany.

Ibsen listened to him quietly, nodded his head deliberately, and then said, "Ah, well, that will come some day!"

Signs of the coming of this day were already at hand. *Brand*, the *Poems*, and *The League of Youth*, had already been translated into German, and other works soon followed; in 1875 his plays began to appear on the stage. About this time Ibsen asked his friend Dietrichson to write a biographical sketch of him to be published in German papers. In 1872 Edmund Gosse reviewed Ibsen's *Poems* in the *Spectator*, the first article in the English language on Ibsen.

Friedrich Hegel, who was Ibsen's true friend as well as his publisher, took over a number of the earlier plays of Ibsen, previously published in very cheap editions in Norway. When in 1871 a Norwegian printer, Jensen by name, attempted to pirate *Lady Inger* and *The Vikings*, Ibsen protested energetically against this "impudent effrontery" and warned him, "if you dare persist in your intention I shall show you, both in the columns of the newspapers and in open court, what the consequences of such rascality are." Ibsen had the satisfaction of seeing Jensen forced to pay a fine and compensation, while the court ordered his whole stock of the two plays confiscated and destroyed. In Ibsen's letters to Hegel one finds in these years references to 1,000 or 2,000 dollars to be invested in bonds; there is as frequent mention of money as there had been during his days in Rome, only now it is not a question of needing it, but of investing it.

Thus Ibsen became economically independent. He used this independence to retire to his study and to lock the door

behind him. He was free to be true to himself, which meant
that he devoted himself exclusively to his poetry, as almost
no other figure in world literature ever did. At approximately
biennial intervals he sent a new drama into the world, and all
the rest of the time he spent with his characters. From this
time forward the association of the poet with the personages
of his plays practically sums up the remaining annals of his
biography.

3

In the fall of 1872 Dietrichson stopped a few days in
Dresden to visit his old friend Ibsen, and while there received
a rare treat. The poet who always guarded the secrets of his
workshop absolutely, even from his family, invited Dietrichson to a reading of the first part of *Emperor and Galilean*.
After dinner thirteen-year-old Sigurd was sent into another
room to study his lessons for the next day, chiefly an assign-
ment in religious instruction. The boy would have preferred
to hear his father read the play, and when Mrs. Ibsen returned from the other room she reported with a smile that
Sigurd had exclaimed, "I believe there is just as much religion in father's play as there is in my lesson!" Ibsen had
no special talent as a reader, but he had a pleasant voice and
a forceful, absolutely unaffected manner. When he finished
at midnight, closing with the chant of the church choir so
ominous for Julian about to ascend the throne: "For thine is
the kingdom, and the power, and the glory!" Dietrichson
felt that he had heard one of the greatest historical dramas
since Shakespeare's day; later the wonderfully drawn characters of the tyrant Constantine and the lustful Helena
haunted him in his dreams.

Sigurd was right—the play was an intense effort on the
author's part to clarify and give expression to his own religious experience. Christ had made Julian's youth one long

dread; in this statement as well as in the following the author is probably speaking through his hero:

> Oh, he is terrible, that mysterious—that merciless god-man!   At every turn, wheresoever I wished to go, he met me, stark and stern, with his unconditional, inexorable commands. . . . Always "Thou shalt." If my soul gathered itself up in one gnawing and consuming hate towards the murderer of my kin, what said the commandment: "Love thine enemy!" If my mind, athirst for beauty, longed for scenes and rites from the bygone world of Greece, Christianity swooped down on me with its "Seek the one thing needful!" If I felt the sweet lusts of the flesh toward this and that, the Prince of Renunciation terrified me with his: "Kill the body that the soul may live!"—All that is human has become unlawful since the day when the seer of Galilee became ruler of the world.   Through him, life has become death.   Love and hatred, both are sins.   Has he, then, transformed man's flesh and blood?   Has not earth-bound man remained what he ever was?   Our inmost, healthy soul rebels against it all;—and yet we are to will in the very teeth of our own will!   Thou shalt, shalt, shalt!

The boy who had grown up in Skien with a yearning for beauty and an ardent desire to become an artist, but who had also in his home, school, and church been continually under the shadow of pietism, had fought out in his own breast the struggle between the pagan and the Christian view of life. Neither could satisfy him; he knew all about "the old beauty that is no longer beautiful and the new truth that is no longer true." Ibsen, as a poet of the future, could not deal with the subject of Julian the Apostate as a romanticist, Schiller for example, might have done; the royal lover of Greek beauty in such a drama would have struggled to restore the day when Pan was not yet dead, fought against the inevitable fate of all beauty on this earth, and fallen a victim of an idealist cause, exciting pity and fear in the spectators, who, while knowing the hopelessness of his struggle from the first, would yet applaud the chivalrous fight of the hero.

On the contrary, Ibsen's hero—in whom there is to be found "much self-anatomy" as the poet wrote to Edmund Gosse—knows that a return to "the first empire" of pagan sensualism is no ideal worthy of his day. Equally impossible is "the second empire" of Christian self-abnegation; the poet knew from observation in his own family the obscurantism and medievalism of such a course. Julian endeavors to establish "the third empire," the day of the free, striving man restrained only by an innate sense of nobility—much the same ideal Nietzsche a decade later preached as the coming of the Superman. Men were to find God not on Mount Olympus nor on Calvary but in their own souls, wills, and senses. The noble spirit of Christ was to inspire men whose flesh was not starved, whose minds were not bound by superstitions, and whose wills were not thwarted by other-worldly considerations. Men of "the third empire" were to realize themselves fully, rising high above either of the previous ideals by combining Greek freedom of the spirit with Christian readiness for self-sacrifice. This was the positive message Ibsen gave to the world; to be sure, an ideal that lay in the far distance. He knew that just as Moses never entered the Promised Land so would he never see "the third empire" realized. But this was a matter of no regret to Ibsen, because he felt that as soon as a group or a party set about to realize an ideal, by this very fact was it travestied, as worthless followers of Julian made a mockery of his high aims. And didn't Björnson dispose of Ibsen's noble yearning for a vital religion of the future with the simple judgment: "Atheism!" Ibsen preferred to be ahead of his time and to stand alone.

No drama in world literature, probably, contains a conflict on a grander scale—the Emperor pitting himself against the Galilean—against God himself! But into the high pathos of this theme there is mingled a bitter mockery making the play a tragi-comedy, as indeed all human life appeared to Ibsen.

From the splendid mob-scene in the first act with the quarrel of the "pious," to the end, there are scattered through the whole piece many examples of mordant humor. When Julian has commanded that the ignorant Christian population is to worship Apollo, the citizens discuss it as follows:

A CITIZEN: Who is this Apollo that people begin to talk so much about?
THE OTHER CITIZEN: Why, 'tis the priest of Corinth—he who watered what the holy Paul had planted.
FIRST CITIZEN: Ay, ay, to be sure, I think I remember now.
PHOCION: No, no, no, 'tis not *that* Apollo; 'tis another entirely;— this is the Sun King—the great lyre-playing Apollo.
THE OTHER CITIZEN: Ah, indeed; *that* Apollo! Is he better?

There is bitter self-irony in the figure of the pedantic Julian, who, full of ridiculous anger, threatens to change the world by his writings; Ibsen knew but too well how little effect a book has on the course of the world! Small wonder that he yearned with his hero for the "road to Eleusis"—toward mysticism. But at the same time Ibsen shows a firm belief in the "one increasing purpose" running through the ages: "there is One who reappears, at certain intervals in the course of human history. He is like a rider taming a wild horse in the arena. Again and yet again it throws him. A moment, and he is in the saddle again, each time more secure and more expert; but off he has to go, in all his varying incarnations, until this day. Off he had to go as the God-created man in Eden's grove; off he had to go as the founder of the world empire; off he must go as the prince of the empire of God."

But in spite of the tragic force, the vast theme, the wealth of poetry, a number of striking characterizations, and ten years of labor, *Emperor and Galilean* does not have the verve of many other Ibsen plays. When Emperor Julian meets his end on the field of battle where there appears to him "the carpenter's Son hammering the Emperor's coffin" and where he exclaims: "I will not be vanquished! I am young; I am invulnerable, the third empire is at hand—," a moment later to sink down mortally wounded with: "Thou hast conquered, Galilean!" we have to a large extent lost interest in the hero. The reason for this perhaps is that the poet himself had tired of him. While in all other cases Ibsen practiced the severe self-discipline of never printing a play before it was as perfect as he could conceive of its being, and never hesitated to do over again the work that he had already finished, in this one case he sent the second part to the printer before it was a finished play in the sense in which his other dramas are. Evidently on this occasion he wished to avoid the intense mental strain of recasting the whole in a more unified structure. And the reason probably was, that he was working in the unknown milieu of the fourth century which he had to reconstruct painfully from ancient authors, while in his other plays, such as *The League of Youth* or *Brand* he moved in a setting that he knew as well as his own pocket.

It was in this little country of Norway where Ibsen was ever at home, no matter how far he wandered or how long he stayed away. In the poem *Burned Ships* he tells how his thoughts nightly fly back to his native land. Every day he read Norwegian papers from the first page to the printer's trade mark at the end of the last; in advertisements or reports of crimes he often discovered the "characteristic" touches that meant so much to him. When his country in 1872 celebrated a festival in honor of the union under King Harold a thousand years before Ibsen sent home a poem in which he admonished his people to unite with the other Scandinavians into one union, just as Italy and Germany had recently become united under Cavour and Bismarck. The striking thing about this poem is the personal note that introduces it:

HENRIK IBSEN'S MAGIC MIRROR

Ibsen is represented with his poet's pension of 400 dollars and a beer glass, humble and un-
kempt, standing opposite a mirror in which he appears many times enlarged and with a glorious
halo. "Herr Ibsen is to write a poem for the 1000-year anniversary and in looking for inspiration is gazing on the greatest that, in his eyes, the country has produced in the last thousand
years. What wonder then that he will end by writing the poem about himself rather than about
the 1000-year anniversary."

—From *Vikingen*, August 3, 1872.

My countrymen, who filled for me deep bowls
Of wholesome, bitter medicine, such as gave
The poet, on the margin of the grave
Fresh force to fight where broken twilight rolls,—
My countrymen, who sped me o'er the wave
An exile, with my griefs for pilgrim-soles,
My fears for burdens, doubts for staff, to roam,—
From the wide world I send you greeting home.

I send you thanks for gifts that help and harden,
Thanks for each hour of purifying pain;
Each plant that springs in my poetic garden
Is rooted where your harshness poured its rain;
Each shoot in which it blooms and burgeons forth
It owes to that gray weather from the North;
The sun relaxes, but the fog secures!
My country, thanks! My life's best gifts were yours!

Since his country inspired him with such bitterness it is not surprising that on a visit to Norway in the summer of 1874 he felt as he later described it to Björnson: "When, ten years ago, after an absence of ten years, I sailed up the Fjord, I felt a weight settling down on my breast, a feeling of actual physical depression. And this feeling lasted all the while I was at home; I was not myself under those cold, uncomprehending Norwegian eyes at the windows and in the streets." He felt that he could not do any writing at all in Christiania; his former years there had implanted in him an ineradicable inhibition.

This cramping feeling persisted in spite of the fact that he was definitely recognized as a great dramatist in Norway and was no longer considered a *poète manqué;* in spite of the many performances of his plays in the National Theater; and in spite of the cordiality shown him on numerous occasions. For Ibsen, the most touching symptom of this changed feeling was a demonstration on the part of the students, who on the afternoon of September 10th marched with flags and music to Ibsen's dwelling to express their admiration and affection. Among other things a song composed for the occasion was sung. It touched the poet's heart, so that he took this occasion to speak freely—as he rarely found it possible to do—about his inmost feelings. For this reason the speech to the students is a very important biographic document.

Ibsen, now approaching his fiftieth birthday, was quite a different man from the desperate, debt-laden poet who had so eagerly left Christiania ten years before. He had won confidence in himself through the position his work had definitely brought him in Norway, Sweden, and Denmark, and was beginning to gain for him in Germany and England as well; this incipient world importance manifested itself in his outward appearance; he had by this time begun to wear the long black frock-coat and the tall silk hat that are so inextricably connected with the Ibsen of world fame. He felt therefore that he might give the students a definition of what constitutes a poet:

As for me, it was a long time before I realized that to be a poet, is chiefly to see, but mark well, to see in such a way that the thing seen is perceived by his audience just as the poet saw it. But thus is seen and thus is appreciated only that which has been lived through. . . . All that I have written, these last ten years, I have, mentally, lived through. . . . Partly, I have written on that which only by glimpses and at my best moments I have felt stirring vividly within me as something great and beautiful. I have written on that which, so to speak, has stood higher than my daily self. . . .

But I have also written on the opposite, on that which to introspective contemplation appears as the dregs and sediments of one's own nature. The work of writing has in this case been to me like a bath which I have felt to leave me cleaner, healthier, and freer. Yes, gentlemen, nobody can poetically present that to which he has not to a certain degree and at least at times the model within himself.

After this very frank and illuminating confession concerning his methods he unlocked his heart and showed for once the real warmth of feeling usually so carefully hidden under the mask of sardonic wit:

> And now, my dear countrymen, in conclusion a few words which are likewise connected with something I have lived through. When Emperor Julian stands at the end of his career, and everything collapses round about him, there is nothing that renders him so despondent as the thought that all which he has gained was this: to be remembered with respectful appreciation by clear and cool heads, whereas his opponents lived on, rich in the love of warm, living human hearts. This motive has proceeded from something that I have lived through; it has its origin in a question that I have at times put to myself, down there in the solitude. Now the young people of Norway have come to me here tonight and have given me the answer in word and song, have given me the answer so warmly and so clearly as I never had expected to hear it. . . .

Loud applause greeted Ibsen's speech, and with ringing hurrahs for the master the students marched off. In the evening the poet and Mrs. Ibsen were guests at a performance of *The League of Youth,* the play that had so enraged the people ten years before, that riots ensued. By this time the Norwegians were ready to enjoy the play for the clever comedy that it was, rather than to resent the poet's satirical thrusts. As the curtain fell there was a unanimous call for the author and Ibsen appeared behind the footlights as a storm of applause rang through the theater.

Now the prophet was not without honor, even in his own country! Even in Christiania!

IX

THE SOCIAL PLAYS

1

The poet whom the Christiania students came to honor was the author of *The League of Youth,* the play that had dealt so harshly with Björnson and the radicals of the peasant party. Ibsen realized very well that these young men from the conservative section of Norwegian society had serenaded him because they considered him—the extreme individualist —an adherent of their party! This sad fact dampened somewhat Ibsen's great joy in the honor shown him. He felt that if he should write anything not in conformity with the views of these conservatives, they would all pounce upon him like a pack of wolves. Thus Ibsen came to know the emotions of the man who is being publicly honored as something that in reality he is not. He alluded to this in his sardonic manner when he said in closing his speech: ". . . it is my hope and my belief that what I experience tonight is an inner experience which sometime shall find its reflection in a coming work."

This coming work was to be a thrust at the very party who had come to honor him by (literally) singing his praises. Ibsen did not intend to have his windows smashed by a mob of conservatives—as happened to Björnson—but in exercising his mission as "state satirist," as he called himself, he preferred to live at a distance. Therefore he made but a brief visit to Norway, because physical courage was not one of Ibsen's virtues.

In the course of his sojourn in Norway several social injustices came to Ibsen's attention, causing him to turn from

—From a contemporary caricature.

AASTA HANSTEEN

A pioneer suffragist in the days of Ibsen.

great dramas that were to revolutionize the spirit of man by means of a call to the third empire of God on earth to dramas that were to make the lives of men more bearable by combating social evils. For example several cases came to light at this time of ruthlessly greedy owners of dockyards who repaired ships in a very slipshod fashion, insured them heavily, and then sent them out to sea, causing the death of the crew in the first storm that happened along. The subject of the "floating coffins" caused a great deal of discussion in the British Parliament, in the Norwegian press, and even in mass-meetings in Christiania. Another burning question of the hour in Norway arose out of the case of a Swedish lady of nobility who came to Christiania to accuse a Norwegian student in pamphlets and from the lecture platform of having seduced and then deserted her; she tried to arouse the interest of Norwegian women in the great injustices that the egotism of men could inflict on her sex under existing laws. The Norwegian painter Aasta Hansteen courageously took up cudgels for this Swedish lady and for all victims of man's brutality, whereupon quite an agitation for the cause of woman ensued. Miss Hansteen had about her some uncouth and mannish ways that caused all pillars of society to turn in scorn and disgust from this "unwomanly woman" and her indecent agitation. The humorous weeklies made endless sport of the lady's short figure, homely face, stubbornly impertinent expression, and the riding whip she always carried, presumably to defend herself against the vile menfolk.

Shortly after the Ibsens' return to Germany they moved from Dresden to Munich (in April, 1875) largely for the purpose of finding a more suitable school for Sigurd. Here *A Bankruptcy*, a new social play by Björnson, dealing with the reform of an unscrupulous capitalist, reached Ibsen. His friend, Georg Brandes, through his letters and books had been steadily influencing Ibsen to go further in the direction he had already entered upon in *The League of Youth;* the Danish critic preached that the literature of the future should present impartial studies of reality, should show the author in an objective attitude toward his theme, and should discuss the problems of the hour. And now that his old rival Björnson had come forward with the first Scandinavian play making business a subject for poetry, Ibsen resolved to outdo him at this game. It always irritated Ibsen when he found in the cartoons of comic weeklies that in a sketch of Norwegian artists Björnson invariably stood at the head, drawn as a much more important figure than himself. German critics, too, considered Björnson the greater dramatist.

Thus he began work on the *Pillars of Society* in the summer of 1875. While in Björnson's play a dishonest business man is reformed after he has been unmasked by an honest lawyer backed by a moral public opinion, Ibsen's capitalist makes a voluntary confession of his misdeeds in the face of a corrupt and corrupting society. The involuntary reformation of Björnson's hero Ibsen considered of very little advantage to society; while the inner change in Consul Bernick, leading to a freewill confession, meant a revolt against the prevailing stuffy morality and the opening of the way toward a new order based on Truth and Freedom. This is very characteristic of the two men; Björnson was optimistically conservative and wished to build up on the past and the present, while Ibsen was ever ready to throw overboard the whole game and to call for a new deal. Equally characteristic is Ibsen's sarcastic title: *Pillars of Society.*

The new spirit in society was to come from the New World, from the United States. Previously Ibsen had used the term "Americanism" as an insult to describe the lack of idealism and the love for the dollar that had caused Norway to remain neutral in the Danish War. Now, along with many of his progressive contemporaries, he saw in America the country untrammeled by stuffy conventions, where everyone was free to realize his personality, and where everyone—even a woman —could do any sort of work. On the eve of her departure for America Dina, the despised and pitied illegitimate child, says to her future husband, that before she marries ". . . first I will work, and become something for myself, just as you are. I don't want to be just a chattel which is being taken possession of." This was in sharp contrast to the position of woman in Norway, where at that time she was an absolute zero so far as vital interests were concerned—as an illustration of this we find Consul Bernick saying to his wife in answer to a question regarding his business affairs: "But of what possible interest can that be to you?" Lona Hessel, one of these untrammeled individuals from the "land of un-limited possibilities," returns to Norway to let fresh air into the stagnant atmosphere of her native town. This play, like practically all of Ibsen's previous works, is a call for the realization of personality; but instead of the Utopian "all or nothing" there is a more realistic presentation of the demand with America serving as the ideal.

This truthful realism took Germany by storm. In Berlin five theaters played *Pillars of Society* at the same time, February, 1878. The young men, as Paul Schlenther wrote many years afterward, felt that it was a joy to be alive when among them there was living a great poet who took the content of the time into his hands and moulded it into a world that appeared at once truthfully presented and idealistic. What an optimistic belief in the regenerating power of love lay in the conclusion of the piece, and what delicious satire in the picture of "Pastor" Rörlund and his Society for the Moral Regeneration of the Lapsed and Lost! What a courageous, noble woman was Lona Hessel, modelled on the uncouth, but generous-hearted Aasta Hansteen! Ibsen became for the youth of Germany the man who let fresh air stream into their lives, and practically every dramatist of the succeeding decades was influenced by the spirit of the master. The great opposition to the innovations and the "immoralities" of Ibsen's dramas was steadily overcome, his plays became the sensations of every season and the number of Ibsen performances increased annually until in the year of his death as many as 932 took place in one season in Germany. *Pillars of Society* was the first Ibsen play to be performed in England —one performance at the Gaiety Theater, December 15, 1880, in William Archer's adaptation.

Even before *Pillars of Society* was published *The Pretenders* had been played by the company of the theater-loving Duke of Meiningen. This was a troupe which under the very intelligent direction of the Duke played in all larger cities of Germany during the years 1874 to 1892, substituting for the empty pathos previously in vogue a greater realism and in general setting a high standard in dramatic art. Naturally it was exceedingly gratifying to Ibsen when at the first of nine performances in Berlin he was called out by the enthusiastic audience, when the Duke invited him to be his guest at his castle, and when he decorated him with the Cross of the First Class of the "Sächsisch-Ernestinische Hausorden"! More substantial rewards came to him from the performances of *The Vikings* at the best theaters in Vienna, Dresden, Munich, Leipzig and other cities—all of which paid the author ten percent of the gross receipts of each performance. No wonder that with all this money to be carefully invested in bonds, steamships, tramway lines, and other undertakings Ibsen cast the suspicion of Bohemianism and poetry from him, as Edmund Gosse puts it, and with his gold spectacles, his Dundreary whiskers, his long frock-coat and tall silk hat, his quick staccato step, he adopted the pose of a gentleman of affairs, very positive and with no nonsense about him. With ironical glee Ibsen noted that on his visits to the Tyrol the

—From *Vikingen,* Christmas, 1878.

THE CONTEMPORARY AASGAARDS CROWD

Norwegian authors are shown riding their books through the air wielding quills. It is interesting to note the prominent position given to Björnson, while the author of *Brand, Peer Gynt, Emperor and Galilean, Pillars of Society,* etc., comes distinctly in second place.

innocent maidens would come to kiss his hand and ask for his blessing because they considered the man with the long black coat a Catholic priest!

In Norway too his plays were steadily gaining ground, frequently due to a clever suggestion made here or there by the dramatist himself. Thus in 1874 he wrote to Edvard Grieg, asking him to compose suitable music for *Peer Gynt*. During Ibsen's years in Bergen Grieg had been a sort of "wonderchild" who was later, on the advice of Ole Bull, sent to the Leipzig Conservatory. When Grieg, at the time 31 years old, received Ibsen's letter, he at first thought it impossible to produce so philosophical and skeptical a poem in the theater, much less to write music for it. But as he re-read the drama and wandered about in the woods and mountains near Bergen he came to the conclusion after four days that there lay an enchanting appeal in the poetry of *Peer Gynt*. Therefore he rented a very lonely cottage overlooking both the sea and the mountains—a place so lonely that the trolls would never be frightened away, he said—and, after having had a piano sent there he spent the rest of the summer in composing the work by which he is now most widely known. In the year 1876 the play was performed in Christiania 37 times before crowded houses attracted by the beautiful poetry of the play, the charming music of Grieg, and the splendid scenery painted by Norwegian artists. Truly, now the Norwegians could feel that a great national art was arising in their country, winning the admiration of all the world.

When Ibsen came to Munich he called on Paul Heyse, the dean of German men of letters of his day, by whom he was received cordially and introduced to the literary club of *The Crocodile*. This was a circle of poets, artists and scientists that had been formed through the desire of King Max II to assemble about his court in Munich a large number of distinguished men; in Ibsen's day the new king, Ludwig II, favored Richard Wagner almost exclusively, but Munich continued to be an important literary center. At the meetings of this club Ibsen generally was very quiet, but he was the very spirit of wit in the more intimate meetings in Hotel Achatz at the Maximiliansplatz with Paul Heyse, Moritz Carrière, professor of esthetics, Dr. Oswald Schmidt, a young physician, and Professor Dietrichson, at the time also living in Munich. These *Frühschoppen* were held daily from twelve to one so long as Ibsen was only planning a new drama; but once he had begun to write it he concentrated absolutely on the work, took his walks alone, and often wrote from dawn to dusk.

When the Swedish University at Upsala decided to award an honorary doctor's degree to Professor Dietrichson the latter suggested that Ibsen ought also to receive this honor, a proposal to which the university readily assented. It was an exceedingly happy day for the poet when on September 7, 1877, in Upsala, he was crowned with laurel and awarded a doctor's degree! In a little group consisting of the most distinguished authors and scientists of Sweden that met on the same evening Ibsen was so lively, good-humored and witty that Dietrichson in telling of it remarks that he finds it hard to understand how this man acquired a reputation for silence. Another incident Dietrichson enjoyed more than Ibsen. This happened at a big dinner in Stockholm where all the guests rushed forward to be introduced to the famous poet as he entered the room, except one Finnish scholar, distinguished in his branch but oblivious of everything else in the world. Finally the host brought the two together: "May I introduce my Finnish friend Dr. X?—And this is Henrik Ibsen."

"Ah, I am delighted to make the acquaintance of Professor Ibsen!" (There was a scientist by that name in the same branch as the Finnish professor.)

"No, no!" replied the host, "this is not Professor Ibsen, this is Dr. Henrik Ibsen!"

Then a light of understanding gleamed in the professor's eye. "Ah, the painter—"

"No, no; the poet, Henrik Ibsen!"

"Hm! Is that so?"

It had been the first time for many years that Ibsen entered a circle where he met someone who had never heard of him. He looked outwardly calm, but none too pleased.

One of the chief reasons that Ibsen took such a deep satisfaction in the doctor's degree awarded him was, of course, that his father had been able to afford him only such a very meagre education. This was what he thought of when, in the fall of 1877, he read in the Norwegian newspapers and in a letter from his sister Hedvig the news of his father's death. With a smile he could now recall his father's disgust at the prodigal son who ran away from a good position to write pieces for the theater! He thought of this man, a bankrupt, one who had lost all social standing for himself and his family, yet a very gifted and witty man feared for his sarcastic tongue—all in all the model for Daniel Heire in *The League of Youth*—and he wrote to his uncle that the latter's fulfillment "of what was my bounden duty, has been a great support to me during my toils and endeavors, and has furthered the accomplishment of my work in this world." But while Ibsen's father had thrown him upon his own resources at the age of fifteen, he himself spared no pains, inconvenience, or expense to afford Sigurd the best education obtainable and he had the satisfaction of seeing his son graduated from a Munich *Gymnasium* with the highest grade in all branches.

The letter of Henrik Ibsen to his uncle Christian Paus on the occasion of the death of his father marks as does nothing else the fact that he had become a stranger to his family.

For almost a quarter of a century he had been away from home and had allowed every tie to break; except for two or three letters to Hedvig he had not sent any news of himself, so that his photograph appeared to his relatives as the picture of a total stranger whom they could not possibly be expected to recognize.   But this was not only an external separation; the genius Henrik Ibsen stood out among his relatives as a tall cedar among the underbrush.   His brothers did not even attain in their lives what might be called mediocrity.   His sister Hedvig was a follower of a devout but obscurantist religious sect.   But of this group of children one became a world-famous poet; the associate of the greatest men of his day, the most vital force in modern drama, the guest of kings and princes, the recipient of orders and honorary degrees—Dr. Henrik Ibsen!

2

It is nothing short of a miracle—in fact "the miracle" in Nora's sense of the term—that a pompous gentleman like Ibsen, so intent on his dignity as a man and an author, should have written the classic drama of woman's emancipation. He had been brought up in the Lutheran environment that held St. Paul to have been divinely inspired when he wrote: "Let women be silent!"   In his earlier works and in his own life he had cherished the ideal of the Romanticists; woman was to be her hero's companion, devoting her energies to his work and firing him to strife and manly deeds.   Thus thought Hjördis and Svanhild; likewise the model of the two—Susannah Ibsen.   When Georg Brandes translated John Stuart Mill's *The Subjection of Women* in 1869 this plea for the equality of women went quite against Ibsen's grain; he did not speak of the immorality of the book, as did most reviewers, but he called Mill a philistine, comparable to his *bête noire* Cicero! Mill's words in dedicating the book to his wife: "Like all that I have written for many years, it belongs as much to her as to me," repelled Ibsen. "Just imagine," he said to Georg Brandes in ridiculing this, "that one would have to read Hegel or Krause with the thought that one could not know definitely whether it was Mr. or Mrs. Hegel, Mr. or Mrs. Krause who was speaking!" Ibsen always preferred to converse with men rather than with women, because he thought the latter illogical.

Ibsen was in the same boat with the rest of Mill's opponents whose opposition was based on *feeling*. "So long as an opinion is strongly rooted in the feelings," says John Stuart Mill, "it gains rather than loses in stability by having a preponderating weight of argument against it." But Ibsen was one of those reasonable persons whose minds are not closed to the weight of argument from a number of sources.

There was in the first place the woman with whom he read and discussed Mill's essay, Susannah Ibsen. At the very time the book appeared he described her in a letter as just the sort of wife needed by him—"She is illogical, but has a strong poetic instinct, a broad and liberal mind, and an almost violent antipathy to all petty considerations." Ibsen found in his wife what "the pillar of society" missed in Mrs. Bernick: "And yet she might have met me, might have shared my interests, might now and then have thrown upon me a ray of that disconnected, spasmodic way of looking at things, which a man cannot exactly make use of in his work, but which nevertheless has an inspiring and purifying effect on his whole course of conduct." It is easy to see how in conversations with such a woman Ibsen came to see the logic of extending his demand "be thyself" also to members of the female sex whom society was thwarting in their efforts at self-realization.

Another marked influence came from Camilla Collett, the

sister of the poet Wergeland and wife of a professor of esthetics. In 1851 at the age of 38 she became a widow, and after that devoted herself to the cause of woman's rights. Ibsen in *Love's Comedy* had paid her the tribute of adopting from her novel *The Sheriff's Daughters* (1855) the famous "tea simile" satirizing philistine love. In her novel Camilla Collett describes how Sophie, a sensitive young girl, observes with horror and repulsion how her older sisters are forced by their parents into marriages with men who inspire in them only loathing. The position of woman being what it was, Sophie saw as the only alternative to such a fate for herself the spinster's life of eternal knitting of stockings. As the lesser of two evils she finally decides—after a disillusioning experience with a young man—to marry a respectable widower old enough to be her father. This novel, as well as later works—for example the somewhat paradoxically named *From the Camp of the Mute* (1877)—were filled with sarcastic thrusts at the "superior" men who continued to be a source of annoyance throughout the lady's octogenarian life; in fact, she became exasperated so often that, as she said, she finally came to enjoy the sensation. This was what Ibsen noted when she paid them a long visit in Dresden in the sixties. Her mocking attitude on the subjects of love, marriage and the conventions was of great influence on Ibsen's work, as he frankly acknowledged to her; while she was grateful to Ibsen for the fine figure of Hjördis. When *The Vikings* appeared Ibsen received an anonymous letter full of enthusiasm for the heroic Valkyrie; he later realized it must have been from Camilla Collett.

Most potent probably in inspiring Ibsen to write a drama on the position of woman was his "armor-bearer" Georg Brandes, who not only introduced him to Mill's essays, but in 1869 actually suggested the writing of a drama in which the character of the minor figure Selma in *The League of Youth* was to be expanded into the central theme of the work. Selma's speeches on being asked to help her husband bear their financial ruin show in their very phrases the germs of *A Doll's House:*

How I have thirsted for a single drop of your troubles, your anxieties! But when I begged for it you only laughed me off. You have dressed me up like a doll; you have played with me as you would play with a child.

At about the same time the woman who was to become the model for Nora entered Ibsen's life. In 1869 there appeared a very pious book, *Brand's Daughters,* in which two daughters of the preacher were depicted as true exponents of Christian devotion. The twenty-year-old author, Laura Petersen, dedicated her youthful work to Ibsen, probably under the illusion that *Brand* had been intended as devotional literature. She received in return a charming letter full of kindly irony:

DEAR MISS LAURA PETERSEN,

For the compliment you have paid me by dedicating your book to me, I beg you to accept my sincerest thanks. If I were asked to express any opinion in regard to the work itself, I should be, in a way, in a difficulty. You desire to have the book regarded as a religious work, and of that kind of literature I am no judge. What has appealed to and interested me in reading it is the description of character—in combination with your unmistakable imaginative gift. Whether you regard such praise as a compliment or not, I have no idea.

The impression conveyed to me is that you would probably be horrified by the idea that you had written a "novel." . . . And perhaps you have not yet clearly realized what art and poetry really are; in which case, pray believe meanwhile that they are not of the Evil One!

What continued to occupy me as a problem long after reading *Brand's Daughters* was the personality of its authoress—was your inner, psychical relation to your book. . . .

In conclusion Ibsen expressed the hope that he might make the lady's acquaintance in the course of his projected journey to the north, a wish that was realized when he went to Copenhagen in the summer of 1870. He gave to Miss Petersen the kindly encouragement and friendly advice he was wont to extend to all young authors whom he considered promising, while at the same time he studied and pondered over her character. A few years later the lady married a Danish high school teacher, and under the name of Laura Kieler gradually won a certain amount of recognition as a novelist. In 1876 she and her husband visited the Ibsens in Munich. When Ibsen had seen her in Copenhagen in 1870 she had appeared to him a "lark" or a "song-bird," and later her marriage was called by him "a doll's house." But it did not remain so long, for her husband became ill and she was obliged to earn money, a fact which she kept from her husband, however, during his illness. When after his recovery her husband learned that his wife had gone out to earn money he became very angry and a quarrel ensued which affected Laura Kieler so severely that she had to go for a while to a sanitarium. These later happenings Ibsen heard from the husband, while he knew the preceding events from the wife. This story gripped Ibsen and he dwelt in his imagination on a marriage in which during an illness the wife takes up the economic burden—yes, even commits a forgery for the love of her husband. In addition to some of the external events for his plot Ibsen found in Laura Kieler a trusting belief that good intentions justify some actions that the law condemns—a trait embodied in the character of Nora.

With the problem of woman's legal and social disabilities on his mind Ibsen left for Rome in the autumn of 1878. Since his purse now permitted it he went in for buying old paintings with the idea of decorating his future home in Munich with valuable works of art. By the spring he had acquired twenty or so and it is amusing to note how in a letter to his publisher Hegel he speaks as one business man to another: "You would hardly believe what bargains are to be had in Italy in this line when one is lucky; and I have been lucky. I am certain that if I should ever be obliged to part with these pictures, I could sell them here or elsewhere in Germany, for two or three times what I paid for them. But I hope to be able to keep them, even though they represent so and so much unemployed capital, and therefore with each year cost me more."

In the Scandinavian Club in Rome Ibsen found a splendid opportunity to make a practical test of the reception of ideas on the equality of women. He proposed that women be given the right to vote in the club, and on February 27, 1879, the matter came up for discussion. Ibsen had carefully prepared a speech in favor of the motion in which he pointed out that the women were paying dues just like the men, that they were no less intelligent and no more given to secret intrigues than the men, that their status was being raised in most countries and that they would feel it as a great injustice if the men did not grant them this their natural right. But he did not stick to his manuscript; in his great excitement he launched out on an enthusiastic improvisation in favor of the proposition. The vote was nineteen in favor and eleven against Ibsen's motion; however, since a two-thirds majority was required to effect a change in the constitution the proposal was lost. Ibsen was beside himself with rage and demanded that another vote be taken. When the presiding officer explained to him that such a proceeding would be impossible because contrary to their constitution, Ibsen stepped up to each one in turn, pointed his finger at him, and demanded fiercely, "Did you vote for or against it?" Rather than face

Ibsen's glaring eyes, most of the men preferred to slink out of the club before they were confronted by this terrible question.   Ibsen himself left in high dudgeon and was not seen by his friends for weeks.

But on the evening of the club's annual ball to the surprise of everyone Ibsen entered the hall, dressed in elegant evening clothes and wearing his resplendent orders.   For a moment he sat down, surveyed the festive scene, then stepped up to a table, and amidst the dancing couples began to deliver a speech.   With deadly seriousness he explained that he had tried to present a great gift to the club by introducing new ideas, ideas that no one had a right to disregard any longer, not even the petty old gentlemen living in the stuffy, musty atmosphere of this club.   But how had they received his gift? Like a criminal act!   And what position had the women taken, the women for whom this present was particularly intended?   They had intrigued and agitated against him!

"What sort of women are these?" he shouted.   "They are simply parasites, worse than the lowest creatures, worse than the scum of humanity, ignorant, immoral, on the same level as the lowest, vilest creatures, the—"

Just before the terrible word was spoken a countess fainted and was carried out.   But unmoved by this occurrence Ibsen continued, intoxicating himself, so to speak, by his own eloquence, to discourse on the wickedness of mankind in general and the immorality of women in particular, on their opposition to new ideas destined to make humanity greater, richer, and better.   When he had finished, he put on his overcoat and silk hat, and the great poet disappeared into the night leaving consternation behind.

In this mood Ibsen proceeded to write *A Doll's House* in the spring and summer of 1879 at Rome and at Amalfi.

The same consternation which Ibsen's speech cast over the Scandinavian circle in Rome his new play spread in

Norway, Germany, England, and gradually throughout all countries where there are theaters on the European model. The keen logic of the dramatist put the matter so squarely before people that there was no avoiding the question. At the same time there was so much feeling and prejudice on the subject that a discussion of it frequently led to quarrels and ill-feeling. Scandinavian hostesses are reported to have issued invitations with the request that guests refrain from discussing *A Doll's House;* this was a precaution that simply had to be taken if social life was to remain social. In the Christiania Theater alone there were twenty-five performances in the winter of 1879-1880 before packed houses of excited, trembling spectators who left the theater discussing hotly the problems so vital to their lives.

With truly desperate dialectic woman's dependent position was shown; living apparently under the protection of chivalry which, however, failed to operate at the two critical moments when Helmer was tested, forced to employ her sexual charms to gain any point, relegated to the kitchen and nursery, regarded as illogical and inferior, and treated by the lord of creation with a humorous condescension. In the "superior" husband Ibsen satirizes his own former attitude with his usual courageous sincerity. There were catchwords that made the play unforgettable:

HELMER: No man sacrifices his honor, even for one he loves.
NORA: Millions of women have done so.

HELMER: Before all else you are a wife and mother.
NORA: That I no longer believe. I believe that before all else I am a human being, just as much as you are—or at least that I should try to become one.

HELMER: You no longer love me.
NORA: No, that's just it.
HELMER: Nora!—Can you say so!

or the haunting force of the "miracle" that Nora hoped for and dreaded, or the eloquent shutting of the door at the very end. The play seemed to shake the very foundations of social life that men—and most women—had believed absolutely secure; it seemed to put a torpedo under the ark, or as Georg Brandes put it, on the stormy sea of life Ibsen seemed to have extinguished the light-houses.

But it must be said it *seemed* only. Ibsen's thoughts were long, long thoughts, and his Nora was an idealist like Brand who dreamed a beautiful dream; and as Brand goes forward to perish in the ice church, so little Nora goes out alone into the world—all or nothing! With almost religious ardor Ibsen had aimed at a very distant goal, the coming of "the third empire," or in the words of Nora: "That communion between us shall be a marriage."

Instead of comprehending Ibsen's aim the critics, the managers, and even the actors in the main refused to accept the ending. Ibsen, knowing full well that once more he was far ahead of his day and content to bide his time, wrote a temporary alternate ending in which Nora consented to remain because of the children. But very soon the theaters ceased to do to Ibsen's play what he had called a "barbaric violence."

In Munich, to which city Ibsen returned in the fall of 1879, the play was put on in its correct form March 3, 1880, with Frau Ramlo as Nora. Ibsen had attended most of the rehearsals and found that the well-selected cast was playing excellently. But it was a matter of grave doubt how this revolutionary play would be received in Germany—where women were still excluded from the universities. Mrs. Ibsen therefore preferred to stay at home, and Ibsen planned to witness the play from behind the scenes. He gave a ticket to John Paulsen, a young Norwegian author whom he was befriending, as he and Mrs. Ibsen did in real heartfelt kindness with many young compatriots who were travelling abroad. In fact, on the very evening of the play as Paulsen called to thank him for the ticket, Ibsen gave him a sum of money with the request that he take it to a poor sick Norwegian painter living in another part of Munich. This deed, thought Paulsen, will bring Ibsen luck!

Later, as he sat with Sigurd in the box reserved for the Ibsens, he noted that many military men present received the play very coldly, and as the curtain fell on the first act things looked none too well for Ibsen. Sigurd ran home in the *entr'acte*, as had been arranged, to tell his mother how the play was going. After the second act, however, Ibsen was called out. But the third act, with Frau Ramlo presenting in a very convincing way the real Nora, no longer the "squirrel" or "lark" but the brave pioneer who pits herself against all the world: "I must make up my mind which is right—society or I"—this act took the audience by storm. The applause was wild. Ibsen's masterful play had won a great victory. There was some hissing—but that stopped when the author appeared. The applause rose like the waves of the sea toward the poet who bowed repeatedly. Sigurd ran home to tell his mother the final result, while Paulsen went to the stage entrance to wait for Ibsen. Finally he came, alone, evidently very much moved. Paulsen congratulated him, but in silence Ibsen supported himself on the younger man's arm and walked home.

This drama had made Ibsen a world-famous playwright. The greatest actresses—among them Eleanore Duse—played it in all the capitals of the world before crowded houses. When some years afterward Madame Réjane put on *La Maison de Poupée* Ibsen telegraphed her in his charming manner: "My most beautiful dream has come true; Réjane has created Nora in Paris."

3

When in the autumn of 1880 the Ibsens were once more settled in Rome a Scandinavian lady of their acquaintance suddenly appeared in the city with her lover. Having found her marriage unsatisfactory she had left her husband and her little daughter—an act that the Norwegians in Rome condemned as "unnatural." "It is not unnatural," said Ibsen, "only it is unusual." The lady sought Ibsen out at a public function, but was treated rather coolly by him. "Well, I did the same thing your Nora did," she said with some asperity. Ibsen replied significantly, "But my Nora went alone."

The cry of the "unnatural" in Nora's desertion of her children was the chief point of attack of the hostile critics, especially of the clergymen, who varied it with such other adjectives as "immoral" and "godless." The Norwegian Lutheran clergymen were very bitter in their denunciation of *A Doll's House*, but this clerical wish to keep women in subjection was quite international and interdenominational; the following typical utterance on *Woman's Rights*, for example, comes from some Helmer writing for an American Catholic paper of the eighties: "1. A woman has a right to sew buttons on the shirt of her husband. 2. A woman has a right to take care of her children and to whip them when they do not behave. 3. A woman has a right to go out into company when her husband accompanies her. 4. A woman has a right to be quiet when it is not her business to interfere. 5. A woman has a right to be kind to her husband, even if he is a scoundrel. 6. She has a right to bear her lot in Christian patience and to earn her reward in Heaven." It is not surprising that Ibsen—who loved the clergy about as much as Dickens did—made the unreasonable position of a pastor a particular theme in his next play.

—From *Vikingen*.

TWO DOLL'S HOUSE CARICATURES

(*At top*)

Text:

Daughter (on Nora's final speech): "You will not do as she did, Mamma, and leave your children?"

Father (laughing): "Oh, no, Mamma is not so highly gifted, child."

(*At bottom*)

"How Nora came home again." *Vikingen*, July 23, 1881, ridicules the sequels of *A Doll's House*. Ibsen refuses to take her back.

The genus of literary folk who write continuations of great works of fiction found *A Doll's House* irresistible, and by German, English and American authors Nora was restored to her husband and children. This was done in moral earnestness, not in a spirit of burlesque. The German fourth act perhaps is the one to deserve the prize. It takes place about one year after the third act. Mrs. Linden, who has married Krogstad and is supporting the family by means of her sewing machine, comes to her friend with a newly finished dress for a recently arrived citizen of the world lying in Nora's lap. The scene breathes peace and happiness, only at times a shadow passes over Nora's brow; she is thoughtful. Then Helmer, who as formerly is the director of a bank and generally respected, enters the room. Nora regards him with a timidly questioning glance and whispers: "Have you now really forgiven me?" For some moments Helmer does not reply, but merely looks at her in a quiet and friendly manner. Finally he takes out of the pocket of his frock coat a huge bag, and he who had formerly so sternly forbidden his Nora to eat sweets now places in her mouth with his own hand— a macaroon! Nora, frightened and rejoiced at once, chews it and calls out aloud: "The miracle!" The curtain falls slowly.

Since the moralists were so eager to have Nora return to her husband or better still to stay at home, Ibsen's thoughts naturally turned to what might happen to a woman who suffered whatever her husband chose to inflict on her and remained dutifully in the place assigned her by society. He was getting ready an answer for his critics who saw in *A Doll's House* only an attack on "marriage, which is represented as an institution that, not to say always but often, ruins the individuals who therefore have a moral right to dissolve it the moment it does not satisfy them any longer." This rather typical criticism came from the Danish editor, Carl Ploug, a liberal later turned conservative.

John Paulsen, a somewhat flattering admirer who was later to become the poet's Boswell, soon followed the Ibsens into Italy on a travelling stipend granted him by the Norwegian government, largely on Ibsen's recommendation.   He was fast becoming a close friend of the family, treated with motherly kindness by Mrs. Ibsen, who invited him to Christmas and other festive dinners, and regarded by Ibsen with kindly interest, not unmixed with irony.   When he arrived in Rome, knowing that Ibsen was not at home, he asked the Italian maid to tell Mrs. Ibsen that her "amico" had reached the city and would call in the afternoon.   The maid, understanding the situation in her Italian way, took Mrs. Ibsen aside and whispered: "Your amico just called to say that he would be back in the afternoon.   But then *il signor commendatore* will be at home—how careless of him!"   Because he had at the time of the dedication of the Suez Canal received the Turkish Order of the Commander Ibsen really had the servants use this martial title for him!   The story of the maid's solicitude in regard to Mrs. Ibsen's clandestine affair with the innocent Paulsen became a family joke, a pendant to the one about the gift of a little negro girl made to Ibsen by the Khedive in Egypt, "my concubine" as he would call her with a roguish glance at his wife.

One afternoon at tea Ibsen was in very bad humor and one of his guests, an elderly gentleman, unfortunately began to discuss the host's chief weakness.   He said that it was ridiculous how freely orders were being given nowadays; that, in fact, the one sure way of recognizing King Umberto was by his manner of appearing like an American, without any orders whatsoever.   Poor Paulsen, wishing to smooth over the situation, made some further remark about orders, but he only drew down on himself the terrible wrath of his host: "I'll beg you to spare me in future your allusions to my decorations. For the life of me I cannot see why just you should occupy yourself with this question, because it is not likely that you will ever be led into the temptation of having one offered to you!" Paulsen was deeply offended, left Rome for some weeks; but after he had apologized to Ibsen on his return all was forgiven and forgotten!

Madame L. de Hegermann-Lindencrone, a New England girl who married a Danish diplomat, gives a very vivid pen-picture of Ibsen in Rome at this time. Since it has a distinctly American flavor I shall reprint it here:

> The celebrated Ibsen honored this feast (Scandinavian Club) with his presence, and especially honored the Chianti and Genzano wines, which were served copiously in *fiascos*. When you see Ibsen, with his lion face and tangle of hair, for the first time, you are fascinated by him, knowing what a genius he is, but when you talk with him, and feel his piercing critical eyes looking at you from under bushy brows, and see his cruel, satiric smile, you are a little prejudiced against him. We met him often at our friend Ross's studio at after-noon teas, where there is always a little music. Ibsen sits sullen, silent and indifferent. He does not like music and does not disguise his dislike. This is not, as you may imagine, inspiring to the per-formers. In fact, just to look at him takes all the life out of you. He is a veritable wet blanket.

One day in the course of a walk about the city Ibsen called Paulsen's attention to some beautiful temple ruins, which the latter confessed never to have noticed before. "You must learn to use your eyes instead of dreaming as you walk along," said Ibsen, looking at the young man over his gold-rimmed spectacles. "For a person who wants to be an author that is doubly necessary. Tell me, what is the color of the wall paper in your room?"

Paulsen blushingly confessed that he did not know.

"You see," said Ibsen highly pleased, as he always appeared whenever his worst fears came true, "I was right. You notice nothing. But how can a normal human being live in a room for months without noticing the color of the walls! Whenever I enter a strange house I take notice of the minutest objects, nothing escapes me. Yes, I see *everything*," he continued quietly as though speaking to himself. Paulsen adds that Ibsen did not have to tell him this, because his plays were ample testimony to his powers of observation.

One field toward which Ibsen's powers of observation had been directed for some time was the realm of science opened up through the work of Darwin. *The Origin of Species* appeared in Norwegian translation in the early seventies; there were lectures at the University of Christiania on the new discoveries; and a great deal of discussion of heredity and environment, the survival of the fittest, and allied subjects filled the columns of the newspapers. The rôle the clergy played in these discussions did not impress Ibsen very highly; in a letter to Brandes he speaks of "that enfeeblement of judgment which, at least in the case of the average man, is an inevitable consequence of prolonged occupation with theological studies." It is quite possible that Ibsen was also somewhat influenced by Zola's series of novels, begun in 1868, in which the laws of heredity were to be illustrated; Paulsen states that Ibsen was very fond of Zola. In the first sketch of *A Doll's House* there are many lines that might have been written by Zola; for example the doctor says in congratulating Nora on her expensive new carpet, which he does not consider a luxury: "The race is ennobled in beautiful surroundings," or later: "Study the natural sciences, ladies, and you will see how there is one law pervading everything. The stronger tree deprives the weaker of the conditions of life and turns them to its own use. The same thing happens among animals; the unfit individuals in a herd have to make way for the better ones. And that is how nature progresses. It is only we human beings who forcibly retard progress by taking care of the unfit individuals."—But in contrast to Zola Ibsen was too much of an artist not to eliminate such scientific preachments from the final version of his drama.

In Dr. Rank Ibsen had exemplified a very striking and tragic case of heredity; a son suffering innocently for the dissipations of his father. Feeling that in a full discussion of the rights of the individual in marriage the matter of venereal diseases must be taken into consideration he made this a central theme in his next play, achieving through the use of this insidious disease a modern, effective counterpart of the *Nemesis* of the classical Greek drama. Connected with this theme he found so many outworn beliefs, ideals, and conventions, no longer applicable but yet containing a haunting force, that he decided to make these "ghosts" the chief object of his attack. He knew that he was striking in the face of the "impure hush" surrounding all these subjects, but he decided courageously that it was time "to move a few boundary posts."

The heroine of his new drama was a Nora grown up, confronted with the worst in her husband, crushed by the very seamiest side of marriage, and hounded by the outworn ideals of society until she became a Mrs. Alving. The story of this *mater dolorosa* who gives all for mother love is told with a fine breath of poetry pervading the sombre realistic action. Ibsen managed to give his drama all the traditional force of the tragedy of fate and the uncanny eeriness of the haunted castle theme, but in a form that was convincing to the modern mind. The window of the room in which the sad tale is told to the end just as the sun rises a second time faces a fjord and mountain landscape wrapped in a gloomy fog. Incessantly falling rain serves to sustain the dominant mood of nervous depression. Only at the end the glacier and the snow-peaks glow in the rosy morning light, but they glow on a "haunted palace"—in Poe's sense of the term, while the "ghosts" in

> A hideous throng rush out forever,
> and laugh—but smile no more.

The whole ends with a gruesome irony: the "ideals" of Pastor Manders appear as hideous lies to the accompaniment of the mocking, raucous laughter of the gods. As the curtain falls the spectator is uplifted by the human dignity of the bowed but heroic figure of the noble Mrs. Alving, Ibsen's greatest character.

In this play he developed completely for the first time what has been called the "Ibsen technique." This is generally taken to refer to the "evolutionary" type of drama in which the action does not take place in the play but the past action is gradually revealed, so that the drama, compared to, say a Shakespearean play, constitutes only a fifth act, so to speak. But there is nothing new in this—Sophocles employed this method in *Œdipus Rex,* for example. Nor is the absence of monologues or "asides," the non-obtrusion of the author's self, the breaking up of long speeches into terse, natural dialogue, the return to a literal observance of the unities, and the avoidance of "artificialities" exactly Ibsen's invention. But the marvel about his work is that as a consummate master of his craft he used all of these and other means so skillfully that everyone felt he had created a new type of drama. The tenor of the whole is realistic, "a picture of life," as Ibsen wrote in his sketch for *Ghosts;* but dramatic moments are by no means absent, catchwords are employed in the manner of a *Leitmotiv,* e.g., "the joy of living," and over the whole there hovers a poetic, non-obtrusive symbolism. Above all, the master-hand of Ibsen showed itself in the creation of vital, individual characters. And the author's keen sense of humor is not dormant by any means.

The objectivity of the author did not prevent a certain bent in the play that causes very grave questions to arise: Are not our morality and our religion outlived, and therefore pernicious institutions requiring a radical making-over? Is not a well-meaning pastor upholding this morality a ridiculous as well as a pernicious force? If the state forbids the marriages of lepers, what about those afflicted with syphilis? Could there arise a situation in which it would be permissible for a man to marry his half-sister? Would a mother ever have the right to put a merciful end to her son's suffering? And most striking perhaps the dramatic question after Pastor Manders had upbraided the sodden carpenter Engstrand for marrying Chamberlain Alving's maid, "for a miserable three hundred dollars, to go out and marry a fallen woman": Mrs. Alving: "Then what have you to say of me? I went and married a fallen man."

It is very natural that Mrs. Alving should ask this question. It is logical too, that this woman whose tragic fate has descended on her out of her very efforts to comply with the current law and morality, should condemn all laws. Because Mrs. Alving's unhappiness has arisen out of her failure to marry the man she loved, it is quite conceivable that she should think of the possibility of a marriage even between half-brother and half-sister if they are in love. Therefore Ibsen could say with a certain justification that he could not be made responsible for the opinions expressed by personages in the drama. On the other hand it is certain that Ibsen, at the time of the writing of this play at least, inclined toward anarchistical ideas. This is shown, for example, by the fact that he considered the news of the assassination of Alexander II—the liberator of the serfs and not one of the worst tsars by any means—as an event to be hailed with joy. Paulsen tells that on the evening of this day he found the Ibsens and their guests in a festive mood, because there was now one tyrant less in the world. At the very time when he was composing *Ghosts* Ibsen wrote to Frederic Hegel that he was going to settle a personal grudge with the "black band of theologians" in Norway by erecting a fitting monument for them in one of his plays; they had aroused his anger particularly because the educational board, then largely controlled by clericals, would not make an exception in Sigurd's case in the matter of admitting him to the University without certain formalities. It is therefore safe to say that Ibsen probably was not so objective as he thought he was.

A Doll's House had aroused a good deal of opposition, and had earned for Ibsen many hard names, but on the whole it was just the reception with heated discussion pro and con that the poet desired for his plays. But the reception of *Ghosts* was entirely different. It was as though in a fashionable gathering Ibsen had spoken aloud some natural monosyllable that was taboo; "a dirty act done publicly," an English reviewer called it, and Ibsen's friend, Paul Heyse, named it "die Carbol-Comoedie." The theater managers refused to have anything to do with the play, actors and actresses stated that nothing in the world could induce them to act the parts of Oswald or Regina, and the Norwegian book-sellers sent their copies back to Hegel, preferring not to sell the book. The liberals too turned against Ibsen; one of them, Henrik Jaeger, later Ibsen's biographer, travelled about in Norway lecturing against *Ghosts*. Worst of all, much more was expressed by nasty insinuations than in word or print. All of this can serve to give an understanding of Georg Brandes' word that *Ghosts* was Ibsen's noblest deed.

Ibsen's courage called forth the admiration of his rival Björnson. He had been deeply offended by the attack on him in *The League of Youth* and later by a poem in which Ibsen called him a "weather-vane." Because Ibsen refused to join with him in a petition to have the union mark struck from the Norwegian flag Björnson in 1879 coldly refused to call on Ibsen in Munich although the whole family, including at the time Björnson's old friend Magdalene Thoresen, awaited him with tense expectation; Sigurd, in his pitiful eagerness at least to catch a glimpse of his god-father, posted himself in a café where he knew Björnson came to read Norwegian newspapers. But when *Ghosts* appeared Björnson's voice arose loudly in praise of it amidst all the cowardly and hypocritical slander of Ibsen. "The only one in Norway who has stepped forth and defended me boldly and courageously is Björnson," Ibsen wrote on January 24, 1882; "It is just like him. His is in truth a great and kingly soul, and I shall never forget what I owe him for this." Ibsen wrote a letter of heartfelt thanks to Björnson and a few years later they renewed their old friendship by a personal meeting in a summer resort in the Tyrol. But they never became exactly congenial cronies, and the letters of congratulation they exchanged on festive occasions were about as heartfelt as notes between two neutral powers during a war.

In the great rivalry between the two dramatists Ibsen had won definitively. Twenty-five years before Björnson—fresh from his stage triumph *Between the Battles*—had said in reviewing *The Feast at Solhoug* that Ibsen was not a dramatist, but a lyric poet; now both in a Norwegian and in an American publication Björnson wrote: "I do not hesitate to say that in my opinion, Henrik Ibsen possesses the greatest dramatic power of the age." It was a generous tribute, but nobody doubted its truth. Björnson, far ahead of Ibsen at first, had now become a follower of his rival; while Ibsen, moving at a comparatively late age from Romanticism to Realism, advanced to the masterpiece *Ghosts*, which was "modern" in its technique, its subject-matter, and its symbolism. At an age when most men of letters have written their best works and have arrived at a well-established style, Ibsen was *the* modern poet about whom the young dramatists gathered as their idol and inspiration. As he advanced in years he steadily progressed in art, due to the seriousness of purpose with which he devoted himself to the one field of drama and to his great capacity for taking pains, which caused him to recast and rewrite his plays again and again until they were as exquisitely finished as the work of a jeweler.

One of the youthful moderns to see the greatness of *Ghosts* was a young Viennese dramatist, Felix Philippi. He travelled to Munich in 1886, in spite of warnings that Ibsen would not receive him, or would act with frigid formality if he did. But one morning Ibsen did receive him in his home furnished with ugly rented furniture and decorated with fine oil paintings. The dramatist appeared in solemn garb in which he might have gone straightway to a ball.

Full of enthusiasm Philippi said what he felt about *Ghosts,* while Ibsen listened to the praise with evident embarrassment. Then he looked at his youthful admirer with his clear, steel-blue eyes—such eyes Philippi thought he never could forget —and stretched out his hand saying in his distinct, gentle voice: "I like you. I find that you have understood me."

Encouraged by this Philippi asked Ibsen's permission for a performance of the play. "You are a bold man," said Ibsen, but after some hesitation he consented. A few weeks later the first German performance—there had been some performances by travelling companies in Scandinavia—of *Ghosts* was given in the picturesque old Bavarian city of Augsburg, 35 miles northwest of Munich. Since a public performance of this "revolutionary play with destructive tendency" was forbidden by the authorities, the promoters of the venture were forced to make it a private performance with admission by invitation only. Contrary to the habit he had formed recently of never going to the theater, not even to see his own plays, Ibsen came to the performance. The play was presented with consummate art, and the effect on the silent audience was startling, overwhelming. At the end there were calls upon calls for the author until finally Ibsen was prevailed upon to appear on the stage protesting and murmuring, "This is terrible." But when he faced the cheering auditorium a gleam of happiness lighted up his features and tears came into his eyes. The Grimstad apothecary boy's dream of becoming an immortal man was now realized, for this drama would, as Georg Brandes had written some time previously, forever link the name of Ibsen with that of Sophocles.

4

In the winter of 1881 a young English dramatic critic, William Archer, applied for membership in the Scandinavian Club in Rome, that he might have the opportunity of meeting Henrik Ibsen. He was at the time twenty-five years old, and had heard of Ibsen in the course of his frequent summer visits to his uncle, a naturalized Norwegian, who was a shipbuilder in Larvik, a town on the east coast of Norway but a short distance from Ibsen's birthplace. In the course of these visits Archer had learned a good deal about the Norwegian language and literature, and in the previous winter he had made an adaptation of *Pillars of Society* which was given one performance at the Gaiety Theater, as mentioned in a previous chapter. The constitution of the club did not permit non-Scandinavian members, but since the Norwegians were charmed with the young Englishman who spoke their language, they made him an associate member.

Thus William Archer was privileged to attend the Christmas celebration of the club. He recognized Ibsen the moment he entered, but found himself disappointed by his short stature which caused the poet to appear as a rather insignificant individual. Archer asked the president of the club to

introduce him, whereupon Ibsen spoke to him quite cordially
—not at all ruffled about the unauthorized translation of
which he had already heard.   After the dinner and the
speeches Ibsen stopped to chat a bit with this progressive
critic who had arranged the first Ibsen performance in England.   *Ghosts* had just come off the press, and Archer, who
had received his copy on that very day, was reminded by it
of Ibsen's poem addressed to a young revolutionist in which
Noah's flood was described as the best revolution up to date,
though it too was limited; Ibsen would gladly have put
a torpedo under the Ark in order to make a clean sweep of
everything.   At this allusion Ibsen cast a look of extreme
surprise at Archer.   In that look lay the germ of his next
play, *The Enemy of the People*.   At this moment Ibsen
lived through Dr. Stockmann's surprise on finding that his
demonstration of the rottenness of society was regarded by
society as something less than a cause for unmixed gratitude.
Even though Ibsen had just said in his after-dinner speech
that he was not looking forward to a peaceful Christmas
season, yet he was by no means prepared for such a tempest
as Archer seemed to forecast.   Ibsen invited Archer to call
and showed great courtesy and kindness to the young Englishman who had absolutely no claim on him.   But Archer also
had the pleasure of seeing a loud-mouthed, asinine Dane
wilted by Ibsen in his gruffest and most crushing manner.

In a few days the club was littered with papers in which
critics scoffed at Ibsen as "a pale ghost of his former self,"
and poets bewailed him as a "fallen star."   Georg Brandes
stood out as one critic who preserved his sanity and courage.
Ibsen and Archer had a hearty laugh over the article by Carl
Ploug in which this critic attacked Ibsen because it seemed
very improbable that Oswald Alving could have acquired the
disease merely from smoking his father's pipe!

After "the anonymous poachers and highwaymen" had

"shot dirt" at Ibsen from the ambush in "shopkeepers' news-papers" the poet retired from the company of his friends and associated only with Dr. Stockmann.   Mrs. Ibsen told that at such times her conversation with her husband did not exceed a "good morning" and a "good night."   Punctually every day Ibsen went to the Café Aranjo to read the papers.   One day he read in *Aften-Posten* the stenographic report of a public meeting in which a strange rôle was played by a Christiania pharmacist, Harald Thaulow, a queer genius and reformer, patriotic and public-spirited, but continually quar-reling with friend and foe.   To mention one example of his many crotchets, he stated in his will that he hoped he would be burned at the stake, but that if this did not take place he wished his ashes preserved in an urn bearing as inscription the words of Goethe: "Er ist ein Mensch gewesen, und das heiszt ein Kämpfer sein."   He was a man after Ibsen's heart and he paid the poet the compliment of entitling the pam-phlets in which he ruthlessly attacked all abuses and hypocrisies: *Pillars of Society in Prose*.   The meeting de-scribed in the paper was concerned with the affairs of a soup kitchen designed to furnish inexpensive meals to the poor. Herr Thaulow read a long report, abusing the board of directors: "No one will succeed in juggling away the fact that no establishment in Christiania is a greater humbug than this soup kitchen, and the board of directors have no right to send the manager into the desert as the scapegoat for their own stupidities."   He continued in this vein for three-quarters of an hour, while repeated requests were heard that the chair-man silence the speaker.   The newspaper account continues:

THAULOW: I will not have my mouth stopped.   (*Continues his reading.*)
CONSUL HEFTYE: Make Mr. Thaulow stop!
    (THAULOW *continues to read.   Several persons manifest their indignation by demonstratively walking about in the hall.*

THE CHAIRMAN *asks the assembly whether they recognize his right to withdraw from* MR. THAULOW *the privilege of the floor. Unanimous* "Aye." THE CHAIRMAN *again requests* MR. THAULOW *to stop.*)

THAULOW: I will not have my mouth gagged.

CHAIRMAN: In that case I proceed with—

THAULOW: I'll make it quite short. (*Continues to read.*)

HEFTYE: Is he permitted to read on?

THAULOW (*continuing*): The glorious results of the Christiania Soup Kitchen . . . I'll be done in a minute.

HEFTYE: At this rate this general meeting will be broken up.

CHAIRMAN: I regret to have to interrupt Mr. Thaulow. Your remarks—

THAULOW *goes on reading.*

HEFTYE: Silence—or you will have to leave the room.

THAULOW: All right. (*Sits down, exhausted.*)

THE CHAIRMAN *thereupon resumes the reading of the board's official report.* THAULOW *accompanies the reading with grunts and tries several times to obtain another hearing. At last, the opposition having grown too strong, he gives up the fight and leaves the hall with these words:* "Now I'll have nothing more to do with you. I am tired of casting pearls before swine. It's an infernal abuse that is being inflicted on a free people in a free country. So— and now good-bye . . . you ought to stand in a corner and be ashamed of yourselves."

In bluff old Herr Thaulow's actions Ibsen found very suggestive material for his next play. But he knew also from his own experience how it felt to have the "damned compact liberal majority" attempt to silence an unwelcome speaker, for just this group had suppressed his poem sent to Norway in 1872 on the occasion of the millennial celebration. More than two years previously, in writing to Professor Dietrichson, he had suggested that not much could be done for Norway "before the intellectual soil has been thoroughly turned up and cleansed, and the intellectual swamp drained." From his experience with *Ghosts* he knew how the people thank the man who sets out to drain and cleanse the bogs of society. What he thought of himself in this connection is to be seen from the answer he gave to someone who compared him to Zola: "Only with this difference, that Zola descends into the cess-pool to take a bath, I to cleanse it." As the figure of his hero grew in Ibsen's mind he endowed him with some autobiographical traits, for example his descent from an old pirate from Pomerania and a name derived from Ibsen's original family home, Stockmannsgaard. He used this hero to express his own attacks on the "truths" of democracy, e.g., that the majority has right and truth on its side, that the lower classes are the true kernel of the nation, and that culture demoralizes; he asserted that the minority is always right, that the lower classes are only the raw material that must be fashioned into the People, and that the demoralizing forces are stupidity, poverty, and miserable living conditions. Furthermore, Ibsen put into the mouth of Dr. Stockmann all his accumulated hatred of the liberals, "the worst enemies of freedom," and the "free press" which is ruled by the subscribers. Small wonder that, as Ibsen wrote to his publisher, he and Dr. Stockmann got on very well together.

But a poet, especially an Ibsen, rarely speaks his opinions directly, and therefore he fashioned a spokesman to whom the public would lend a more ready ear than to his caustic self. He had just been impressed with Björnson's noble heart and determined courage in the face of opposition. Björnson had once described the occasion when he felt most fully the joy of being a poet: "It was when a party from the Right in Christiania came to my house and smashed all my windows. For when they had finished their assault, and were starting home again, they felt that they had to sing something, and so they began to sing 'Yes, we love this land of ours'—they couldn't help it. They had to sing the song of the man they had attacked." Björnson had at this very time spoken courageously for *Ghosts* at the cost of having a number of papers close their columns to him, and Ibsen thanked him by giving his external traits to the intrepid Dr. Stockmann. For the wrong he had done Björnson in making him the model of Stensgaard in *The League of Youth* he now made ample reparation. He brought on the stage Björnson's boyish enthusiasm, his kindness, his impulsive, changeable nature, his hail-fellow-well-met traits, his qualities of a good husband and father, his love of a rousing fight, and all the other characteristics that made him the popular hero of the Norwegian nation. With this he mixed some of the naïveté and never-say-die spirit when aroused to a fight that he had found in the charming novelist Jonas Lie, with whom he had spent the previous summer at an Alpine resort. The latter was a somewhat helpless individual very much liked but regarded with a slightly ironic air by Ibsen; from one of Lie's poems Ibsen had borrowed the phrase of Hilmar Tönnesen in *Pillars of Society:* "There must be someone to hold high the banner of the ideal."

When the days of the sirocco approached the Ibsens left Rome for a cooler climate, Gossensass in the Tyrol. Both Mrs. Ibsen and Sigurd knew that Ibsen was engaged upon a new play, but neither of them had any idea what it was about, because Ibsen preserved an absolute secrecy about his plays until he had finished them; then he read them to his family. Naturally enough, they were both very curious.

They were riding in the train through the Italian countryside, no longer third class, as Mrs. Ibsen had previously insisted they do—despite the protests of her husband who found it somewhat humiliating. With her economical management of affairs, so necessary in their earlier years of marriage, she had done her full share to achieve the prosperity they now enjoyed. As the train stopped at a station Ibsen left the carriage for a few moments. As he did so he dropped a scrap of paper. His wife picked it up and read on it only the words: "The doctor says . . ." Nothing more.

Mrs. Ibsen showed it laughingly to Sigurd and said, "Now we will tease your father a bit when he comes back. He will be horrified to find that we know anything of his play."

When Ibsen entered the carriage his wife looked at him roguishly and said after a few seconds: "What sort of doctor is it that figures in your new play? I am sure that he must have many interesting things to say."

But if she could have foreseen the effect of her innocent jest, Mrs. Ibsen would certainly have held her tongue. For Ibsen was speechless with surprise and rage. When at last he was able to recover his speech it was to utter a torrent of reproaches. What did this mean? Was he not safe in his own house? Was he surrounded with spies? Had his locks been tampered with, his desk rifled?

Once his imagination was set free on this subject, he began to see things in broad daylight.

Mrs. Ibsen, who had listened with a quiet smile to the rising tempest of his wrath at last handed him the scrap of paper. "We know nothing more of your play than is written on this slip which you let fall. Allow me to return it to you."

There stood Ibsen crestfallen. All his suspicions had vanished into thin air!

At Gossensass Ibsen continued to receive more evidence of the hostile reception of *Ghosts,* and in the fury of his anger he worked more rapidly than usual on *An Enemy of the People,* finishing it in one year whereas most of his plays had required two. In this summer resort the poet's life was as regular as in the city. Every forenoon he worked, at a definite hour every day he took his walk, arrived punctually at the meals, after dinner took a short nap, then copied what he had written in the morning. In the evening he chatted with friends over a glass of beer or wine. At meal time he was very quiet, and God help the misguided person who took the liberty of intruding his company on Ibsen! In the same way a business letter or visitor could quite upset him. For in intense mental labor he was building up his play scene by scene, adding touches here and there as he strolled along the banks of the Eisach or sat at the writing table in the hotel room. Didn't he explain to his disciple Paulsen that a speech had to be cast differently depending on whether it was delivered in the morning, or in the evening?

And he built a masterpiece of dramatic technique, not in the evolutionary manner of *Ghosts,* but a drama that might serve as a classical example of the "well-made play." In the first act there is a skillful, gradual development of the theme with the mention of the baths, of a letter, with the arrival of the letter, of the great discovery. The act ends with the ominous toast: "I hope you may have nothing but joy of your discovery!" And the genial host dances about the room with Mrs. Stockmann—laughter, applause, and cheers for the doctor! With the second act the difficulties begin, but Stockmann with right on his side defies the powers of evil unflinchingly. At the very height of the action in the third act his defeat is foreshadowed symbolically when he is forced to doff the mayor's cap and lay down the cane which he had mockingly assumed a moment before in his cocksure spirit of victory. The fourth act contains a masterful mob scene ending in the crushing of the doctor's revolt; while in the last act the hero must face a triple, soul-trying temptation before he rises to the ringing final defiance, denoting a glorious inner victory: "The strongest man in the world is he who stands most alone!" What a muddle-headed man— yet what a poetic halo there is about him!

On September 9, 1882, Ibsen sent the meticulously finished manuscript to his publisher, saying that he felt quite lost and lonely after parting with the doctor. But this same

—From *Vikingen*, December 9, 1882.

HENRIK IBSEN AS DISCIPLINARIAN

In the first picture Ibsen is satirizing the Radicals in "Steens-gard" (League of Youth) while the Right applauds. Next he attacks Consul Berwick (Pillars of Society) while the Left grins. Lastly in "An Enemy of the People" he attacks impartially Right and Left.

doctor was received with joy in the theaters of Christiania, Bergen, Stockholm and Copenhagen, where *An Enemy of the People* became *the* play of the year. The crowds applauded the priceless humor of the jovial scientist telling his "plebeian" brother home truths in public meetings and receiving his defeat with a stiff upper lip: "A man should never put on his best trousers when he goes out to battle for freedom and truth." They recognized at last that Ibsen belonged to no party, but delivered his blows impartially to the Right and to the Left. The doctor's Ibsenian paradoxes gave rise to much discussion, in which the scathing satire of the poet attracted most attention. Above all the unflinching idealism in the face of martyrdom of Stockmann, of Petra, and of that real Ibsenian woman, Mrs. Stockmann, appealed to the younger generation who were not flesh of the flesh of Stensgaard and Aslaksen, here revived from *The League of Youth* as men of affluence, the due reward of their political spinelessness.

The play ends with Dr. Stockmann recruiting a "dozen" disciples "to drive all of the wolves out to the far west, boys!" Boycotted on all sides, his windows smashed, the doctor does not look like a man who would have much influence. The story does not tell how these youngsters responded to Dr. Stockmann's teachings; but Ibsen had the gratification of learning soon of the actions of some of his young disciples. The timid middle-aged directors of the Christiania Theater had found reasons why it was not "advisable" to stage *Ghosts*. In October, 1883, a Swedish company presented Ibsen's great tragedy at a minor theater of the city, while the official theater put on an erotic French farce. The result was that young men interrupted this performance with whistling and blowing of horns, with calls of "Put on *Ghosts*" and "Down with the Directors" and with repeated full-throated shouts of "Hurrah for Henrik Ibsen!" It seemed like a realization of Dr.

Stockmann's words: "I shall help you grow into free, high-minded men!"

On his seventieth birthday Ibsen received a striking personal confirmation of the influence of his idealism. Norway's greatest hero, Fridtjof Nansen, on that day sent him the following telegram:

I send my thanks to the man who has stamped my youth, and determined my development, who has pointed out the demand of the ideal and the nobility of will.

X

THE WORLD'S GREATEST LIVING DRAMATIST

1

"Ibsen is terribly radical," a Scandinavian friend of the poet wrote home from Rome, January 4, 1883. "I have now become rather well acquainted with him and his views. One evening I went to a café with him and the poet X who is also spending the winter here. Late at night—about the sixth glass—Ibsen's tongue was loosened, and then you should have heard him! Poor X, by the way, is a Norwegian liberal, friend of Björnson's, etc. You should have seen him, when Ibsen got under way! . . . For over an hour, while X was struck dumb with surprise and terror! Ibsen refuses to recognize nationality or anything like that; he is an absolute anarchist, wants to make *tabula rasa,* lay the torpedo under the ark; mankind must begin again at the beginning to build up the world—and begin with the individual. . . . The great task of our time is to blow up all existing institutions— to destroy!"

On another occasion Ibsen was very sharply attacked because he was working only to tear down and was offering nothing constructive—certainly a terrible responsibility he was loading upon himself. Ibsen gave his attackers the slip with this remarkable utterance: "Different people have different duties assigned them by Nature; Nature has given the one the power or the desire to do this, the other that. Each bird must sing with his own throat and thus fulfill the task assigned him by Nature, and his justification must be that he can in truth say like Luther: 'I *can* do no other! Here I stand. God help me. Amen!'"

"A remarkable, a splendid personality!" exclaimed this same friend. "I mentioned the sixth glass: I do not mean to imply that Ibsen gets that far often. But once in a while when he is in the company of someone with whom he likes to chat he goes to a café to sit and wrangle till late into the night. But this happens only on rare occasions and does not in the least influence his life and his serious work."

While Ibsen thus appeared often as an anarchist he was very much of a bourgeois in many other respects. It was precisely with the play, *An Enemy of the People,* in which he defied his cowardly and hypocritical opponents, that he was able to drive a good bargain with the Christiania Theater; he forced them to pay him four thousand Kroner ($1,000) for the right of producing it, instead of getting only the receipts of one performance, or about fifteen hundred Kroner, as had been the agreement in the case of previous plays. Just a month before the anarchistic tirade described above he had asked his friend Hegel to invest a large sum for him in Norwegian State Securities. Brandes in an article on Ibsen had remarked on the ironical situation of this exiled critic of Norway receiving an annual state pension from the very state he was constantly lampooning; on March 27, 1881, Ibsen wrote to an influential member of the Storthing that this pension of sixteen hundred Kroner was not sufficient and suggested four thousand Kroner as an acceptable sum. Ibsen argued that since Norway did not belong to the international copyright union the people on the whole profited by getting their books more cheaply through pirated editions of foreign authors, while the Norwegian authors paid for this by not having their books protected outside their own country— therefore the state pension would be a compensation for the insufficient legal protection; the Storthing rejected the proposal since Ibsen was legally a Danish author and therefore his losses were due to the fact that Denmark and not Norway

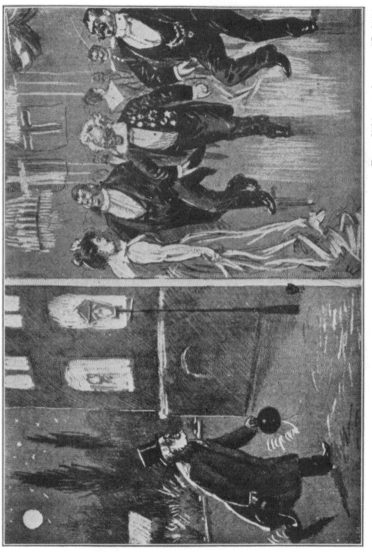

HENRIK IBSEN AS POLITICIAN

1. Seen with the spectacles of socialists or anarchists.
2. Seen with the spectacles of truth.

—From *Vikingen*, January 27, 1894.

had failed to sign the Berne convention.   Another reason—
probably the chief one—for this refusal was that the "anarchist and atheist Ibsen" was very unpopular among the
conservative and clerical circles in Norway.   Furthermore,
in spite of his views of the state and its servants Ibsen used
all his influence to aid his son in entering the diplomatic
career; in 1885 he had the pleasure of seeing Sigurd appointed attaché at the Swedish-Norwegian legation in Washington.

Ibsen, who at this time summed up his philosophy:

> To live is to war with fiends,
> That infest the brain and the heart;
> To write is to summon oneself
> And play the judge's part.

—was quite aware of these and other incongruities in his
character; but in his case, if ever, the saying applied that
consistency is the virtue of small minds.   Many people, to
be sure, can bring their words and their actions into greater
harmony than did Ibsen, but not one man in centuries can
create anything to equal *The Wild Duck*.   Much of Ibsen's
own soul-life went over into the character of Hjalmar Ekdal,
a great talker but not much of a doer.   Externally this character is modelled largely on Ibsen's eccentric instructor in
painting during his Christiania days, Magnus Bagge, a man
who saw fit when he later came to Germany to style himself
by his own right Magnus *von* Bagge.

Hjalmar Ekdal in *The Wild Duck* is the object of the missionary zeal of the reformer Gregers Werle, who wishes to
stir him up out of his fatal contentment, "an effect of marsh
poisoning."   To these efforts Hjalmar replies:

Now, my dear Gregers, pray do not go on about disease and
poison; I am not used to that sort of talk.   In my home nobody
ever speaks to me about unpleasant things.

Just as Peer Gynt had met in play the unpleasant scene of his mother's death, so Hjalmar does not wish to be robbed of his comfort. Again Ibsen satirizes his own nation in the character of a dreamer and braggart. In a letter to Georg Brandes written January 3, 1882, he tells how the reception of *Ghosts*—one of the great crises of his life—had affected him:

When I think how slow and heavy and dull the general intelligence is at home, when I notice the low standard by which everything is judged, a deep despondency comes over me, and it often seems to me that I might just as well end my literary activity at once. They really do not need poetry at home; they get along so well with the *Parliamentary News* and the *Lutheran Weekly*.

Thus ended the chapter of Ibsen, the reformer. *The Enemy of the People* was the last of his social plays. Without drawing any absolutely hard and fast line, one can say that he now turned from his efforts to influence conduct to the study of souls. Above all, however, he continued to be a poet as he had been in all his previous works.

In *The Wild Duck* Ibsen rises to a high vantage point above the battle and with a humorous grin views himself trying to make over the world by presenting his demand for the ideal, for sacrifice, for marriage founded "upon entire and unreserved candor on both sides," for the cure of society's ills by telling the truth about them. With amazing frankness, with a devotion to truth and to his art that mark him as a man of marvelous strength of character, Ibsen caricatures himself in the idealist Gregers Werle—or as one critic puts it: In writing *The Wild Duck* the author of *Brand* and of *A Doll's House* and of *Ghosts* kneels in his quiet chamber and flagellates himself with a scourge into which he has woven iron barbs.

Ibsen had seen some of the effects of his preaching; his ideals were burlesqued by people who claimed to be his followers. From Gregers' speeches it is evident that he has read *Brand, A Doll's House, Ghosts,* is in fact an Ibsen disciple. In a letter of June 27, 1884, in which Ibsen states that he has finished the play in the rough draft, he says resignedly: "I gave up universal standards long ago, because I ceased believing in the justice of applying them." Out of this resignation came *The Wild Duck* which, like no other drama in the world, views with irony and pity Destiny's "little children stumbling in the dark." The curtain falls on a scene unparalleled anywhere in its mixture of tragedy and humor— unless it be in real life. Hedvig's sacrifice of her life has been made merely to supply a subject for fatuous declamation; a profligate and a woman of unsavory reputation enter upon a marriage founded "upon entire and unreserved candor on both sides"; and the telling of the truth turns out to be a wicked, caddish and despicable act! Dr. Relling, the incarnation of cynicism, substitutes for ideals the good native word "lies" and sums up the whole story: "Rob the average man of his life-illusions and you rob him of his happiness at the same stroke."

After a summer in the Tyrolean mountains, spent in "energetic individualization of the persons and their mode of expression," while his wife and son made a visit to Norway, Ibsen sent the manuscript of *The Wild Duck* to his publisher:

> For the last four months I have worked at it every day; and it is not without a certain feeling of regret that I part from it. Long daily association with the persons in this play has endeared them to me, in spite of their manifold failings; and I am not without hope that they may find good and kind friends among the great reading public, and more particularly among the actor tribe—to whom they offer rôles which will repay the trouble spent on them.

Many great actors have found fame in portraying these creations of Ibsen. There is Gregers Werle, the idealist who hates himself and his very name—perhaps because of that other Gregory who demanded of the poor clergy the ideal of celibacy about which Ibsen probably had a sturdy Lutheran skepticism; this rebellious son begins by winning our sympathy, but at the end vis-à-vis Hedvig he appears a sadistic fiend.   Gina's is a hard rôle to play, but a good actress can convey to the audience the same sympathy the author felt toward this sensible, kindly woman, as Ibsen always did toward everything genuine.   The sturdy clear-seeing Dr. Relling and "the old man in silver locks," Lieutenant Ekdal with his red wig, are also fine parts.   But the greatest of all is Hjalmar Ekdal—denying his father, handing Hedvig the menu card, strutting up and down playing his flute, pasting together Hedvig's torn letter, returning for his bread with thick butter after it had been "all over," or clenching his fists and crying upwards before the child's corpse "O Thou above—! If Thou be, indeed! Why hast Thou done this thing to me?"

Hjalmar is uncannily real, revealing the very innermost thoughts that the mind's censor generally is in the habit of suppressing the instant they arise; but these very thoughts do not escape Ibsen's search.   Who has not found in himself traits of Hjalmar Ekdal, emotions or feelings that he would not mention even to his closest friend?

Ibsen gave his plays such a life-like appearance because he saw and observed life so closely.   He often preferred to leave unsettled questions such as baffle us in real life.   He does not tell us definitely who Hedvig's father is, nor yet whether Gregers carries out the threat of suicide.   To William Archer's question as to whether or not Mrs. Alving gave Oswald the tablets, he answered that she probably did not as long as there was the slightest hope of a recovery.   To someone who asked whether carpenter Engstrand had set fire to the orphanage he replied, "Quite likely.   At least I shouldn't put it past him."

Many personal recollections of the playwright found a place in this drama. Poor old Ekdal, who had formerly been wealthy and honored, was modeled on Ibsen's father. It is told of Magdalene Thoresen, the vivacious pastor's wife of Bergen, that she used to say jokingly to her black-bearded, silent son-in-law: "Come here, Ibsen, let me kiss you! You are so dæmonic!"—one personal reminiscence employed in the character of the drunken theologian Molvik; perhaps there were others too. Gregers' principle of doing things for himself, brought into play when he pours water into his smoking stove, draw comments from Gina such as Mrs. Ibsen may have employed when her husband insisted on polishing his own shoes or sewing on buttons for himself. But for Ibsen the rarest memory was that of Hedvig in the attic poring over heirlooms left there by ancestral sea captains. In this play he erected for his sister, for whom Hedvig was named, a beautiful monument that makes the charming, devoted little girl of Skien immortal. Among all the tame, rabbit-souled folk of the Ekdal ménage she is the only one who shows the unbroken spirit of the wild duck, preferring when wounded to die rather than to live just for the sake of living.

Without making the plot any the less sufficient in itself the wild duck hovers over this realistic play, shedding a poetic glow over the drab scene; a symbol that, like many words, has several meanings and connotations. Ibsen's great devotion to the reading of newspapers has perhaps served to give his character a prosaic touch in the eyes of many, but throughout his life he read poetry and sensed poetry wherever he was. He gave up verse quite definitely at this time, since he felt that as a medium of dramatic expression it was as obsolete as the Dodo; but, if anything, he made *The Wild Duck* all the more poetic because of this. Wherever you touch the play there lurks a deeper meaning. The attic, for

example, stands for the land of dreams. Hedvig finds there
a childhood paradise. A lazy man like Hjalmar finds in it an
escape from the work and worry of real life. For the old
lieutenant it is the dream of past glory; in there he assumes
the cap of the officer again and kills bears as of old. Gina
and Relling never enter the attic—such as they live without
dreams. Hjalmar Ekdal with the false picture of himself
and the world that he has built up in his imagination, with
the subterfuges that hide his real motives, with his escape
from work to the play and pretense in the attic is—every man.

Ibsen was fifty-six years old when he wrote this play, and
he felt that at his age he had to make use of his time to achieve
the literary immortality he craved with every fiber of his
being. He has told the method of working to which he had
advanced after a life-time's devotion to his craft: "As a rule
I make three drafts of my dramas which differ very much
from each other in characterization, not in action. When I
proceed to the first sketch of the material, I feel as though
I had the degree of acquaintance with my characters that one
acquires on a railway journey; one has met and chatted about
this or that. With the next draft I see everything more
clearly, I know the characters just about as one would know
them after a four weeks' stay in a spa; I have learned the
fundamental traits in their characters as well as their little
peculiarities; yet it is not impossible that I might make an
error in some essential matter. In the last draft finally I
stand at the limit of my knowledge; I know my people from
close and long association—they are my intimate friends,
who will not disappoint me in any way; in the manner in
which I see them now, I shall always see them." It is because Ibsen studied his characters so well, from the cradle
to the grave, that they continue to present to the reader different and profounder aspects after each re-reading of a
play. It was in this summer of 1884 when Ibsen made an

intense effort in the fulness of his experience and on the height of his mental power that he achieved a symbolical drama that seems most typically Ibsenian, *The Wild Duck*. This symbolical play, the romantic *Peer Gynt*, and the realistic *Ghosts* will probably stand as his three greatest works.

With his usual clearness Ibsen himself judged prophetically about the drama, realizing not only that he had created a different type of play, but that *The Wild Duck* would probably "entice some of our young dramatists into new paths." When enthusiastic young men with special permission from the police gave a private performance of *Ghosts* in Berlin an eccentric Ibsen enthusiast, the Danish professor, Julius Hoffory, strode up and down the aisles between acts, shouting in the manner of the sybils and prophets: "This day marks the beginning of a new literary era." And as Ibsen with *Ghosts* inspired the naturalistic problem play in the modern literature of all nations, so too he is the pioneer who stands behind the modern symbolical play with his masterpiece, *The Wild Duck*.

2

"Ibsen is nothing but a pessimist, he is forever tearing down, he is an anarchist, he is destroying the people's faith." These and similar accusations the poet read or heard on every hand, especially after the "hopelessly pessimistic" *Wild Duck*. Naturally enough these criticisms challenged Ibsen to determine just what were his positive, constructive proposals.

In the summer of 1885, after an absence of eleven years, he visited his native country for the second time since his voluntary exile in 1864. In Christiania on June 10th he attended a session of the Storthing where the proposal to give to the poet Alexander Kielland a state pension similar to Björnson's, Ibsen's and Lie's, was being debated. The

liberals had in the previous year won a decisive victory in a
bitterly fought struggle against the conservative ministry and
the king.   Ibsen's sympathy, on the whole, was with them,
but he felt a very great disgust when he heard liberals oppose
the measure on the ground that Kielland was a free-thinker;
probably, like the editor Hovstad in *An Enemy of the People*,
these "leaders" were themselves free-thinkers, but because of their constituents they took this hypocritical attitude
in public.   This debate did not tend to alter Ibsen's pessimistic attitude toward salvation through parliamentarism and
legal reforms; the "third empire" was not yet at hand just
because another group of politicians was in power.

Four days later when Ibsen had reached Trondhjem a
labor union greeted him with a torch-light procession.   In
addressing them Ibsen stated that during his eight days in
Norway he had found "immense progress in most lines," but
that he had also met with disappointments, since "the most
indispensable individual rights are not as yet safeguarded as
I believed I might hope and expect under the new form of
government."   Then he continued, presenting his positive
credo in a masterful little address:

So there is still much to be done before we may be said to have
attained to real liberty.   But I fear it will be beyond the power
of our *present* democracy to solve these problems.   An element of
nobility must enter into our political life, our administration, our
representation, and our press.

Of course I am not thinking of the nobility of *birth,* nor of that
of *wealth,* nor of that of *knowledge,* neither that of *ability* or *intelligence.*   But I think of the nobility of *character,* of the nobility
of will and mind.

That alone it is which can make us free.

This nobility which I hope will be granted to our nation will
come to us from two sources.   It will come to us from two groups
which have not as yet been irreparably harmed by party pressure.
It will come to us from our women and from our workingmen.

The reshaping of social conditions which is now under way out there in Europe is concerned chiefly with the future position of the workingman and of woman.

That it is that I hope for and wait for; and it is that that I will work for, and shall work for my whole life so far as I am able.

With such thoughts in mind Ibsen proceeded a little to the south of Trondhjem to Molde, the charming sub-arctic town he had chosen for the year's summering-place. In this spot, amidst rugged mountains and on the marvelously colorful Romsdalfjord Ibsen found much of the raw material for his next play. The setting, for example, was derived from an ancient family estate near Molde, which in the play became Rosmersholm.

Furthermore Ibsen met here his old friend, Count Carl Snoilsky, the Swedish poet. Since their first meeting in Rome twenty years previously the Byronic youth had changed a great deal; in 1867 he had married a wealthy lady, entered the service of the foreign office, and become one of the members of the Swedish Academy. But his life was made very miserable by the snobbishness of his wife's family, who brought to bear all possible pressure to make him give up writing verses—an occupation in their opinion unbecoming a nobleman of a line so famous for its soldiers and statesmen as was his. After publishing a volume of sonnets in 1871—recognized everywhere as the finest sonnets in the Swedish language—he bowed to the prejudices of his family, a renunciation that drained all the happiness out of his life. One of his old-time friends visiting Snoilsky in these years reports that as they spoke of former days the poet wept while telling of the cramped life he was leading.

Suddenly in 1879 all Scandinavia was thrilled or shocked by the news that Count Snoilsky had left Stockholm, thrown up all appointments and engagements, and that he was accompanied in his flight to Italy by one of the leaders of aristocratic Swedish society, Countess Ebba Piper. This lady offered him the spiritual companionship and the sympathy for his work as a poet that had been so sadly lacking in his wife. The latter had been for years in poor health and died of tuberculosis shortly after her husband's elopement; of a broken heart, the gossips said, heaping bitter reproaches on the Count. In 1880 the lovers were married in Marseilles and the oppression of the last ten years seemed removed from the poet's inspiration. After a journey through Algeria and Tunis, described in a vivid volume by his wife, the poet settled in Florence and entered upon a second creative period.

Snoilsky was originally of Polish extraction, his family having settled in Sweden early in the seventeenth century. His heredity showed itself in his poems, which were aristocratic in form and content. His philosophy was Epicureanism, described by critics as being of a tender sobriety, of a seriousness that robs the pursuit of pleasure of all its coarseness. The following winter Ibsen wrote to him: "It was a great gain to us to be with you, and to make acquaintance with the noble and high-minded lady who is your wife. The recollection of those days is the most inspiring of all the memories of our stay in Norway." Count Snoilsky became the model for Johannes Rosmer of Rosmersholm.

After passing the summer at Molde amidst the snow-covered mountains Ibsen went by steamer to Bergen to revisit the scene of his poverty-stricken apprenticeship in Ole Bull's Norse Theater. Quite properly he could feel a certain pride in returning after these many years as Norway's leading man of letters and the greatest living dramatist. Expecting that Peter Blytt and other leading citizens would meet him at the pier, he put on formal dress and his orders as the ship wound its way through the rocky islands outside the harbor of Bergen. But as he gazed expectantly at the landing place there was no brass band and no citizens' committee;

only his bibulous, down-at-heel bar-room acquaintances, Peter Kieding, the broker, Dahl, the sexton, and Parelius, the musical tailor had come to meet him. For the sake of auld lang syne they had already taken many a cup and greeted him: "Welcome, old Henrik—how about a little brandy?"

Ibsen returned to his cabin and did not go on shore until much later!

But Bergen, the city of his early poetic dreams and youthful love affairs brought some pleasanter moments too. In the old theater dating back to the eighteenth century Ibsen had an opportunity of reflecting vividly on his ambitions now realized; he was asked to direct the actors at a rehearsal of *Lady Inger of Oestraat,* the play he had timidly submitted as the work of a "friend in Christiania." What a dramatic scene, with the sharp contrasts of then and now! And as more than thirty years before Henrikke Holst had presented the black-bearded, pale, "dæmonic" theater-manager with a bouquet of wild flowers, so the same lady, now Mrs. Tresselt, brought a similar gift to the world-renowned poet in his hotel —her grandmother's heart beating like that of a young girl at her first dance!

Ibsen recognized her immediately and was highly pleased at seeing her. Mrs. Tresselt, with a smile just as roguish as in the days when she had teased the Herr Student more than a generation before, said, "You may believe me, Ibsen, that today I examined my old physiognomy in the mirror, because I wanted to appear the least bit pretty on coming to see you. I wished so much that you should find me not too greatly changed, so that you'd like me a bit as in the old days."

The gray-haired poet paid her a fitting compliment and grasped her hands in deep emotion. The lady standing before him had been the shy young dreamer's ideal of all that is lovely in woman.

When Mrs. Tresselt, who for years had been very active in amateur dramatics, told him how much she had enjoyed his plays, he asked whether she had found in them any traces of their youthful love affair.

"Let me see," laughed Mrs. Tresselt, "probably Mrs. Strawman in *Love's Comedy*—the one with her dozen children and her eternal knitting!"

Ibsen protested that there were other more poetic reminiscences; then he told her of his life and his family and inquired what she had been doing all these years. At last he asked, "Well, why was it after all that nothing came of our love affair?"

"Why, you remember, Ibsen, you ran away!"

"That's right," said Ibsen, and added with his customary honesty in looking at his own motives, "Yes, face to face I've never had any courage."

This was not their last interview. Ibsen, always socially correct, returned the call. Later Mrs. Tresselt also visited the Ibsens during their Christiania years. Bergen left a very pleasant memory in the poet's mind; not least pleased was he to note the charmingly rococo statue of Holberg the citizens had erected to honor the town's most famous son, Ibsen's beloved master in comedy.

In contrast to the jovial city of Holberg, Christiania once more proved to Ibsen that he could be happier in a foreign country. During his stay in Molde he had unexpectedly met Professor Dietrichson, who was likewise spending the summer there; but this old friend of many pleasant meetings in foreign countries markedly avoided Ibsen when they met in Norway, and associated only with distinctly conservative people. In the previous summer Mrs. Ibsen, who was a very calm and sane person, had written her husband from Norway: "I could never have believed that we were in such utter disrepute with the Right as numberless signs prove us to be." Very naturally Ibsen felt that Dietrichson, now professor at the University of Christiania, was acting in a cowardly manner unworthy of their long-standing friendship.

The conservatives felt very bitter toward the liberals (including Ibsen in that party) because of their political defeat, and they also could not forgive *Ghosts*. An ironical fate caused the plays of the austere, ascetic Ibsen to be interpreted or imitated in a manner illustrated by Shaw's saying that in the Odyssey heroes are made into swine and in many modern works swine are made into heroes. "If we had free love," said Hans Jaeger, who attempted to introduce Zola's naturalism among the Christiania students, "then in the course of our lives we could get into a completely intimate relation with—well, perhaps it is difficult to say with how many, it may be different with different people, but let me say, for example, with twenty women. In that case I am cheated in the present state of society out of nineteen-twentieths of my life's content." Such men were classed by the conservatives as disciples also of Ibsen, the man who had said, "But Nora went alone!" Probably it was because of such sensual views held by many of his would-be followers that the dramatist made Rosmer and some of his other figures especially austere. But the conservatives interpreted Ibsen in this manner, and in the students' club where Dietrichson was the chairman the majority were conservative.

Now in this students' club a motion was made to greet Ibsen with a torchlight procession; the *enfant terrible* who suggested it was Fritz Thaulow, afterward famous as a landscape painter, incidentally the son of the bellicose pharmacist who served as model for Dr. Stockmann. The conservatives were anything but pleased; they suggested that a man of Ibsen's retiring disposition might not enjoy a noisy demonstration, or that it would be difficult to procure a sufficient number of torches in the short time at their disposal—but no one dared to oppose the plan openly. Willy-nilly Professor Dietrichson and other members of a committee had to call on Ibsen to ask whether he would accept this homage from the students. Ibsen realized from Dietrichson's manner, if not his words, just how sincere the offer was and declined with thanks. He motivated his decision by stating that he had recently declined a similar demonstration offered him by the labor union of Christiania, asked the committee to convey his hearty thanks to the students, and added with a smile that since the students did not pay any attention to him on his arrival he did not care particularly to hear their cheers on the occasion of his departure! Afterward Ibsen remarked to some callers that the greatest kindness the students could do him would not be a torch-light procession, but the election of liberal leaders in place of Professor Dietrichson and his colleagues. A student who was present took it upon himself to present this at the next meeting of their body as an official statement directly from Ibsen. This proved to be a veritable bomb exploded in the meeting. Dietrichson telegraphed Ibsen at Copenhagen asking whether this was true, and received the answer that Ibsen felt he had nothing in common with the students' organization under Dietrichson's leadership.

Thereupon Dietrichson delivered a speech before the students which he ended with the following words: "Ibsen said that he had nothing in common with us. Then let *our* answer be that *we* feel we have something in common with him. Not with the little Henrik Ibsen who in a weak moment forgot the very spirit of which his whole work bears the stamp; not with that illiberal spirit which by reason of a difference of opinion refuses to receive the respectful thanks and greeting of his countrymen; not with that overbearing tyranny which demands that we agree with him for the price of enjoying his favor, that we lay our free conviction in the dust before

the throne of his greatness; but with that Henrik Ibsen who
has given our country some of the greatest and best in all
our literature. And if Ibsen has lost his faith in the Norwegian students, then our answer is that we will not lose our
faith, neither in him, nor in the great teaching that he has
left us, and that also in future we shall hold fast to what we
consider truth and right, no matter whether it finds grace in
Henrik Ibsen's eyes or not. If we act in this manner, then,
that will be the most worthy, the only right answer from the
Norwegian students to Henrik Ibsen."

This patronizing hypocrisy was scarcely the tone of old
friendship, but the result of a very human desire for revenge.
Dietrichson went further in showing his animus; when the
students were assembled about the punch bowl he distrib-
uted some verses he had written in praise of the free student
and in mockery of Ibsen:

> But let the poet be great as he may,
> A *man* must stand back of all he shall say.

Ibsen was shelved as a "has-been":

> Norwegian students feel sorrow and grief
> Whenever a star is sinking.

"The sorrow and grief that intelligent people feel," com-
mented *Dagbladet*, "is because of this offence of the Students' Club against the proudest name this nation owns. The
fathers voted in the Storthing with Lars Aftedal against
Alexander Kielland; the sons vote in the Students' Club with
Professor Dietrichson against Henrik Ibsen."

As a result, the Students' Club was split into a radical and
a conservative group, while a violent expression of opinion
filled the papers. "Finally," wrote Camilla Collett, "the
shell of phrases that covers everything in our city has been

thoroughly cracked open. It will continue to burst more and more, and then it will become evident that it is hollow in its interior. But an Ibsen had to come to deliver the first blow."

Yet, it must be said, Ibsen's rôle does not seem to have been particularly heroic. "Face to face" with Dietrichson he had used polite phrases and had then spoken the provoking words behind his back, permitting a young student to say them in the meeting. The affair shows very clearly why the thin-skinned Ibsen preferred once more to go into voluntary exile. When he wrote *Rosmersholm* in Munich he erected a "fitting monument" to Professor Dietrichson and numerous others in Norway, among them the intolerant Björnson, in the figure of Peter Kroll, who holds the principle: "Whoever is not with me in the essential things of life, him I no longer know. I owe him no consideration." But to show that he was impartial as regards the Right and the Left Ibsen satirized the unprincipled liberals in Peter Mortensgaard, "the lord and leader of the future, . . . for Peter Mortensgaard has the secret of omnipotence. He can do whatever he will. . . . For Peter Mortensgaard never wills more than he can do. Peter Mortensgaard is capable of living his life without ideals."

Rosmersholm was largely the result of the "disturbing effect" of the impressions and observations in Norway. Of these Ibsen wrote to Brandes, November 10, 1886: "Never have I felt myself less capable of understanding and sympathizing with the 'Tun and Treiben' of my Norwegian compatriots than after the lessons taught me last year—never have I been more repelled, never more disagreeably impressed. Nevertheless, I do not relinquish the hope that all this crude immaturity may some day clarify into both the substance and the outward form of genuine civilization."

Such an ennobling of a savage, scheming murderess goes on before our eyes in this play through contact with a noble personality; just as historically people have changed their characters through contact with a Buddha, a Socrates, or a Christ.   This is the message of Ibsen who is "writing for eternity" and therefore not concerned with ephemeral alleviating measures.   This "call to work" in the ennobling of the world is distinguishable throughout *Rosmersholm,* as Ibsen writes in a very friendly letter to a students' debating club, consenting for once to explain one of his plays.   Furthermore, he says, the play deals with the struggle which all serious-minded human beings have to wage with themselves in order to bring their lives into harmony with their convictions; the heroine Rebecca West after such a struggle rises to the standards of a true nobility, preferring to die rather than to win by cheating.   But first and foremost, Ibsen writes to his youthful admirers, the play is a poetic work of art— a story of human beings and human fates.

How true this is becomes apparent when one stops to compare Ibsen's raw material with the finished product.   All is blended harmoniously in the shadows of the moribund house of Rosmersholm, "sad in the fruit, bright in the flower."   The human beings who move across the stage are drawn with such consummate skill, entire biographies condensed into a few short acts, that they continue to present new facets the more profoundly the reader penetrates into their histories, each of which might fill a three-volume novel.   Ulrik Brendel's strange fate is unrolled as this uncanny ghost of his former self twice walks in the old country estate.   Rosmer's wife Beate, long dead in the mill-race, also must be counted among the *dramatis personæ* in *Rosmersholm,* where the children do not cry and the grown-ups never laugh.   "To understand the play," Ibsen remarked to a friend from sunny Vienna, "you ought to know the North.   The grandiose, but severe nature that surrounds the people up there, their solitude and separation forces them to look into themselves.   This makes

them thoughtful, serious, ruminating, doubting, often de-
spairing." In the spiritualized, tradition-laden family-seat
"the Rosmer view of life ennobles—but it kills happiness."
The White Horses appear, as Johannes Rosmer and Rebecca
West voluntarily meet their death.

The whole play sounds like a dirge on the old theme that
beauty and goodness pass away all too soon. *Rosmersholm*
calls up Landor's lines "On Music":

> Mind how at every touch, at every tone
> A spark of life hath glistened and hath gone!

3

Gradually Ibsen became a traditional feature of Munich
life. Every evening, no matter what the state of the weather,
his striking figure was seen to enter the Café Maximilian
between seven-thirty and eight-thirty, never at any other time.
He regularly sat down at the second or third table at the
right of the entrance. From this point of vantage he could
overlook the whole café and at the same time see the reflection of all who entered, as he glanced upward along his
paper into the large mirror opposite the door. On the table
before him he had a glass of dark Munich beer or a cognac
with a Seltzer water bottle; beside him he had a stack of
newspapers. He observed human nature in the news items
or even more frequently he glanced beyond the paper observing a character, a trait, a turn of phrase, or some psychological nuance for his dramas. Often too he sat like a
marble figure, his glance turned inward, his lips pressed together, his fingers in a position as though they were holding
a pen, deeply absorbed in creative activity. And few were
the intrepid souls who ever dared to interrupt him! At the
end of an hour he paid the waitress without saying a word,
took up his ever-present umbrella, his silk hat, his gloves, and

walked out of the door with his characteristic short, quick
steps.   Always the same hour, the same dress, the same café
—accomplishing his daily round in systematic concentration.

Among the few who did dare accost Ibsen at his café was
Georg Michael Conrad, the tall, curly-haired, goat-bearded
editor of *Die Gesellschaft,* the rousing weekly that fought for
Zola and Ibsen, Wagner and Boecklin, for the modern, the
truthful, the art related to life, and which burst the bubbles
of many pompous literary reputations.   Conrad tells of an
interview he had with Ibsen during the latter's working hours.
At Zola's request the *théâtre libre* had a translation of *Ghosts*
made and wished to get Ibsen's authorization.   When weeks
passed and they failed to get an answer, they turned to Conrad, asking him to act as an intermediary.   He went one
morning to the building where Ibsen lived, finding on a door
two flights up a card inscribed *Dr. Henrik Ibsen* in the poet's
own handwriting.   He rang three times; finally Ibsen opened
the door, a steel pen in his hand. Conrad explained his er-
rand, excusing his untimely arrival by the urgency of the
matter—Paris was to have an opportunity of seeing *Ghosts!*

"Of course I received the letter," said Ibsen as he admitted his visitor and led him to his study, "but I have not yet
answered.   Correspondence is such a terrible thing, it takes
up so much time.   I am at work on a new play.   What can
I do?"

Conrad offered to transmit Ibsen's wishes to his French
friends.

"That is fine.   Do whatever you consider best," said Ibsen.
"Write in my name to Paris."

"Would you like to examine the translation?"

"No, no," he declined energetically, "every translation
is good and every translation is bad.   Therefore, authorize
the performance in my name; I agree to everything."

When the business was thus settled Conrad took the opportunity of asking a few questions concerning the new drama. Ibsen had laid his pen down and stretched comfortably in his arm-chair.

"Yes, that is very difficult," said Ibsen, glancing at the sheets of manuscript.

"The setting is in Norway, of course?"

"Yes, of course; I know that country best. There I am certain in regard to every point. Uncertainty is terrible. Before I write down one word I have to have the character in mind through and through, I must penetrate into the last wrinkle of his soul. I always proceed from the individual; the stage setting, the dramatic ensemble, all of that comes naturally and does not cause me any worry, as soon as I am certain of the individual in every aspect of his humanity. But I have to have his exterior in mind also, down to the last button, how he stands and walks, how he conducts himself, what his voice sounds like. Then I do not let him go until his fate is fulfilled."

"How is it then, Herr Doktor, when you see your creations bodily on the stage? How do the pictures in your imagination compare with the real actors?"

He smiled a bit of a wry smile.

"I seldom go to the theater. I am satisfied so long as the public is satisfied. That's a fact, but please do not draw any evil conclusions from it."

"Perhaps this," laughed Conrad, "that in writing your play you think of the public or of the effect?"

"For God's sake, no! In that case my new play might as well not be written at all. I couldn't possibly imagine what position the public would take in regard to it, least of all a non-Norwegian public."

"Could you give me a hint as to the nature of the conflict?"

"That is impossible to state in a few words; it would give

you a distorted picture. Only after everything is finished. I have not yet completed the fifth act."

"Does nature play a part in the background as in *Rosmersholm* and *The Wild Duck?*"

"Yes, especially the sea. It's very peculiar how intensively the people in Norway are affected by the sea. I do not believe that in other countries this will be understood."

"Then we'll simply take it as symbolism or mysticism. Our critics will know how to deal with the situation."

"Yes, to be sure, the critics—they are often far from adequate. They like to symbolize, because they have no respect for reality. And if one really gives them a symbol, then they reduce it to a triviality or they revile the author."

"Have you already selected the title for your new piece, Herr Doktor?"

Ibsen explained that he always selected his title after the play was finished. He told Conrad that simultaneously with the Norwegian edition a German translation was to appear in the new and progressive publishing house of S. Fischer in Berlin. Thus the two men continued to chat for a while. Ibsen seemed to welcome the pause in his work, quite contrary to his usual habit in the face of interrupters, probably because he enjoyed the vividly genial personality of Conrad.

As he was about to leave Conrad noticed Ibsen's attire; over his collarless shirt he was wearing a double-breasted black frock-coat.

"But my dear master," said Conrad with a smile as he patted Ibsen's hand, "you don't always sit at your desk in a frock-coat, do you?"

"God forbid! In shirt sleeves. Only because you surprised me I quickly put on this coat." And with a hearty hand-shake Ibsen bade his caller farewell.

In Munich Ibsen found the faithful friend who was to be

his chief translator and interpreter in Germany, as William Archer was in England. An earnest, brilliant student of Germanics, Julius Elias, had gone to Norway to pursue the study of Icelandic and had discovered there Ibsen's dramas which came to interest him much more than philology. On his return to Munich young Elias began to give readings from the social plays in his own translations. He was later instrumental in arranging the authorized German edition of the poet's works and also in furthering the epoch-making performance of *Ghosts* in Berlin that brought the dramatist wide recognition in Germany. Ibsen, who, like his wife, shunned society, preferring the peace and comfort of his home to useless gregariousness, nevertheless made Elias happy by attending his "Doktorschmaus" and draining many a glass to the success of the young scholar's career, staying on till the small hours. As the bakers' boys delivered their wares the next morning they saw with some amusement before Ibsen's door a small group taking repeated solemn farewells with profound assurances of mutual esteem.

About the time of the publication of *Ghosts* Ibsen had planned to issue an autobiographical work entitled *From Skien to Rome;* but on the advice of his publisher he abandoned the project at this period of his extreme unpopularity. In 1882 a Finnish professor, V. Vasenius, had written a biography of the poet, and this was followed in the next year by another one by the German, Ludwig Passarge. As Ibsen approached his sixtieth year, the Norwegian critic Henrik Jaeger prepared to issue a more extensive biography, and for this work he was furnished a great deal of material by the dramatist himself. In addition to this there were, of course, an ever-increasing number of articles on Ibsen in all parts of the world showing that he was beginning to receive universal recognition. But the one event that probably more than any other pleased the poet was that *Ghosts* was performed at Meiningen while Ibsen was the guest of the Duke, who invested Ibsen with the insignia of a knight of the "Sächsisch-Ernestinische" order—"the third class, with the Star." About this time he wrote to Hegel, January 5, 1887: "Please do not think that it is vanity that makes me tell you this. But I do not deny that the honor gives me pleasure when I think of it in connection with the stupid denunciation of which the play was so long the object in Scandinavia."

A little vignette of Ibsen by a journalist, Gotthelf Weisstein, present on this occasion, shows him as he appeared in public at the formal festivities which he tried to avoid as a usual thing; the third-rate dramatist Paul Lindau serves as a foil: "In the course of the soirée," he writes, after mentioning the "nerve-racking" performance of *Ghosts*, "we met also Ibsen. The Norwegian poet, who with his snow-white head looks older than he is in reality, by means of his stiff silence makes the impression of a small-town German professor—in spite of his many orders. It was very comical to observe this Moltke among the poets by the side of Lindau. Our countryman chatted and sparkled like fireworks. Ibsen measured out to us even the minutest pearls of his wisdom with an amount of emphasis and an impressive mien, as though he wished to write for eternity on the tablets of our minds the fact that he had communicated to us: 'Tomorrow I shall take the train for Munich!' "

Since he met with all this recognition, it is not surprising that the world-famous poet of mellow age began to see life a bit differently from the youthful, embittered, starving author of *Brand*. Ibsen himself expressed in so many words his change in attitude, for example, in a speech in Göteborg, September 12, 1887, at a banquet tendered him by the literary club "Gnistan" (the spark). He thanked the members for all the kindness and friendship they had shown him, stating that he appreciated this all the more because his polemic interest was decreasing and he had the feeling that his literary activity was about to enter upon a new phase; the friendliness and sympathy shown him on every hand were very significant and serviceable in furthering the more optimistic mood of his next drama.

On another occasion he stated that on his summer journey to Denmark and Sweden (not Norway) in 1887 he had discovered the sea; that from this summer he was carrying away memories of the sea that were going to be of great significance for his life and his writing. However, perhaps his discovery of the sea as a poetic subject was due to the Swiss painter Arnold Boecklin, whose painting *Triton and Nereid,* showing a mermaid lying in the shallow water by a rock, was exhibited in the seventies. In 1883 appeared his even more famous *Play of the Waves.* Ibsen's letters show that he took great interest in the Munich art exhibitions, and even if he did not see the originals he could hardly have escaped seeing reproductions of these widely discussed works in magazines or in the Munich shop windows. At any rate there is a striking parallelism in the work of the two men whose birthdays were less than half a year apart. Both introduced mythological figures into rather realistic settings, both inclined toward the somber and macabre, both felt the attraction of the sea, and both employed a great deal of symbolism. Boecklin too "worked for eternity," himself mixing the colors that effectually prevent his paintings from cracking or fading. However, from his Grimstad days onward Ibsen independently shows considerable interest in the sea, although it is rather striking that he wrote *The Lady from the Sea* at the very time when Boecklin had made the sea with its mythological figures a fashionable subject.

But Ibsen, always independent in his effects, used all the poetic romanticism of the sea only to repudiate it in the end, in order to do some "freeing of minds" in the spirit of

Rosmer. Many a romantic soul has been disappointed by the ending of *The Lady from the Sea*. Throughout this play the sea stands for freedom and the land for tame, dull conventionality; the carp in the pond are contrasted with the wild fish in the sea who like the wild duck are unbroken by civilization. The heroine bears the name Ellida, so meaningful to every Scandinavian as the name of the magic vessel of Frithjof in Tegnér's *Frithjofssaga*. The hypnotic lure of the sea—recalling Goethe's *Der Fischer* and many other romantic ballads—is embodied in an episode recalling a picturesque tradition of Venice: the bold sailor took his own and Ellida's ring, strung them on a key-ring and tossed them far out into the sea as an unforgetable symbol of their eternal union; this ceremony was biographical—Ibsen and Rikke Holst performed it in Bergen. But just as Ibsen's ending shows that what the sea hath joined together man can put asunder, so the poet would seem to say it is with many other romantic or traditional vows or ceremonies.

Ellida chooses "in freedom and on her own responsibility" under conditions such as every self-respecting woman ought to enjoy; but as a profoundly significant contrast Ibsen introduces the story of her step-daughter Bolette who "sells herself" in a loveless marriage of convenience to a bald, middle-aged pedagogue as the only means of escaping a dreary spinsterhood in the stifling small town where all the straits are ice-bound in winter. This story is, so to speak, a repetition of Ellida's own marriage, and it seems to disclose an endless vista of women who for untold generations have been forced into such dreary unions in violation of their emotions. The condemnation of the marriage of convenience Ibsen took over from Camilla Collett, as mentioned previously, but the Norwegian authoress influenced the play more directly—she was the model for the heroine in her relation to "the stranger." When Camilla Wergeland in 1879 came to

Christiania as a girl of seventeen, she and the poet Welhaven felt a mutual attraction. Welhaven, then twenty-one and the lion of Christiania society, wrote of her in his *Soirée-Billeder*

> There was a pause in the soirée
> When she, the parson's daughter, came
> And gossip, passing with the teacups,
> Was silenced by her airy tread.

The great controversy between Welhaven and Wergeland, Camilla's brother, broke out about this time, but in spite of the family feud Camilla corresponded with and secretly met her brother's enemy. She loved him, but for a woman to declare her love would have been considered, as someone has put it, *lèse-virginité;* and he never spoke the words, "I love you," but always held her at a tantalizing distance, at the same time addressing ardent poems to her. This duplicity on Welhaven's part tore the young girl to pieces physically and psychically. Her father took her to Paris to break this spell, but immediately on her return she was attracted again by the lure of her poetic lover. This went on for many years until finally the spell was broken after the lady had become engaged to another man. When fifty years later *The Lady from the Sea* appeared, Camilla Collett recognized herself in the heroine and wrote to Ibsen about it; he acknowledged the relationship in a letter dated Munich, May 3, 1889:

Allow me, then, today to send you a few words of very sincere thanks for your comprehension of *The Lady from the Sea.*

I felt pretty certain that you in particular would understand it; but it gave me inexpressible pleasure to be confirmed in my belief by your letter.

Yes, there are suggestive resemblances—indeed, many. And you have seen and felt them, seen and felt that of which I could have only a vague premonition.

But it is many years now since you, by virtue of your characteristic spiritual and intellectual development, began in one form or another to make your influence felt in my writings.

You may be sure that my wife and I do not forget you; we both think and talk of you.

At the same time Ibsen immortalized in the figure of Ellida a free-hearted, forceful woman whom he had admired since his Bergen days, and to whom some of his finest letters are addressed, his wife's step-mother, Magdalene Thoresen. She was a fisherman's daughter and passionately attached to the sea. She was adored by a young step-daugher, Susannah Thoresen, to whose intense affection she showed nothing but indifference, at least in the years when Ibsen first met them. She had an elderly husband who was very much in love with his wife and treated her with great consideration and self-effacement. Ellida thinks and conceives in images, in poetic pictures; Georg Brandes, who met Magdalene Thoresen for the first time on the beach of a Danish sea-side resort, tells that this lady, who had led a full and vivid life romanticized everything that she had experienced, was rather high-strung and extravagant in her speech, making a translation of her conversation into the language of everyday very difficult. He found in her also all of the warmth of color and sensuous appeal with which Ibsen has endowed Ellida Wangel.

In addition to the poetic story resolved in a very practical way there is a mass of profound thought in this play well worth pondering over. Ibsen plays with the idea that at one point in our evolution we might have chosen to live in the sea rather than on land and that thus we might have been "better and happier" as Ellida puts it; but in the end, this, like other romantic ideas of the heroine, is shown to be of very dubious value. "It is too late now to rectify the error," says Arnholm, and the poet seems to imply that while the "wild" life may be more picturesque and heroic we are now committed to "tame" civilization and can do best by developing the qualities of cooperation and kindness. Ibsen's reading of evolution distinctly does not result in a preaching of the "big, blond beast," but in presenting as a hero the sympathetic character of Dr. Wangel, in whose conduct "the miracle" is translated into reality.

Satirical elements are not absent from the play either. The figure of Ballested who in the narrowness of his environment has been forced to compromise with his ideal of becoming a great painter by spending his time also in acting as guide, barber, cornetist, actor and dancing teacher, seems to convey Ibsen's notion of what the narrowness of Norwegian life makes out of the artist. No doubt this Jack-of-all-trades and master of none is drawn with a side-glance at Björnson, the dramatist, lyricist, novelist, orator, politician, and country gentleman. In Lyngstrand the fatuous, self-satisfied male is satirized. His idea of marriage is that the woman should sacrifice all her interests and all her time for the husband who thinks only of his work (and perhaps of another woman for inspiration). Full of enthusiasm Lyngstrand paints the picture of such female self-effacement and adds: "It seems to me that must be such a delight for a woman!"

Since *The Lady from the Sea* is a play with a happy ending and a message as positive as Ibsen ever gave, it is interesting to note how the generation of Norwegians who absorbed Ibsen-enthusiasm in their formative years were influenced by it. In 1910 the marriage and divorce laws in Norway were reformed on the principle that marriage is "a union between two free individuals with a mutual duty to respect each other's needs and desires." The laws of the new code were framed to create "complete legal equality between husband and wife," but with the freedom accorded the wife she is likewise given an equal responsibility for all her actions as well as for the support of the family. The assumption on which the laws permitting divorce by mutual consent are based—"it is morally indefensible to maintain a marriage relationship by legal statute where all bonds between the parties have been broken"—recalls very vividly the breaking down of Dr. Wangel's legal claims in the last act of the play. "Vows bind no one; neither man nor woman," says Ibsen; and the Norwegian government does not consider it a duty to chain together two free adult individuals who do not feel that they belong to each other. And statistics show that with the easy, inexpensive divorce by mutual consent Norway has only about one-seventh as many divorces in proportion to the number of inhabitants as the United States, largely because the "freedom and responsibility" effectually prevent the economic exploitation of one party by the other through alimony and other means. The whole matter has become one conducted with privacy and self-respect.

Such ennoblement of humanity as Ibsen attempted in the message of *The Lady from the Sea* had been the goal of Johannes Rosmer, the character among all those in Ibsen's plays who in his ideals as well as in his dignified bearing and retired manner of life most closely resembles the author. Rosmer, in speaking of his life's ideal says, "What a joy it would be to let a little light into all this gloom and ugliness." But he adds sadly that such happiness would not come through him. A similar pessimism was often felt by Ibsen, but events after his death have shown that he did have a share in banning much gloom and ugliness by freeing the minds of men and women.

4

On March 20, 1888, Ibsen's friends and admirers used the occasion of his sixtieth birthday to show their gratitude for what he meant in their lives. Georg Michael Conrad was one of the throng of callers who came to offer congratulations in Ibsen's home in Munich, where for the first time in his life the Norwegian exile was surrounded by furniture that he owned, having previous to this time always lived in furnished apartments. He tells that bouquets, wreaths, and flowers in pots stood everywhere; on the chairs and tables other presents lay spread out: works of art, books, painted fans and embroideries. Letters and telegrams continued to arrive from all parts of the world. A bright March sun shone through the high windows, the flowers glowed and shed their fragrance, and the sixty-year-old birthday-child beamed with joy over this unending kindness of his friends. "This is too much, I don't know what to say!" he exclaimed again and again, pointing to the abundance of presents. Mrs. Ibsen moved about among the guests in joyous amazement. Conrad felt that there was something solemn and something comical in the sight of these two old recluses routed out of their peaceful seclusion by this happy throng of well-wishers. Björnson summed it up in his telegram: "To-day the world comes to the recluse."

Among the telegrams that pleased Ibsen most was one from the Danish pastor, Christian Hostrup, Ibsen's senior by ten years. As a young man he had written some amusing *vaudevilles* (among others *The Neighbors* to the tune of which young Ibsen in Grimstad had composed the verses making sport of a young dude), then he had been a pastor for over twenty years; when Ibsen's *Doll's House* appeared it inspired him to return to literature as a determined follower of the great fighter of social lies. It was a shocking thing to be a clergyman and an Ibsenite, and the aged pastor made many enemies through his fearless liberalism. The heartfelt tone in which Ibsen thanked this clergyman shows that his supposed animus against the clergy, manifested in the portrayal of Strawman, Rörlund, Manders, Molvig and other theologians, did not extend to sincere and courageous preachers.

A little later another, but a very bigoted preacher, unwittingly paid Ibsen a noble compliment by publishing a book in Christiania with the title *Christ or Ibsen?*

About this time Ibsen was made to feel that he was growing positively historical when he read in a literary journal a sketch of the life in Botten-Hansen's circle in Christiania, containing a description of *The Hollanders* and their Patron Saint Holberg. He wrote immediately to the author, his old friend Ludvig Daae: "It affected me strangely and powerfully to be so vividly transported once again into surroundings which have exercised such a decisive influence on my subsequent development, and from which I have never in my innermost soul separated myself—never could nor wished to do so."

Paulsen tells how another reminiscence of his early days came to Ibsen one day in Munich. A great many Norwegians called on their famous countryman as they travelled abroad. As a general thing Ibsen was very reserved in the presence of these strangers, but one day Paulsen was surprised to see him showing enthusiastic cordiality to a young man, patting him on the shoulder and displaying genuine joy at seeing him. Later Paulsen learned that it had been young Schulerud, the son of the Grimstad friend who had shown his faith in Ibsen by advancing his few dollars for the printing of *Catiline.*

Among his Norwegian guests Ibsen found some splendid models and often too he heard from them many delightful stories that helped to round out the plots of his plays. About the time he was writing *Hedda Gabler* he heard of the wife of the composer Johan Svendsen who in a fit of jealousy burned the manuscript of a symphony her husband had just finished. He found another *motif* for the play in the account of another lady whose husband had conquered the drinking habit to which he had been addicted; whereupon one day she wished to test his self-mastery and her power over him, so she put a large quantity of brandy in his room; the result was that later she found him helplessly intoxicated. Another story, not utilized in the play, but one that brought a broad grin to Ibsen's face, was told him about Björn Björnson. This son of Ibsen's rival, a brilliant and forceful actor, returning home one day on a Norwegian steamer, discovered that he had not been treated in a manner conforming to his dignity. In high anger he protested to the captain: "Do you know who I am? I am the son of Norway's greatest author!" "Please excuse it, Herr Ibsen," answered the captain, "I shall see to it personally that you get what you wish."

When he was in the mood Ibsen himself could tell delightful stories to his guests. One day when Paulsen appeared with a cut in his face inflicted by a careless barber, Ibsen told him of a Munich barber, one of whose patrons protested that it made him nervous the way a large Danish dog, sitting three feet from the chair, kept staring at him continually. "Oh, never mind that dog," answered the barber, "he's just waiting to pick up some of the meat-scraps that occasionally fall down while I'm shaving." Paulsen tells that even in a group of men Ibsen never made a remark that was in any way vulgar, though he could tell or enjoy stories such as the following about Ole Bull. The great violinist and heart-breaker was appearing in Madrid, and as usual the women were wild over him, not least the young Isabella the Second, Spain's hot-blooded queen. After one of his concerts he was called before the queen. With southern vivacity she expressed her enthusiasm for his divine music and then asked that he play at the castle the next evening before her alone. Such a musical tête-à-tête would be charming, she thought. When royalty commanded, Ole Bull could but obey. But after this musical hour before the queen, he was presented by a chamberlain with the Spanish order bearing the inscription: "Pour la vertu." Later on in Stockholm at a court festivity he wore this order. Scarcely had Queen Desideria, who knew the Spanish court well, seen it when she began to laugh and asked Ole Bull to tell her why he had received that particular decoration. With a profound bow and with diplomatic seriousness the violinist answered, "Because of my virtue, Your Majesty!"

In spite of the fact that Dietrichson speaks of Ibsen's home as a very hospitable house in these Munich years, it seems from most accounts that he led a very retired life. In the evenings Mrs. Ibsen read many novels to him; if the book did not please him Ibsen's comment would be: "Lay that book aside, I cannot *see* the characters." One little picture revealed in a letter of November 10, 1886, shows this old and now lonely couple reading together and being immensely amused over an essay by Brandes discussing Luther's attitude on marriage and celibacy; the Danish critic shows that Luther held a woman with an illegitimate child to be better than a nun, that marriage is not for the sake of mental or spiritual companionship (this ideal was developed by the Romanticists), and that the great reformer even permitted bigamy in cases where an invalid wife gave her spouse cause for a certain complaint with which Luther shows very great compassion—all ideas that are perhaps a bit surprising to present-day Lutherans. Ibsen prized very highly the companionship of his wife; he spoke of her as being "inwardly quite free and a complete personality"—high praise that he accorded very few people. She was mentally very much alive, a greater reader than her husband, whom she informed about many books that he did not read. She had a strong, almost passionate belief in him, but this did not in the least prevent her from giving energetic expression to her opinions

when they differed from his. Ibsen talked over with her all
his literary affairs, and his poem *Thanks* shows what she
meant to him as a source of inspiration.

> Her grief was when perils
>   Obstructed my road,
> Her joy when good spirits
>   Made lighter my load.
>
> Her home is the boundless
>   Free ocean that seems
> To rock calm and soundless
>   My galleon of dreams.
>
> Her race is the changeful
>   Elfin-like throng
> That trip through the morris
>   Dance of my song.
>
> My fires when they dwindle
>   Are lit from her brand,
> Men see them rekindle
>   Nor guess by whose hand.
>
> Because she expects not
>   That I should repay,
> I pen and have printed
>   This thanksgiving lay.

In the later eighties Skien experienced a terrible fire, as
most Norwegian cities consisting in the main of wooden structures periodically do. When Ibsen was told that the place
of his birth, the Stockmann house, with the adjoining church,
Latin school, town pillory, jail and madhouse had all been
consumed by the flames, now never to serve as the goal of
pilgrimage for his admirers, he remarked grimly, "The inhabitants of Skien were quite unworthy to possess my birthplace." He knew how willing and eager they were now to
exploit his fame, while at a time when they might have

helped him they had done everything to make him feel his poverty. A popular saying in Skien had been: "The Ibsens have the brains and the Pauses have the money," and it would have been a very easy matter for his uncle Paus to have enabled his nephew Henrik to receive a schooling that would have raised him in social status above the servant girls—his only associates in the first dark years in Grimstad. But the spirit of these small-town souls forbade any noble impulse. These same Pauses, shocked at the withdrawal of Ibsen's sister Hedvig from the state church to join a devout sect corresponding roughly to the Quakers, had attempted to exert pressure on her by discharging her husband, Hans Jacob Stousland, a sea-captain in their employ, just as in *The Enemy of the People* the owner of Captain Horster's ship had discharged this brave man because he befriended Dr. Stockmann. After Ibsen's return to Norway he never visited Skien, even though it is but a few hours by rail from Christiania.

In 1889 the Ibsens again went to Gossensass, their favorite summer resort, to which allusion is made in *Hedda Gabler* as that little village just below the Brenner Pass of which Tesman says: "It was there that we passed the night"—whereupon Hedda cuts off possible indiscreet revelations regarding their honeymoon by adding quickly—"and met that lively party of tourists." Ibsen himself avoided the tourists as much as possible except as objects of study. When the hotel dining room was opened to the guests the Ibsens at their reserved table were already eating their dessert; thereafter he sat buried in a paper observing the guests with the customary glass of beer before him. He guarded his privacy jealously. One day when two ladies sat down at his table with their beerglasses intending to start a conversation Ibsen simply arose and left. He did not rebuff them in his famous manner, because it was contrary to his spirit to speak rudely to women.

Ibsen was very friendly toward the guests whom he knew, and even took part in the Gossensass custom of accompanying departing friends to the railway station. Mrs. Ibsen fitted her life wholly to his; if he wished to be alone she went on long walks either by herself or with Sigurd, who had meanwhile returned from America.

In Ibsen's sketches for *White Horses* (which later became *Rosmersholm*) dating from December, 1885, there are mentioned among the *dramatis personæ* an elder and a younger daughter of Rosmer. These two figures were later eliminated and did not appear until the next play, *The Lady from the Sea,* but not even in Bolette Wangel did the playwright develop the characteristics of the elder daughter: "highly gifted, without any application for her talents." This interesting problem of female psychology, and likewise a development of the younger sister, Ibsen preserved for still later plays; the former was developed in *Hedda Gabler,* written in the summer and autumn of 1890, and Hilda Wangel reappeared in *The Master Builder.* With these problems in mind there was nothing more natural for Ibsen than to observe young women at first hand. In Saeby in 1887 he had frequently talked with a young Danish actress, later Madame Engelcke-Friis. In Gossensass he met a young girl from Munich, Helene Raff, later distinguished as a painter and novelist, who reports that Ibsen often spoke of the weaknesses in the methods of training for women in Society. "It is the misfortune of women," he used to say, "that they are trained to wait in idleness and longing for something uncertain. In the case of hopes unrealized, potentially useful personalities often are crushed by their bitter disappointment. The sane thing would be to point out to them how they can win happiness through an exertion of their own wills."

When the chill autumn winds swept down on Gossensass most of the guests deserted the hotel for warmer regions.

One day as Ibsen approached the stairway of the hotel he saw a woman slip and fall down a few steps. He assisted her to her feet, led her to a chair, and then met the lady's husband, who turned out to be Professor Wilhelm Dilthey, the well-known German historian. After this informal meeting the two families frequently sat together in the evenings after dinner. There generally took place a heated discussion on the state in which the anarchically inclined Ibsen enjoyed attacking the views of the nationalistic historian. Then two more guests arrived, an elderly physician with his daughter who had come to this Austrian resort to meet the young lady's fiancé, an Austrian army officer. The professor and Ibsen were asked to act as witnesses at the wedding, while Frau Dilthey made some preparations to render this hotel wedding as festive as she could. She noted that Ibsen on a number of occasions asked the bride many questions about her life, as though he wanted to use her as a model for one of his characters. On the evening before the wedding, the whole party, augmented by the bridegroom and his brother, sat together over Tyrolean wine in great gayety of spirit. Suddenly Ibsen said to Frau Dilthey, "Why all this gayety?" She replied in great astonishment that this was self-evident on the evening before a wedding, only to be shocked into speechlessness by Ibsen's paradox: "On the contrary, it seems to me one ought to weep at weddings and rejoice at funerals." The lady, in telling these reminiscences remarks that Ibsen had spoken only too true, for the fate of this soldier's bride turned out to be a very sad one indeed.

With another young lady whom he met in Gossensass Ibsen carried on a fairly active correspondence—eleven letters in fifteen months—during the time he was planning *Hedda Gabler*, putting a stop to it when he concentrated on writing the play. This girl "said to have been seventeen" (William Archer) was a Viennese, Emilie Bardach, who, sitting one day on a bench along the poet's customary walk, greeted the lion of Gossensass society with a smile. Ibsen stopped and engaged the young lady in a conversation which became the first of many such talks, usually held in the bay window of the hotel dining room. With the same enthusiasm with which he had argued in the *Brand* days that "one ought to swallow the latch key" or before publishing *A Doll's House* that wives ought not to be merely play-things of their husbands, he now encouraged Miss Bardach to tell him of her life and hopes. Ibsen was rather struck by some of her confidences. The gist of her confessions was that she did not care a bit about one day marrying a well-brought-up young man—most likely she would never marry. What tempted and charmed and delighted her was to lure other women's husbands away from them. She was a little dæmonic wrecker; she often appeared to him like a little bird of prey that would fain have made him too her booty. Love seemed to mean for her only a sort of morbid imagination. Ibsen studied her very, very closely, and found various sides to her nature, including a great deal of heart and womanly understanding. In a talk I had with her in Berne on August 31, 1927, Fräulein Bardach said that Ibsen had asked her an endless number of questions and seemed to be particularly eager to catch her in a lie. She also told me that because she did not consider it æsthetic Ibsen gave up (for the time being) the drinking of beer, but that he had never kissed her.

The testimony of Fräulein Helene Raff is along the same lines, showing that the sensational speculations indulged in by many writers when Fräulein Bardach published her letters at the very time of Ibsen's death were quite absurd. Fräulein Raff writes me in a letter of December 8, 1927: "Ibsen's relations with young girls had in them nothing whatever of infidelity in the usual sense of the term, but arose solely out of the needs of his imagination; as he himself said, he sought out youth because he needed it for his poetic production. I must admit, however, that because of this need of the aging man who yearns for youth, he at times struck a too-devoted tone face to face with young women and that his wife was offended because she thought such things not in conformity with his dignity. For this reason she assumed at times a harsh attitude toward such matters." In one of his devoted moments Ibsen presented Miss Bardach with his photograph inscribed "To the May Sun of a September Life—in the Tyrol. September 27, 1889. Henrik Ibsen."

On his return to Munich Ibsen continued to see Fräulein Raff frequently, and when he visited her in her studio he praised in her temperament "das Gesunde" because she was doing exactly what he considered the aim of human life to be, namely, "to realize oneself." Fräulein Raff was kind enough to compile for me from her diary these details: from October 25, 1889, to April 12, 1891, she saw Ibsen forty times, either on the occasion of her visits to his home, visits on his part to her studio, or on walks about the city. She saw the deep tragedy in Ibsen's position vis-à-vis youth, anent which she quotes Goethe: "Ein alter Mann ist stets ein König Lear." After her first call Ibsen wrote her the following letter:

Late Friday night, Munich, October 29, 1889.

DEAR CHILD,

How kind, how lovable of you to visit us yesterday. My wife is so truly, so heartily fond of you. And I—too. As you sat there in the twilight and told us various things so thoughtfully and under-standingly, do you know what I then thought, what I wished? No, that you do not know. I wished—alas, if I only had such a dear and lovely daughter.

Come and see us again quite soon. But in the meantime you must keep busy at work artist-like in your atelier. There you must not be disturbed for the present.

Blessings on your dear head,

Yours devotedly,

HENRIK IBSEN.

It is interesting to note in the second paragraph how Ibsen speaks of the problem uppermost in his mind at the time, as the sketches of *Hedda Gabler* indicate; it is the misfortune of the well-brought-up young girl that she has no purpose in life or that she has no gift for anything but being bored, or that she must turn her personal advantages to profit "like actresses and others." Throughout his letters to Emilie Bardach he touches repeatedly on this *Hedda Gabler* theme. The most striking thing about these letters is the cautious manner of the writer in expressing himself always in phrases and pauses that might mean much or might again mean nothing at all; in fact they might serve as a letter-writer for an elderly gentleman wishing to express soft sentiments in a form that could be read aloud in court. Probably Ibsen was in love to some extent with the various young girls whom he was wont to address as "my princess," but at the same time he had a very keen sense of the fitness of things; Paulsen reports, for example, that once when someone spoke of the love affairs of the aging Goethe Ibsen exclaimed, "That billygoat!" Fräulein Bardach wrote the first letter, and repeatedly Ibsen begins his reply by thanking her for her *two* letters which he had left unanswered for such a long time; he avoids calling her "dear" by omitting the salutation altogether or writing simply "Fräulein Emilie"; except in the twelfth letter, written almost ten years later, when he wrote on the back of a photograph "Herzlich liebes Fräulein," carefully avoiding the much more usual and more meaningful "geliebtes." When after the first letter Fräulein Bardach protested against the lack of warmth in the term "hochgeschätztes Fräulein" and in the signature "Dr. H. I.," Ibsen consented to calling her "child" and signed his letters "H. I." It is hard not to believe that the dramatist who had such a keen appreciation for humor, especially for unconscious humor, did not write some passages in these letters with a roguish grin—especially when one recalls that he was writing at the same time lines like the following. (Tesman says to Hedda that he must tell his maiden aunt that she has begun to call him by his given name and adds, "Fancy that! Oh, Aunt Julia will be so happy—so happy!")

HEDDA: When she hears that I have burned Eilert Lövborg's manuscript—for your sake?

TESMAN: No, by the bye, that affair of the manuscript—of course nobody must know about that. But that you love me so much (*literally "that you burn for me"*), Hedda—Aunt Julia must really share my joy in that! I wonder now, whether this sort of thing is usual in young wives? Eh?

HEDDA: I think you had better ask Aunt Julia that question too!

Just as he had done in regard to Fräulein Raff so Ibsen urged Fräulein Bardach to cultivate a purpose in life. In the letter of December 22, 1889, he wrote: "Your musical studies,—I hope you carry them on without interruption? I am especially anxious to hear about that. . . ." Evidently what he heard was not very promising, because in the letter of January 16, 1890, he suggests another field of activity: "You seem to have a special talent for the painting of flowers. You ought to cultivate this talent seriously." But rather than the woman with a career Ibsen saw in Fräulein Emilie Bardach the elegant, bored society girl: "In my imagination I always see you adorned with pearls. You do love pearls so very much."—"How gladly I should see you in your winter surroundings! To be sure, in my imagination I am with you. I see you on the Ringstrasse, light, hurried, floating along, gracefully wrapped in velvet and furs. In soirées and at parties I also see you—and especially in the theater, leaning back, with a somewhat tired expression in your mysterious eyes. I should like to see you at home, but there I don't succeed, as I haven't the data. You told me so little of your home life—almost nothing tangible. . . . But more than all I should like to see you now on Christmas Eve in your family home, where I suppose you are spending this evening. As to how you people are celebrating Christmas I have no clear idea. I only imagine this and that to myself. And then I have a dim feeling that you and the Christmas season do not quite fit together."

In a letter dated February 6, 1890, Ibsen asked Fräulein Bardach to stop writing to him; evidently the tone of her letters was such that he felt as a matter of conscience obliged to say to her: "You should occupy yourself with me as little as possible. With your young life you have other duties to follow, other moods to yield to." She respected his wish until half a year later on the occasion of her father's death she reopened the correspondence. Ibsen wrote her a very kind letter of condolence, but when she continued to write he asked her emphatically to cease writing to him; he sent her in return for her Christmas gift *Hedda Gabler* with the injunction: "Receive it in a friendly spirit—but in silence!" This injunction Fräulein Bardach obeyed for seven years, when she telegraphed Ibsen on the occasion of his seventieth birthday. These letters show among other things the dramatist's chivalry and consideration for ladies, for with his men friends he indulged his artistic temperament to an amazing extent. Among the papers of the late Dr. Julius Elias I found telegram after telegram composed in very unpleasant, unreasonable tone. To queries from this scholar, who was translating *Hedda Gabler* for the simultaneous German edition, as to the force of certain phrases or when the next act would be ready, Ibsen would reply rudely: "I cannot be bothered with such matters now!" or "I must have *Arbeitsruhe!*" In one (unpublished) letter Ibsen went so far as to call his friend a "Winkelschriftsteller" (shyster author), an utterly undeserved piece of invective in regard to the scholarly Dr. Elias.

Like most of Ibsen's figures Hedda Gabler no doubt is a composite from several models, but it seems beyond question that he gathered some traits from his observation of the Viennese society girl. The dramatist intended the play in part as a warning against the parasitical position of young women in genteel circles; he always put the demands of art first, but he also had other ends in view, as the following comment on his own plays shows: "All those people who avoid being alone with themselves or thinking, go to the theater as they would go to a seaside resort or into society: they want to be amused. But I for my part think that rejuvenating truths ought to be spoken from the stage just as well as from the pulpit or the professor's chair. Especially since a great many people no longer go to church." In *Hedda Gabler* he showed the hollowness and the lack of character of the world that lives by the words of Judge Brack, the final lines of the play: "Good God!—people don't do such things!" One of the most profoundly ironic words in all dramatic literature!

All of the human beings depicted in this play—the bored Hedda, the smooth Judge Brack, Aunt Julia, such a person as everyone can find among his relationship, the timid yet courageous Thea Elvsted, the temperamental scholar Eilert Lövborg, and the pedantic Tesman—all of these have given the actor-folk such vital rôles that this play, like *A Doll's House*, has been acted around the world. The character of Tesman forms an interesting illustration of the method Ibsen had, of gradually getting better and better acquainted with his characters until he knew their very hearts and reins. In the first sketch he appears to the author (as he might have appeared to him after a railway journey together) as "homely in appearance, but honorable." But after Ibsen had lived with Jörgen Tesman intimately for over a year he knew that he was only outwardly honorable and to a large extent guilty in the destruction of Eilert Lövborg's manuscript. Critics have pointed out Ibsen's amazing subtlety in the portrayal of this weak villain whose crime does not, however, go beyond an almost subconscious connivance.

For Eilert Lövborg Ibsen had an incredibly real model in the young Dane, Julius Hoffory. This great admirer of Ibsen's was the professor of Scandinavian at the University of Berlin, a very brilliant but frightfully dissipated man. He had the misfortune one day in Strassburg to meet with a dishonest baggage carrier who stole his valise containing a manuscript belonging to the philologist, Professor Sievers. This experience gave Ibsen the material for an episode in the drama, while a visit of Hoffory's to Munich supplied a few traits in Lövborg's character. Ibsen found his conduct to be so strange that he inquired of the porter at Hoffory's hotel about the gentleman's habits. He learned, as a matter of confidential information for Herr Doktor Ibsen, that on awaking Hoffory called for a bottle of port wine, consumed a bottle of Rhine wine at lunch, of Burgundy at dinner, and in the course of the evening one or two bottles of port. At the very time when the dramatist was finishing *Hedda Gabler* Hoffory was stranded in Munich with no one but Ibsen to look after him; he was in such desperate physical and mental condition, utterly unwilling or unable to follow rational advice, insisting that he must await in Munich the crisis of a love affair of his, that Ibsen wrote to Dr. Elias the only method of saving the scholar's life was to place him in a sanitarium under the care of physicians who knew the history of his disease. This was done; after a short time his condition improved, but three years later he was again sent to an institution where he died insane.

Some time previously Ibsen had received the following document:

DEED OF GIFT

I herewith bequeath my entire estate, which is administered by Herr Knudson, lawyer in Aarhus, together with my annuity, to Dr. Henrik Ibsen in Munich for his free disposal and ask him, in the case of my death, to provide for my cousin, Caroline Hoffory in Copenhagen and for my friend Alma Rothbart from Grimmen in whatever manner may seem fitting to him.

DR. JULIUS HOFFORY,
Professor at the University.

Berlin,
September 6, 1891.

Ibsen did not profit very much as legatee, because Hoffory's money had melted away long before his death.   But from this picturesque professor with the blond, pointed beard, consorting with Alma Rothbart, the dramatist derived his Eilert Lövborg with vine-leaves in his hair and the red-haired Mademoiselle Diana.   Another very characteristic touch is that when *Hedda Gabler* appeared Hoffory recognized his portrait with glee and adopted Eilert Lövborg as his *nom de plume*.   As a proof of the life-like nature of Ibsen's portrait I might add that when I asked Ibsen's German publisher, S. Fischer, what Dr. Hoffory looked like, he replied with a smile, "Like Eilert Lövborg!"

When *Hedda Gabler* was performed in Munich it caused quite a sensation, but also very much adverse criticism; in general, the critics who had denounced the happy ending of *The Lady from the Sea*, blamed Ibsen for the unhappy ending of this drama.   Fräulein Helene Raff tells of a visit to the Ibsens at this time.   The dramatist made no comment on the reception of his play, but took pride in showing his large collection of paintings and etchings, all originals, to the young painter. He called her attention especially to a half-nude female figure in a frame in late Renaissance style, explaining that he had found it in a second-hand shop in Rome. At first he had been attracted chiefly by the frame, but when he had had the picture restored by a Munich expert he was told that it probably was a Giorgione or at least from his school. Ibsen felt a need for works of art about him, while he rarely enjoyed concerts. "As a usual thing," he said, "music only makes me nervous."

At the present time it seems strange just how much *Hedda Gabler* puzzled critics and spectators at the time of its première in Munich, January 31, 1891. Of the attacks launched on Ibsen the following is a typical example: "The public has no desire to solve the conundrums which the dramatist has manufactured partly out of trickery, partly out of muddled thinking." Certain phrases in the speeches of Hedda, such as "to end it all beautifully" or "with vine-leaves in his hair" caused laughter at the first performance. To some visitors who expressed regret for the boorish cretinism of the critics and the public, Mrs. Ibsen replied calmly: "Sooner or later they will realize what the play is intended to convey. My husband figures on about ten years for the public to arrive at an understanding of his dramas."

XI

THE LAST YEARS BACK IN CHRISTIANIA

1

On March 12, 1891, the younger generation of authors in
Munich held a great banquet to which Ibsen was invited as
guest of honor. After the official speeches the toast-master,
Georg Michael Conrad, called on Martin Greif, a very
distinguished lyric poet, but a man consumed with an ambition to achieve fame as a dramatist; in fact, the sore point
in his life was the judgment of the critics then and now: his
historical dramas on Bavarian kings are not redeemed even
by some beautiful lyrical passages. This man, feared as a
rather caustic after-dinner speaker, made an attack on foreign
dramatists, reserving his most sarcastic shots for Ibsen.

A sensation was caused when Ibsen tapped on his glass and
asked for the floor. A hush fell over the already somewhat
boisterous gathering, for all were eager to hear what the
great master would say.

I wish to sing the praises of Munich, the city of the arts, because
it is hospitable to every talent, whether native or foreign. Munich
surely profits by this, for her glory is spread all over the globe.
It is difficult to understand why Herr Martin Greif singles out for
attack the foreign *dramatists*, since he is recognized far and wide as
a *lyric poet* rather than as a playwright. Personally I do not feel
that Herr Greif was attacking me, because I have the feeling that
for Munich audiences I am not a *foreign* author. My plays are
staged at least as often and as successfully as those of Herr Martin
Greif, and I propose that we share our laurels unenviously and
fraternally.

Loud laughter and cheers greeted the sarcastic ambiguities
of this short speech. Conrad in a final talk called on the

two authors to shake hands before the entire assembly, whereupon he accompanied Ibsen to his home through the nocturnal
streets of Munich.   The latter, just a trifle uncertain of his
steps, supported himself on the arm of the younger man,
and continued to mutter malicious remarks in his very best
vein.

"What did this Martin Greif really wish to say? I don't
understand.   What sort of dramas does he write anyway?
The dramas of people who have long been dead, whom he
never knew.   Can a dramatist write plays about people un-
familiar to him?   What concern of Martin Greif's are these
dead kings?   He ought to let them rest in peace, and drama-
tize the living to his heart's content.   Now he is disturbing
the Bavarian sovereigns in their rest in the grave.   When he
has finished with them, the Hohenzollerns will most likely
be the next in order.   It is true that there are plenty of dead
monarchs.   History is vast.   But surely that is not today the
province of the drama."

After this evaluation of the historical drama he muttered
again, "What concern of Martin Greif's are these dead
kings?"

"But, my dear Doctor," interposed Conrad, "didn't you
write a *Catiline?*"

"Oho!" cried Ibsen, stopping short in his tracks.   "In the
first place, Catiline was not a king but an anarchist.   In the
second place, at that time I was not a dramatist, but a druggist.   *Catiline* was a druggist's first effort.   Has Martin Greif
ever been a druggist?   Well then!"

"This argument was unanswerable," Conrad remarks in
telling the story, and adds, "At least at this hour of the night."

From April 11 to 17, 1891, the theaters of Vienna presented an entire week of Ibsen plays, reaching its climax in
a grand banquet attended by not only the Austrian authors,
actors and critics, but the statesmen as well.   Ibsen was *the*

great poet, an international literary figure of such fame as
no present-day writer possesses, unless it be to some degree
Bernard Shaw. Before he entered the hall where everyone
was awaiting him in breathless expectancy he glanced in a
little mirror in the top of his tall silk hat and carefully
ordered his leonine mane so that it would stand up properly.
In a poetic toast, spoken by the actor Max Devrient, he was
greeted as the great liberator who gave to the world an inner
freedom, who banished "ghosts" and who had the courage
to admit the light of day into places previously kept in darkness. Another speaker called him the greatest living
dramatist—to the cheers of the audience. Ibsen arose and in
his soft, gentle voice replied in characteristic words:

All that moves me, all that I experience, is material for my
poetry, and I shall carry the memory of this hour back with me to
Munich. This is a beautiful hour, a beautiful experience—I do not
yet know exactly—but I believe the beautiful, the clear, the free
that I now see will become part of a work of art.

It was a moment in which the master builder stood on the
top of the tower and heard "harps in the air."

Other capitals, Budapesth and Berlin, fêted Ibsen during
the same spring. On this his final visit to Berlin, Ibsen felt
that he would like to give a party for his friends and asked
Dr. Julius Elias to arrange for a private dining room, a
supper and large quantities of champagne. The other guests
were a half dozen critics and actors; Dr. Julius Hoffory sat
at the table wearing black eyeglasses and black gloves, a
veritable Banquo's ghost. Ibsen in his expansive mood acted
not only the host, but the waiter as well, walking around the
table with the champagne bottle filling the glasses of his
guests. Finally they induced him to sit down and even to
talk, when the following dialogue between him and Paul Marx
occurred:

IBSEN: But, my dear friends, here you sit and talk of the future, passive and hopeful. Arise, assert yourselves as individualities, and forge the future. Mould it to your heart's desire! Formerly there were political revolutions—the future will bring the humane revolution. Then the recruits will no longer come to the drill-ground; they will simply say, "No, thank you, we don't care to do that!"—and they'll repair to some nearby saloon.

MARX: But . . . then they'll be shot as deserters.

IBSEN: My dear friends, what harm is there in that?

MARX: To be sure, the individuals sacrificed would probably not weigh very heavily. But then, dear Ibsen, it must be the superior men and autocrats, as for example Bismarck, who appeal to you most.

IBSEN: Ah, no! Such men ought to be killed first; like those recruits they ought to be placed before a firing squad.

MARX: Is that so? Why?

IBSEN: Because they enslave and hold down the individualities of others.

MARX: But that is in direct contradiction with what you said before!

IBSEN: My dear Marx, have you ever thought a thought through to the end without meeting contradictions?

Thus spoke Ibsen and resumed his champagne rounds. Of course, this was a whimsical argument in lighter vein, but it was quite characteristic of the author who had created Dr. Stockmann, the apostle of truth at all costs, and then Gregers Werle—another apostle of truth.

Some time after this party Ibsen remarked to Dr. Elias: "I must get back to the North."

"Is this a sudden impulse?" asked his friend.

"Oh, no," was the reply, "I want to be a good head of a household and have my affairs in order. To that end I must consolidate my property, lay it down in good securities, and get it under control—and that one can best do where one has rights of citizenship."

Just a short time previously sixty-year-old Ibsen and his

wife who had always lived with rented furniture, had gone about in Munich buying household goods like a newly married couple. This seemed to indicate that they intended to make their home in Munich permanently. But there were probably various reasons in addition to the one mentioned to Dr. Elias that caused him now to return to his native land. Sigurd was carving out his career up there, having relinquished his diplomatic post in 1890 to become a writer on political and sociological questions. A letter from Ibsen to his sister Hedvig on March 13, 1891, seems to show that his thoughts were dwelling on a return to his home. It is interesting to note in this connection the remark addressed to his French translator, Moritz Prozor, November 20, 1890, anent *Hedda Gabler:* "But it is a good thing, too, to have done with it. The constant intercourse with the fictitious personages was beginning to make me quite nervous." Previously he had regretted parting with the characters of his plays, and had found Dr. Stockmann or the folk in *The Wild Duck* very stimulating. It seems like a sign of old age to find Ibsen "quite nervous." Mrs. Ibsen said after Ibsen's death that he had expressed a desire to spend his last years at home and to be buried in his native land.

Thus in 1891, after Ibsen had remained in Munich the previous summer to work on *Hedda Gabler,* he left for Norway, took the journey to Trondhjem and the North Cape, and then returned to Christiania. For several months the Ibsens lived at the Grand Hotel, then they sent for their furniture from Munich, and rented a large house on "Victoria Terrasse." Norway's capital had welcomed him home; he was now a prophet not without honor even in his own country, and he settled down at home as Norway's most distinguished citizen. He felt that all looked up to and envied him. "Only think—to be Solness the master builder! Halvard Solness! What could be more delightful."

While he was thus being lionized by all Christiania, Ibsen was suddenly given a shock at the hands of youth. A struggling young author, Knut Hamsun, announced a lecture on modern Norwegian literature, and asked Ibsen to be present. With his usual kindness toward young authors he agreed to come; the presence of the great poet would sell out the house at two kroner a seat.

Hamsun, now in his thirty-third year, had just arrived at recognition through his novel *Hunger*. He was a picturesque figure from the bleak northlands; in his twenties he had spent some time in America as tramp, shoemaker, Unitarian preacher, stone-mason and street-car conductor, after that living as a Newfoundland fisherman for three years—all of which gave color to his personality and writing.

Ibsen entered the hall exactly on time and was conducted to a front seat, while the auditorium rose to greet the great national dramatist. Then Knut Hamsun appeared on the stage, a well-built, powerful young man with black hair and a bristling moustache, wearing pince-nez of English pattern.

He spoke of his life close to the people, close to nature, and began to base on this his demands for a literature grown up from the soil (just as though being a street-car conductor in Chicago was a greater experience than being hailed as the world's greatest dramatist). He attacked theorizing and symbolical works, and then suddenly launched a very direct attack on Ibsen, whose most recent works, *Hedda Gabler*, *The Lady from the Sea*, and *Rosmersholm* he considered clouded in mysterious symbolism. Speaking almost directly to the poet, who sat helpless and nervous where all the audience could see him, he dilated on the artificial and utterly false theory of art that made a certain thing in the drama represent something other than the reality. Besides lacking thus in æsthetic qualities, he went on to say, Ibsen also was full of extreme contradictions, having always followed any current of thought popular at the moment. And he closed the remarks on his victim: "You see, ladies and gentlemen, least of all can Ibsen claim to be a philosopher."

There was some applause from a group of young men enthusiastic for the new and impatient of the older men whose renown dwarfed the attempts of the coming generation. About half the audience, considering Knut Hamsun's half-baked theories and asinine egotism in extremely bad taste, received his message in chill silence. So did Ibsen. But from this meeting he carried away the thought expressed in Solness:

> The luck will turn. I know it. I feel the day approaching. Someone or other will take it into his head to say: Give *me* a chance! And then all the rest will come clamoring after him, and shake their fists at me and shout: Make room—make room—make room! Yes, just you see, doctor—presently the younger generation will come knocking at my door—

Naturally enough as he walked the familiar streets of Christiania Ibsen's thoughts turned to his "rare fairytale fate." The apothecary's apprentice in obscure Grimstad on seeing his first verses in print had indulged in a pipe-dream:

> I will build me a cloud castle. Two wings shall shape it forth;
> A great one and a small one. It shall shine across the North.
> The greater shall shelter a singer immortal;
> The smaller to a maiden shall open its portal.

More than forty years before he had thought of himself as a master builder rearing a castle to shine all over the North—a dream that had been fulfilled far beyond his highly improbable expectations; he found that his fame as a deathless poet shone even beyond the North, all around the world. Here was a subject that now took hold of his imagination to the exclusion of polemical themes. He began to plan *The Master*

Builder, a drama more autobiographical than any he had written previously. A lyric mood began to enter into his work.

The problem of luck and the consequent Nemesis occupied him intently. The new play told of a master builder who had crushed all about him and made himself great till at last Nemesis came to him from youth; not from the brash Knut Hamsun type, but from adoring, idealizing youth who demanded that the master builder, youth's idol, climb higher and higher to the very top—a feat that constituted the impossible for the hero and that caused him to be dashed in pieces.

Ibsen knew very well what his weakness was, the vertigo of the master builder. He had dreamed in his youth of being a man of action, but when in 1855 Abildgaard had gone to prison he had realized that he was not made of the stuff of political heroes, and therefore he chose for himself another goal. In *Olaf Liljekrans,* written during his Bergen days, he had set for himself a different career, and one that his later life fulfilled with amazing exactness:

> The minstrel has neither house nor home,
> Ne'er findeth he rest, his spirit must roam;
> Holds he a soul of song in his breast,
> He is homeless in valley and homeless on crest—
> Be it hill or dale, he needs must sing
> And needs must touch the trembling string,—
> Discover the life that secretly gleams
> In tossing fjords, 'neath thundering streams;
> Must hear the life that ne'er was guessed,
> Then clothe man's dreams that vaguely throng
> And clear his seething thought in song.

This was the ideal that Ibsen realized, living without a real home in foreign countries for twenty-seven years. But Georg Brandes in an essay written in 1882 had placed his finger on the sore spot in Ibsen's soul and had frankly described the weakness of the master builder; he dared not climb as high as he had built:

Even the poet can only express such extremely ideal views indirectly, suggestively, ambiguously, through the mouths of independent dramatic characters who relieve the author of all responsibility. Only vulgar adversaries could take the grim jest of the torpedo under the ark to be literal, bitter earnest.

Such a philosophy entails a separation of the theoretical from the practical, of the individual from the citizen, of intellectual liberty from practical liberty which means responsibility—a dualism which can be carried into practice only by a dramatic poet living in exile, who need have nothing whatever to do with state, society, politics, parties, or reform.

Nor does the ideal of spiritual nobility inherent in this philosophy seem to me to be a very high one. It is quite true that a great author best maintains his personal dignity by never being seen in the thick of the fray; it is true that it gives an impression of distinction to hold back, never to interfere in the disputes of the day, never to write a newspaper article. But it seems to me that there is more distinction still in the action of the legitimist generals who enlisted as common soldiers in Condé's army and fought on foot in the foremost ranks. By so doing they lost not a whit of their inner, essential dignity.

Even without Brandes' explicit statement Ibsen knew his weakness very well and felt it keenly "like a great raw place here on my breast" whenever he received the idolizing plaudits of youth. In spite of occasional attacks on him like the one from Knut Hamsun, it is a testimonial to the vitality of his message that the poet approaching his three score and ten was the leader around whose banner the young and the radical were flocking. Ibsen, like Solness, felt a yearning toward youth and sensed a rejuvenating force coming to him from association with young minds. Circumstances even changed his ideas about the old Goethe, as a letter to Georg Brandes of February 11, 1895, shows:

I cannot resist a desire to send you my thanks especially for your essay, *Goethe and Marianne v. Willemer.* I did not know at all the episode you describe. It may be that many, many years ago I read something about it in Lewes, but then I forgot it again because this relationship had at that time no personal interest for me. Now, however, matters appear somewhat differently. If I think of the character of Goethe's productivity during the years in question, of the rebirth of his youth, then, it seems to me, I might have guessed that without doubt he had been blessed with something that proved as beautiful (deilig) for him as his meeting with just Marianne v. Willemer. Really at times Fate and Chance can be very benevolent, very kindly powers.

Some years previous Ibsen had met and formed a close friendship with a young lady of twenty-seven, Miss Hildur Andersen, just then on the threshold of her career as a pianist. In a letter to Edvard Brandes he calls her "an intimate friend of mine—a good, wise and faithful one." She was the granddaughter of Fru Sontum, who had received Ibsen in such a friendly manner on his arrival in Bergen. To her Ibsen presented quite a number of his manuscripts with the dedication "to Princess Hildur." In the very month when he was beginning to put *The Master Builder* on paper he wrote the following letter to a youthful friend in Munich (the "Solveig" refers to a sketch of a young girl's head, so named by Ibsen, which Fräulein Raff had given him as a birthday present in 1890):

DEAREST MISS RAFF:

Allow me to send you my warmest, my most heartfelt thanks for your kind letter, which reached me on my birthday, and also for your wonderfully charming picture, which I had the unspeakably great pleasure to receive a few days ago. It is now hung in a good place in my study, so that I may constantly satisfy myself by the view out over the broad, open sea—and constantly increase my desire to meet the dear, dear lovely young girl who has created the beautiful little work of art. And who during its execution has thought of me from afar. Oh—if I might only have the opportunity

to render thanks personally, thank you in such a way as I should like
to.   The sea I love.   Your picture carries me in thought and sentiment to what I love.   Yes, you have surely enriched me for life by
what you have given me.   Now little Solveig shall be hung beside
the sea picture.   Then I will have you wholly and altogether before
me—and within me.

Such warm recollections of Munich arose in me when I received
these remembrances in words and colors from you.   How I should
like to be down there again now.   For I belong there so heartily.
But then there are so many things in life which place a restraint
upon a man's wishes and desires.

You have acquired an incredible ability in handling the Norwegian language.   Do you never think of making a summer trip up
here?   To dream a bright fleeting summer night's dream among the
mountains or out by the sea?

Give me an answer to that some time, dearest Miss Raff.   Will
you?   It would make me unspeakably happy—of course at your
convenience—again to receive a few lines from you.

Yours truly and obligedly,

HENRIK IBSEN.

In her years of association with the Ibsens Fräulein Helene
Raff came to know them quite well and to cherish for both a
very great admiration.   Since she herself comes from a family
of artists,—her father, Joseph Joachim Raff was the famous
violinist and composer, her mother an actress—since she has
gained considerable distinction as a painter, novelist and
critic, and especially since reflection and almost four decades have enabled her to see more clearly the strength and
weakness of each, her judgment is of great value in regard to
the marital life of the Ibsens, which must be considered one
of the sources of *The Master Builder*.   She writes me, December 8, 1927: "If I may be permitted to express a quite personal observation, then it would seem to me that Frau Susanne
had only two qualities that perhaps at times made more
difficult an understanding with him: an occasional external
harshness, behind which she concealed her real feelings, and

a not quite wise sensitiveness in matters which in consideration of their value she might have viewed in a more broad-
minded manner. Of this nature was her attitude toward
Ibsen's relationship with young girls and women which of
course had nothing whatever in common with infidelity in
the current sense of that term."

The frequent expressions of jealousy on the part of the
master-builder's wife are probably an exaggerated reflection
of the Ibsens' domestic atmosphere at the time this play was
written; though in no other respect does the vigorous Susannah
Ibsen seem to have served as model for the anæmic Aline
Solness. Further evidence pointing to a temporary rift in
the Ibsen menage is found in a letter of Magdalene Thoresen,
written shortly after Ibsen's return to Norway: "I have been
several times at the Ibsens and have talked much with Ibsen.
They live splendidly and have an elegant home, though all
is pretty much in Philistine style. They are two lonely
people—each for himself—each absolutely for himself."

In the very spirit described by Ibsen's mother-in-law he
began the work on *The Master Builder*. According to his
habit he set out to "crystallize in a poem the mood which
then possessed him":

> They dwelt, these two, in so cosy a house
> In autumn and winter weather.
> Then came the fire—and the house was gone.
> They must search in the ashes together.
>
> For down in the ashes a jewel is hid,
> Whose brightness the flames could not smother,
> And search they faithfully, he and she,
> 'Twill be found by one or the other.
>
> But e'en though they find it, the gem they lost,
> The enduring jewel they cherished—
> She ne'er will recover her vanished faith—
> Nor he the joy that has perished.

—From *Vikingen,* December 17, 1892.

MASTERBUILDER IBSEN

Masterbuilder: "The only thing, as I believe, that can contain human happiness—that I shall build now."

The poem indicates that the drama was begun as one dealing with the theme of marriage, and since Solness (or Ibsen)
was the chief character, it was to be the marriage of an artist.
Thirty years previously, in *Love's Comedy*, Ibsen had presented in a scene remarkable for the moral earnestness with
which the work of the poet was conceived, Falk and Svanhild
parting from each other lest the ties of marriage should
hobble Pegasus:

FALK: Yes, upward is my flight; the winged steed
    Is saddled; I am strung for noble deed.
    And now, farewell! . . .
SVANHILD: Now I can lose thee gladly till life's past!

But in his own life Ibsen had chosen to combine with his
artistic life that of conventional marriage, and had fulfilled
the demands of both; the difficulty of this task is perhaps
best realized by a glance at the life of Byron, Shelley, Hugo,
de Musset, Goethe, or Heine. The struggles that this choice
cost Ibsen can be seen in the relationships of Rosmer and
Rebecca, Solness and Hilda, Rubek and Irene. In his poetic
dreams he went beyond the conventional, but in life he remained quite correct. This must be borne in mind in looking
for analogies between the marriage of Solness and that of
Ibsen; but above all one should remember that both are
afflicted with a tender conscience that finds deep guilt even
in wishes. There was in all likelihood no family tragedy
such as Christiania gossip of the time whispered about, except that Ibsen realized his own marriage fell short of the
high ideal set up in *Love's Comedy*.

In the episode from *The Master Builder*, of the aged artist
and the "bird of prey" one has no difficulty in recognizing
traits of Emilie Bardach, who wrote in her diary at the time
"Ibsen wishes to possess me." But Norwegian critics who
found that in the atmosphere of *Hedda Gabler* Ibsen after

an absence of twenty-five years had grown out of touch with developments of Christiania, remark that the character of Hilda Wangel shows that the poet had used his eyes after his return to observe the "new" Norwegian girl, a product of the late eighties.   Hilda is not the type of Nora prior to her marriage, but she is an independent creature who goes in for sport and is not tired out by a long tramp, who speaks directly to the point without social hypocrisies and doesn't care what people say, who comes in like a breath of fresh air —everything in direct contrast with the frail house-plant of former generations who passed from the authority of her father into that of her husband.   This freedom the younger generation derived to a large extent from the attacks on out-worn conventions and the emphasis on essentials that they absorbed eagerly from the social plays of Ibsen.

That Ibsen himself did anything but over-estimate his own influence is evident from the words of Solness. He tells Hilda that he had begun his career by building churches—symbolic of Ibsen's early poetic dramas—and that he had then turned to building homes for men—the social plays that aimed to make this world a better place to live in. Of these he says —with a quiet, bitter laugh such as was characteristic of Ibsen: "Building homes for human beings is not worth a rap, Hilda . . .   See, that is the upshot of the whole affair, how-ever far back I look.   Nothing really built, nor anything sacrificed for the chance of building.   Nothing, nothing! the whole thing nothing!"

It is very characteristic that Ibsen felt no smug satisfaction with his life's work—the aim of his genius had been too high for that.

From building homes for men Solness turns to constructing "castles in the air"—the new series of dramas which Ibsen said had their beginning with *The Master Builder*.   It is no doubt true, as critics have urged against these plays, that there lies a certain weakness from the dramatic point of view in the fact that they are not wholly intelligible without constant reference to underlying, esoteric meanings. But in his determination once more to strike out for something new Ibsen resembles Ulysses in Tennyson's poem:

Death closes all, but something ere the end,
Some work of noble note, may yet be done,
Not unbecoming men that strove with Gods.
The lights begin to twinkle from the rocks;
The long day wanes; the slow moon climbs, the deep
Moans round with many voices: come, my friends,
'Tis not too late to seek a newer world!

While the tenor of the remarks that greeted the new type of play was pretty generally: "Sense cannot be discovered because there is no sense to discover," later critics have compared the play to Shakespeare's *Hamlet,* in which each succeeding generation can discover new problems and new meanings because of its universal significance. The generation that has passed through the World War, may for example, see in the tragedy of Solness a symbol of the tragedy of President Wilson. Here was a hero to whom idealistic youth looked for great things; on his arrival in Paris millions turned out to shout ecstatically "Vive Wilson!" Wilson then did build a wonderful structure, a super-government comprising almost the entire world. But, seized by the vertigo of all-too-human weakness, he could not fulfill the desire of youth to see him rise higher and higher, and he crashed to the ground because he could not climb as high as he had built.

2

In the eighties Ibsen and Björnson had become reconciled after their long and sharp differences, but the visit in the Alps and the exchange of a few letters did not make them into bosom friends. Therefore, when they were together again in their native land their relations remained distinctly formal and cold. They were men whose natures and whose interests were too divergent to bring them together. Björnson was engaged in active politics, always on the speaker's platform or in the columns of daily newspapers; Ibsen, on the other hand, made himself extremely rare, publishing nothing except one play every two years. But when this play was about to appear there was feverish excitement everywhere such as it is difficult to imagine nowadays concerning the forthcoming book of any author. Telegraphic bulletins announced when the manuscript was sent to the printer, when the type had been set up, and when the book was to be on sale. To ask at a bookshop, "Has it come?" was sufficient request for Ibsen's latest volume; old and young devoured the book and argued about it for weeks afterward. This was so different from the manner of Björnson that when the latter made one of his rare calls on his rival, Ibsen characteristically asked him, "Well, what are you drumming up the mob for now?" Ibsen considered the mob to be always in the wrong, while Björnson enthusiastically believed to hear in the voice of the people the voice of God.

An English man of letters, Richard Le Gallienne, gives an excellent pen picture of a visit in the early nineties to the two great literary men of Norway. He went to Aulestad, Björnson's country seat, to spend a few days with the author and politician, then very active in his fight for separation of Norway from Sweden, in which he of course eventually succeeded. Mr. Le Gallienne arriving early in the morning was met by his host with a towel slung over his back; Björnson asked him whether he would care to join him in his morning bath in the woods. They then walked until they came to a mountain stream falling in a torrent of white water down the face of the rock. Planks had been placed at the foot of the fall.

"This is my shower bath," said Bjornson as he stripped; and there presently he stood firm as a rock beneath the cataract, the water pouring over his strong shoulders, his white head white as the foam, shouting with joy of the morning. So might some huge old water god have stood and laughed amid the sun-flashing spray. It was a picture of elemental energy never to be forgotten; and as one watched him there one could well understand the power that made him the uncrowned king of his country.

At breakfast in Björnson's home Mr. Le Gallienne felt as though he were in the hall of Sigurd the Volsung. The master of the house and his lady, beautiful and commanding like her lord, sat at the end of the long table, royally side by side on a slightly raised dais. There was present also Björnson's daughter Bergliot, named after his greatest poem, "a glorious girl made out of gold and blue sky." The breakfast too was cut on a heroic pattern; roast meats and pungently smoked and spiced fish, bumpers of ale and *apéritifs* of *schnapps.*

In the course of his visit Mr. Le Gallienne had many long talks with his host, pacing up and down in the Aulestad study. One evening, he reports, he committed a frightful *faux pas:*

It was a terrible thing to do, but he generously forgave me, for I was a stranger and naturally didn't know better. I mentioned the name of Ibsen. Then indeed Björnson looked like an old lion. He stopped short, fire in his eyes and nostrils, and shaking his great white mane he thundered out, "Ibsen!" A pause, and then again with withering contempt, "Ibsen is not a man; he is only a pen!"

After this characterization of the dramatist Mr. Le Gallienne was naturally very eager to meet Ibsen. Herr Rosenkrantz-Johnson, the Christiania journalist who had taken him on the visit to Aulestad, was eager to bring this about, but to call on Ibsen as one called on Björnson was a feat requiring more than a journalist's temerity. However, Rosenkrantz-Johnson promised his English friend that they could accomplish the same end by going to the Grand Hotel where Ibsen was wont to appear every day as regularly as clockwork. Mr. Le Gallienne continues his account:

The large café was crowded, but we found a good table on the aisle, not far from the door. We had not long to wait, for punctually on the stroke of one, there, entering the doorway, was the dour and bristling presence known to all the world in caricature—caricatures which were no exaggerations but as in the case of Swinburne, just the man himself. The great ruff of white whisker, ferociously standing out all round his sallow, bilious face as if dangerously charged with electricity, the immaculate silk hat, the white tie, the frock-coated martinet's figure dressed from top to toe in old-fashioned black broadcloth, at once funereal and professional, the trousers concertinaed, apparently with dandiacal design, at the ankles, over his highly polished boots, the carefully folded umbrella —all was there, apparitionally before me; a forbidding, disgruntled, tight-lipped presence, starchily dignified, straight as a ramrod; there he was, as I hinted, with a touch of grim dandyism about him, but with no touch of human kindness about his parchment skin or fierce badger eyes. He might have been a Scotch elder entering the kirk.

As he entered and proceeded with precisian tread to the table reserved in perpetuity for him, which no one else would have dreamed of occupying, a thing new and delightful—to me a mere Anglo-Saxon—suddenly happened. As one man, the whole café was on its feet in an attitude of salute, and a stranger standing near me who evidently spoke English and who recognized my nationality, said to me in a loud but reverent aside, "That is our great poet, Henrik Ibsen." All remained standing till he had taken his seat, as in the presence of a king, and I marveled greatly at a people that thus did homage to their great men.

After a few minutes Herr Rosenkrantz-Johnson took his English visitor to Ibsen's table, having previously instructed him to say that all the English ladies were most enthusiastic about his plays. When the journalist interpreted this banal

BJÖRNSTJERNE BJÖRNSON

"Ibsen is not a man; he is only a pen."

flattery, Ibsen appeared pleased and inquired concerning Mr. Archer and Mr. Gosse. Mr. Le Gallienne told what news he had of English Ibsenites; but, he adds in telling of the meeting, he refrained from mentioning the name of Björnson!

Since their relationship was hardly as cordial as armed neutrality, the engagement of Sigurd Ibsen to Bergliot Björnson appeared to both fathers as nothing to be especially proud of. But since the children were determined in their choice, the marriage had to be gone through with. Great tact was required in all the arrangements, especially in determining which of the fathers was to precede; at last it was decided they were to walk side by side, even though not arm in arm! Ibsen was glad to see his son happily married and liked his daughter-in-law quite well; but Björnson, after the first shock, began to see in the joining of the families of Norway's two great poets a wonderfully romantic event. The son of Ibsen's sister Hedvig, Captain John Stousland of Rutherford, N. J., has told me that on the occasion of one of his visits to Skien he found Björnson calling on his mother. "I saw that big man weeping like a baby," he said, "because Ibsen was taking this marriage in such a matter-of-fact manner." However, when Ibsen shortly afterward became a grandfather he was exceedingly happy. For children he always had a rare understanding and sympathy.

A Christiania gentleman who had compiled an anthology of literature for children sent the volumes—there were five of them—to Ibsen as one man of letters to another. Some months afterward the two men met on the street and Ibsen thanked the editor for his kindness, adding, "Your books have interested me very much."

"What, Herr Dr. Ibsen, you have really read them?"

"I certainly have," answered Ibsen, "I have read each volume from cover to cover, everything—except the preface. I have not entirely lost the soul of my childhood."

The truth of this statement can be seen from *Little Eyolf*, the play Ibsen was writing at the time, in which he went back to a childhood reminiscence of Skien for the figure of the Rat-Wife. He portrayed her with all the mysterious fascination that the childish mind would see in her, exercising a spell on Little Eyolf that lured him to his death, yet at the same time not introducing anything supernatural into the play. Eyolf's speeches are those of an imaginative little boy, full of fears and yearnings such as Ibsen remembered from his own childhood or found in children whom he could meet on their own ground, causing them to feel quite at home with the man whose forbidding glance so often awed adults.

The story also shows that, if Ibsen still had the soul of a child, he also had considerable of the rogue in him who took great pleasure in placing his finger on the weaknesses of pompous souls. He delighted in digging beneath the alleged motives of people to the real feelings that animated them; as for example in this case, making the editor feel that he cared more for literary distinction than for children. How much this unmasking of pretentious personalities delighted Ibsen is told by Georg Brandes:

Finally I remember him from my shorter or longer visits during his later years in Norway: how we would meet by agreement every day at lunch time (and he would always be standing in the entrance of his house at the exact time, waiting for me) either to go for a walk, to view the Viking Ship, or to visit an art gallery. Or how I, invited to his home for dinner, would be received by him rubbing his hands and saying: "Today we shall be merry, drink good wine, drink a lot of wine, and tell stories." Then, "Now you shall hear an edifying tale about Mr. X." Thereupon his face turned into a single satirical smile and the story followed, realistic and burlesque, in which a generally esteemed and praised "man of honor" revealed himself as the comical sinner that he really was.

As a child in Skien Ibsen had painted heads of wolves and monkeys by means of which he portrayed persons offensive to him. In all the dignitaries invited to the dedication of the Suez Canal he had seen the animal features lurking underneath their princely or diplomatic exteriors as he described them in his poem *Balloon Letter to a Swedish Lady*. His cynical eye was ever ready to discover the fox, lamb, bear, donkey or goose in the human beings coming under his observation. Frequently even Ibsen did not discover the secrets of such characters immediately, but only after a long period of intense study.

This happened with Alfred Allmers, the father of Little Eyolf. In the first sketch of the play Ibsen saw him as a successful author, a gentle, noble soul, not unlike Rosmer, endowed with many of the dramatist's own characteristics. Allmers shares with his creator the morbid, self-torturing doubts as to the value of his mission in life. Like the aging Ibsen he feels that thinking is much better than what is put on paper, in a manner recalling the experience of Faust:

> The best thou learnest in the end
> Thou dar'st not tell—

He expresses a Dantesque longing: "Upwards,—toward the peaks. Toward the stars. And toward the great silence."

Truly, after merely a railway journey in the company of this man we should regard him as what his refined exterior proclaimed, a thinker and a poet of noble, spiritual bent.

But Ibsen, according to his habitual method of working, studied Allmers until he knew him as well as he would an intimate friend who could in no way deceive him. He then saw clearly that this poverty-stricken teacher had married for money while he pretended that he did it from altruistic motives, for the sake of his sister. After he had thus sold himself he pretended to be using his acquired leisure for the purpose of writing "the great thick book on Human Responsibility"; but as one might guess from this reference to it, Allmers' authorship is a bombastic pretense. When he finds that his effort at producing a book proves an abject failure, he pretends that he is making a noble sacrifice of his life's ambition for the sake of devoting himself to the education of his son—who, by the way, came to be a cripple because of Allmers' lack of "human responsibility." He mouths would-be scientific language about "the law of change," and he finds himself in a comical predicament when he—the atheist—inadvertently reveals that in a dream he had "thanked God"! There is something hollow about his mourning after his son's death, but even worse is his cruelty and caddishness in placing upon his wife the guilt for Eyolf's drowning. He is so ungrateful and faithless to his wife that he is ready to desert her to go with Asta; yet when the latter rejects such a proposal he is glad to continue living on his wife's money, and to this end joins with some pompous phrases in her resolve to do something for the neglected village boys for the sake of their lost Eyolf.

For this the world, taken in by his well-sounding phrases, will probably praise and admire him. Allmers will probably fare like that other windbag and self-seeker Stensgaard, of whom it is predicted in the last act of the *League of Youth:* "Yes, you'll see, gentlemen! In ten or fifteen years Stensgaard will be either in Parliament or in the Ministry—perhaps in both at once!"

In contrast to the hollowness of Allmers the words of his wife Rita have a true and convincing ring in every speech. She is a healthy, normal, robust, sensuous creature with a heart full of love. Rita is not given to sentimentality or to pretending to feelings that she does not possess. Her very frankness and directness cause her to be misjudged by people who observe only the surface of things. Moreover she is placed in very disadvantageous positions; we see her as a wife whose charms are scorned by her husband because his thoughts dwell on "nobler things" than physical love (though for ten years he had been by no means so spiritual) and also as a mother whose little boy, crippled because of his parents' negligence, limps about the house as a daily mute reproach. She had married for love, frankly and naturally she had chosen the man with the refined features and the thinker's brow who attracted her so strongly, even though he was poor and by no means a catch. When she feels jealousy she is not hypocritical about her emotions, but can *threaten* to throw herself into the arms of the first man who comes in her way, or *wish* that Little Eyolf were not there to come between her and her husband—yet in the end her grief ennobles her, and when she turns to altruism we feel that she is as genuine in this as she had ever been. She is a healthy creature after the poet's own heart.

When Ibsen finished the play, knowing full well how eager the critics were for its appearance and how surely they would again misunderstand, he hid the real inner nature of his characters from even keenly understanding eyes. As he expected, the critics were very much puzzled as to Ibsen's intentions. They called Allmers a "searcher for the Third Empire"—in spite of his weaknesses. They spoke of Ibsen's reconciliation with his native land, because at the end Allmers hoists the Norwegian flag. They mentioned the poet's "atavistic Puritanism" displayed when Allmers "had champagne and tasted it not," some even going so far as to link Ibsen with the Tolstoy of the *Kreutzersonata* as one who considered all physical love as evil; while as a matter of fact Ibsen's feelings in regard to the Russian author were summed up in his words to Gosse, "Tolstoy—he is mad!" They noted that this was in sharp contrast with the usual healthy "joy in life" characteristic of Ibsen, and were at a loss to account for these "flaws" in *Little Eyolf*. Many came to the conclusion that Ibsen was getting old and could no longer draw well-rounded, unified characters; others found fault with the dramatist for the too sudden conversion of Allmers from intellectual egotism to unselfish devotion to the welfare of others.

The key to the understanding of the asinine Allmers, talking about but never writing "the great thick book on Human Responsibility," was given five years later by Ibsen himself in that dramatic epilogue in which the poet more than ever before unlocked his heart—*When We Dead Awaken.* Professor Rubek, the famous artist for whom Ibsen himself served as model, says of his portrait busts, over which "all the world" goes into ecstasies:

> They are not mere portrait-busts, I assure you. . . . There is something equivocal, something cryptic lurking in and behind these busts—a secret something that the people themselves cannot see.— I alone can see it. And it amuses me unspeakably.—On the surface I give them "striking likenesses," as they call it, that they all stand and gape at in astonishment—(Lowers his voice)—but at bottom they are all respectable, pompous horse-faces, and self-opinionated donkey-muzzles, and lop-eared, low-browed dog-skulls, and fatted swine-snouts—and sometimes dull, brutal bull-fronts as well. . . . (Empties his champagne glass and laughs.) And it is these double-faced works of art that our excellent plutocrats come and order of me. And pay for in all good faith—and in good round figures too —almost their weight in gold, as the saying goes.

Little Eyolf stands in the same relation to *Rosmersholm* that the *Wild Duck* occupies vis-à-vis *The Enemy of the People.* Just as Ibsen showed what a parody the demand of the ideal, the fanatic desire for truth-telling, might become when adopted by a Gregers Werle, so he showed in Alfred Allmers an Ibsen disciple who would say with Rosmer that his "view of life ennobles but kills happiness." The self-restraint of Rosmer toward the woman he loves strikes the reader as high-minded and is simply taken for granted on the part of a man of his noble character; while Allmers returns home "so taken up with serious thoughts" and speaks of his "renunciation" for which he had found strength in the infinite solitudes on the mountain peaks "nearer the stars," almost "in sympathy and communion with them," then asks about Eyolf's digestion and sleeps the sleep of the just—this "nobility" is a burlesque. Such travesties of noble ideals the poet found among his own followers, and as he observed them he rubbed his hands in cynical glee while his face became a single satirical smile.

3

Some time after the lecture by Knut Hamsun in which Ibsen had heard youth rudely knocking at the door, another Norwegian author, Herman Bang, invited the dramatist to attend his lectures, one on *Hedda Gabler* and the other on Guy de Maupassant. After the first lecture Ibsen met Bang on Karl Johan Street and said, "Well, at least you treated me politely"—in characteristic fashion denying the lecturer any comment whatever on his interpretation of the drama. Herman Bang, in describing the second lecture, writes that Ibsen did not seem particularly interested until he touched on a certain theme:

I began to speak of de Maupassant's conception of death. There is a passage in *Une Vie* describing how the heroine is shut in a room in which a big bluebottle is buzzing about unceasingly. The fly hums along the ceiling. Its shadow flutters past the light. It is everywhere—like a pain, like a nervous terror, like a horror. She tries to drive it out of the room, but she cannot. She attempts to forget it, but she is unable to do so. She makes an effort to catch it, but she cannot hit it. It is there. It stays there.

The fly—the bluebottle—is de Maupassant's idea of death. I stated as much and had forgotten about Henrik Ibsen, when I suddenly saw him anew—with upturned visage he was gazing straight into my eyes. Never had any man looked at me like that. One time in a distant city I had seen in a zoological garden through

which I had strolled about dusk a gigantic lion gazing with in-
describable melancholy through half-closed lids into the dying light
of the day. The glance of this lion lived during those minutes in
the eyes of Henrik Ibsen. With a peculiar feeling, as it were, of
sorrow and of triumph, I said to myself: "You might have known it.
He who has experienced all and won all still sees Death before him.
He was occupying himself with death and for that reason he
listened. He had nothing else to think of except just death. Life
with all its glory lay behind him. Before him lay only death."
This I read in his face, and it seemed to me this face I had never
seen before.

As the aged Sophocles in *Œdipus at Colonus* pictured
the last hours of his guilt-laden old hero, so Ibsen at 68
presented in *John Gabriel Borkman* a marvelous drama of
old age, of haunting guilt, and of death. The model for this
romantic embezzler, this "Napoleon who has been maimed
in his first battle," this "wounded eagle," who after three
years in detention and five in prison, spent the rest of his
life pacing up and down his gallery from early morning until
far into the night like "a sick wolf in his cage," Ibsen took
from his memories of Christiania days in 1851.

At that time an army officer, the director of the Christiania
commissariat, was accused of fraud, committed in conjunc-
tion with two wholesale merchants of the city. When the
scandal became known he attempted to clear himself by
means of a bombastic denial in the press: "The director
might have expected this sort of treatment, no better than
that accorded all managers of financial departments; dis-
paragement and insulting insinuations without the least
cause." However, the very next day he made an unsuccessful attempt at suicide and lay in the prison hospital for two
months, displaying such taciturnity and apathy that the doctors felt inclined to consider him insane. In the course of
his trial there was no question of insanity and he was condemned to four years in the penitentiary. After he had com-

—From *Henrik Ibsen in Caricature.*

A CARICATURE OF IBSEN DONE IN 1901
BY OLAF GULBRANSSON

pleted his sentence he returned home to lead an absolutely isolated life; it was said that not one word was exchanged between him and his wife.

It is interesting to note what a difference a half century of "war with the trolls" in his brain and heart had made in Ibsen's view of this criminal. In an article of satirical nature printed in the spring of 1851 in *Andhrimmer*, the weekly "for literary satire and political opposition" which he with his friends Vinje and Botten-Hansen had founded a short time previously, Ibsen makes an allusion to the embezzler. It is in the nature of a sarcastic pun: "In combating the petty revolt of the laboring classes our soldiers have not made great advances, while the 'gains' made by a few in the commissariat department scarcely redound to the credit of the army." Forty-five years later Ibsen contemplated the same criminal with profound irony and pity, giving him the name John Gabriel Borkman and a great many of his own traits. He is described as standing "with his hands behind his back," the typical Ibsen pose immortalized in his monument in Oslo, and the stage-directions tell us:

Borkman is of middle height, a well-knit, powerfully built man, well on in his sixties. His appearance is distinguished, his profile finely cut, his eyes piercing, his hair and beard curly and greyish-white. He is dressed in a slightly old-fashioned black coat, and wears a white necktie.

Borkman "smiling bitterly" speaks words of the kind that were always sure to irritate Björnson when he heard Ibsen speaking in a similar vein:

BORKMAN: Then we have been all the time deceiving each other. And perhaps been deceiving ourselves—both of us.
FOLDAL: But isn't that just the essence of friendship, John Gabriel?
BORKMAN (*smiling bitterly*): Yes, you are right there. Friendship means—deception.

It had always been the dramatist's habit to "sound and probe and dissect my own inward parts—and where it hurts most too." In this play he achieves perhaps the supreme self-irony. Like Ibsen who said that to be a poet meant "to summon one's self and play the judge's part" Borkman is examining time after time the record of his life: "I have been my own accuser, my own defender, and my own judge. I have been more impartial than anyone else could be—that I venture to say. I have paced up and down the gallery there, turning every one of my actions upside down and inside out. I have examined them from all sides as unsparingly, as pitilessly, as any lawyer of them all."

Ibsen's visit to Bergen in 1885, more than a quarter of a century after his departure from the "city without plebeians," may have left its traces in this play. The tenderly pitiful scene when upon the knock at the door John Gabriel expects a deputation of bankers coming to offer him the directorship which he alone can fill satisfactorily, only to have his "come in" answered by the humble Vilhelm Foldal, was probably lived through by Ibsen when he appeared on the ship's deck at the Bergen wharf in formal dress and adorned with all his orders, only to find instead of a reception committee of the dignitaries of the city, merely a group of bibulous town loafers. It was in Bergen too that he met again his former beloved, Henrikke Holst, "the maid of sixteen summers" as Fru Tresselt, a grandmother, just as John Gabriel sees Ella Rentheim again after a long lapse of years. That the germs for the scenes in the play lay in these experiences does not mean that Ibsen acted as did John Gabriel—far from it; he showed a tender consideration for his old friends, as can be seen from the following anecdote of the Nineties told by Christopher Due. One day this old friend of Grimstad days saw Ibsen walking along the street in Christiania, whereupon he joined him, stepping up to his left side. Ibsen returned the other's greeting very heartily, but somehow seemed to feel rather uneasy, until he finally stepped to his friend's left side. Christopher Due protested vigorously that he could not "walk at the right hand of the Great Cross of the Order of St. Olaf." "Yes, indeed," returned Ibsen, "you are the older."

The pathetic figure of Vilhelm Foldal dates far back in Ibsen's imagination, and serves as an illustration of the poet's extreme economy in never discarding a character or a motive. Probably the private tutor Evensen from the sketch for *Pillars of Society*, the man with the "extraordinary imagination" who drinks with Hilmar Tönnesen until after midnight was the first appearance of this figure in Ibsen's imagination. In the sketch for *The Lady from the Sea* there is another private tutor or perhaps a clerk: "In his youth he wrote a play which was performed once. Is constantly polishing it, and lives in the illusion of getting it published and making a success. Takes, however, no step in this direction. Reckons himself nevertheless among literary men. Wife and children believe blindly in 'the piece.' " In the first act he leaves the house of the lawyer, on whom he had called to secure a delay in an auction of his possessions: "Thoroughly good-hearted man, that lawyer. Now if only the play is brought out, we are over the worst." After Ibsen had made the acquaintance in his imagination of this character in 1877, and renewed it in 1888, he finally gave him a place in *John Gabriel Borkman* in 1896, enriched and mellowed, as old Vilhelm Foldal who has not made much of a career and whose children despise him.

Foldal's fifteen-year-old daughter Frida plays for Borkman and selects Saint-Saëns' *Danse Macabre*—a piece that with its jangling, mocking rhythms, its mighty crescendo, and its sombre, harmonious close seems like a musical parallel to Ibsen's drama. John Gabriel, listening beside the piano, remarks after the last notes die away that he has heard similar music down in the mines when the hammer-strokes set free the metal which "wants to come up into the light of day and serve mankind." The entire play is filled with similar striking touches. Ibsen makes the two women who have fought a fierce struggle for the hero, twin sisters, a fact that makes their hate far more dramatic, as they recall their feud of the past and then renew it once more over the son of John Gabriel. Poetic and symbolic touches abound, leading up to that final lyrical scene in the snow and the moonlight when the sisters hold out their hands to each other for the first time in a quarter of a century over the body of John Gabriel Borkman:

MRS. BORKMAN: We twin sisters—over him we have both loved.
ELLA RENTHEIM: We two shadows—over the dead man.

The play is not only one of Ibsen's most poetic works, but also a masterpiece of dramatic construction. It seems almost as if Ibsen had intended to answer the critics who had seen signs of faltering old age in *Little Eyolf*, for *John Gabriel Borkman* is a perfect example of dramatic concentration inasmuch as each act follows immediately upon the preceding one; the play therefore consumes less time than is required for its presentation, because in performance allowance must be, made for the shifting of scenery. Another indication of the dramatist's flexibility of mind is the introduction in the last act of the latest wrinkle in stage effects—moving scenery to give the illusion that the characters are going on an extensive walk from the mansion to a stone bench overlooking the fjord. Nor is there any lack of action in this play in which the past is unrolled in an extremely vivid and natural manner. The only traces of Ibsen's near approach to the traditional three score and ten, as far as the technique is concerned, are to be found in his ripe mastery of his craft due to a half century of concentration on this one art.

The play was received enthusiastically by the citizens of Christiania, who revelled in this brilliant work of their greatest poet. Nineteen times the play went over the boards, the first time at quadrupled prices which the Norwegians paid cheerfully because it afforded them an opportunity to applaud Ibsen in person. From every point of view, including the financial, the dramatist had reason to feel perfectly satisfied with *John Gabriel Borkman.*

After the appearance of this play Ibsen's publishers in Denmark and in Germany prepared a new complete edition of his works. Ibsen wrote a brief preface in which he said:

Only by accepting and acquiring my entire production as a connected, continuous whole will the reader receive the intended fitting impression of the individual parts.

It would be hard to find another writer of whom this is as true as it is of Ibsen. Throughout his life-work one finds only variations on one theme; the moral ideals of the individual pitted against the moral conventions and traditions of society—all of which can be summed up in the demand that the individual be unflinchingly true to himself. Sigurd in *The Vikings* lays the foundation for his downfall when he allows friendship to cause him to be false to his best impulses. Firm belief in himself leads Haakon to victory. Falk and Svanhild part to be true to themselves. Brand preaches this theme with prophetic ardor, and Peer Gynt exemplifies the opposite, "To thyself be enough." The social plays take up the same theme. Truth and freedom are declared the true pillars of society. Truth instead of pretense and play is the demand in *A Doll's House. Ghosts* grows out of the hue and cry raised by the former play, and in the same way *An Enemy of the People* is a vitriolic reply to the critics of

Ghosts. *The Wild Duck* views critically the truth-teller—or perhaps the would-be Ibsen disciple. After so much destructive criticism, as his enemies held, Ibsen gives his constructive views in *Rosmersholm*, returning to the old theme of the Third Empire of Emperor Julian. *The Lady from the Sea* presents a positive statement of the *Doll's House* theme: a true marriage founded on "freedom and responsibility." The false position of the woman of Society in which she cannot possibly realize herself is the theme of *Hedda Gabler*. The disparity between life and art is the burden of *The Master Builder* who cannot climb as high as he has built. In *Little Eyolf* a pretentious individual is unmasked and the lie of his life contrasted with his wife's genuine qualities. John Gabriel Borkman, like Sigurd and Consul Bernick, deserted the woman he loved to marry another for ulterior motives, committing that "sin for which there is no forgiveness." Throughout his collected works he preaches with inexorable honesty: "Realize yourself!"

For Ibsen's seventieth birthday a volume was issued under the editorship of Professor Gerhard Gran of Christiania University in which all the leading Scandinavian authors paid their tribute to the dramatist. The first article was by His Majesty King Oscar II; among others who followed were Carl Snoilsky, Verner von Heidenstam, Jonas Lie, Georg Brandes, John Paulsen, Ellen Key, Selma Lagerlöf, and numerous others. Some figures given show that already at that time half a million of Ibsen's books had been issued by his Copenhagen publisher alone, while the list of actors and actresses who had portrayed his characters includes the stars from all over the globe.

A world grateful to Ibsen for the riches he had added to the life of the spirit by the good and faithful increase of his talents sought to express its gratitude to the Master Builder on this anniversary. Sir Edmund Gosse relates that on the

morning of March 20, 1898, he was the first of the very international group of callers who assembled in the poet's home,
where were gathered Henrik and Susannah Ibsen, Sigurd, his
wife Bergliot Björnson, and their little son Tancred. Gosse
presented a handsome set of silver plate given jointly by
himself, Mr. Asquith, James Matthew Barrie, Thomas Hardy,
Henry Arthur Jones, and George Bernard Shaw. Hundreds
of visitors followed during the course of the day, representing many other nationalities, the Norwegian Storthing, the
University of Christiania, the Christiania theaters, and
numerous other organizations. Ibsen was fairly overwhelmed by the tribute of the entire world, while Mrs. Ibsen,
as the Norwegian historian Just Bing told me, moved about
among the guests with a dignity and grace in every way
worthy of the wife of the great man of letters.

On the following evening the Christiania Theater gave a
performance of *An Enemy of the People* in honor of the
dramatist, who was cheered to the echo by the Norwegians
whom he had taught, as the Prologue written by Professor
Dietrichson put it, to think great thoughts. The choice of
this particular play which contained the poet's bitterest satire
on his nation for the rejection of *Ghosts* was a happy gesture
of reconciliation and appreciation. On March 23 the chief
representatives of the government as well as of the arts and
sciences tendered Ibsen a banquet at which the secretary of
state Wexelson addressed a toast to the guest of honor and
Professor L. Dietrichson proposed one to Mrs. Ibsen. Amidst
the loud cheers and acclaim the poet's thought went back to
the bitter years of his apprenticeship in the Sixties when he
was on the verge of starvation, despair and suicide:

How silent and empty it was around me then! How the individual fellow-combatants stood scattered, each by himself, without
coherence, without connecting links between them! Many a time

it would seem to me then as if—once passed away—I had never been here. Nor my work, either!

But now! Now it has become populous round about. Young forces, confident of victory, have joined. *They* do not any longer have to write for a narrow circle. *They* have a public, an entire people to whom they may speak and to whom they may direct their thoughts and feelings. Whether they meet *opposition* or *adherence* —that is immaterial. It is only the *inability*, the *unwillingness to hear* which is of evil. That I have felt.

In conformity with the Biblical saying, "Seest thou a man diligent in his business? He shall stand before kings," Ibsen was honored with invitations from the King of Denmark and from the King of Sweden and Norway. During the course of his visit to Copenhagen the clash between the enthusiastic young Ibsen admirers and the conservative older generation who wished to honor the great poet, but who aimed to do it in measured terms, led to an amusing scene immortalized by an inspired caricaturist. At the banquet the manager of the Royal Theater, Peter Hansen, a man of classical rather than modern tendencies, shocked his listeners by applying to Ibsen the faint praise, "A talent of the first rank." The effect on Ibsen was to cause him to begin his reply: "Professor Hansen's speech has confused me and upset my answer. I must now extemporize," etc. The Minister of Ecclesiastical Affairs, Sthyr, was also present at the banquet, a fact that drew the following comment from *Politiken:* "If one recalls that Ibsen at one time wanted to place the torpedo under the Ark, then one must admire Sthyr. It is an open secret that the clergy opposed the participation of the Minister of Ecclesiastical Affairs in the Ibsen festivities, yes, that barely one hour before the time set for the dinner he received a letter from Pastor Ifversen in which he was implored to avoid this orgy of the godless. But Bishop Sthyr decided to remain faithful and to pursue his chosen path to the end, which is all the easier, since in the first place it was a question only of a good dinner."

In Stockholm Ibsen was received by his own king, Oscar II, and tendered a banquet to which were invited the members of the court, the social and intellectual aristocrats, in short, the élite of Stockholm. The chief address was delivered by Ibsen's old friend, the poet Count Snoilsky, who said in part:

The human heart was your mine, from which you brought to light the gems of your poetry!

> Heavy hammer burst as bidden
> To the heart nook of the hidden!

And one shaft after the other has opened in response to the heavy hammer-blows. Walls which stood in the way of a true understanding of your works have gradually fallen, one after the other. Finally a broad stream of light fell on the old miner—then as another wall of rock falls down—the dark subterranean path leads into a brilliant hall where thousands greet him. If mere splendor and fame had been the goal—surely the victory would have been won. He is the Henrik Ibsen now known and recognized by the whole world. The thinker whose glance has tested and penetrated so much has been mellowed with the years; but he longs to get back to his life-work in the depths in order to search for new veins of metal.

> Hammer blow on hammer blow,
> Till the lamp of life burns low.

Henrik Ibsen! Let us clasp for a moment your hand which has presented us so many poetic gifts, harsh but very salutary. Thanks for the pure, keen air which we have breathed amidst the stern rocks —but thanks also for the lovely, poetry-freighted valleys which met our gaze when the masses of cloud were at times parted. In such a place Agnes smiles eternally her ethereal smile—in such a place sits Solveig patiently expectant.

Thanks and hail to you, Henrik Ibsen!

His entertainment by the King, the orders bestowed on him, and his position as a guest of honor at such a splendid ban-

quet dazzled Ibsen. "My life has passed like a long, long
Passion week, and as I stand here in the real Passion week,
my life is transformed into a fairy play. I the old dramatist,
see my life remolded into a poem, a fairy poem. It has been
transformed into a summer night's dream. My thanks for
this transformation."

The final event in the celebration of Ibsen's seventieth
birthday was a festival given by the Norwegian Woman's
Rights League in Christiania May 26, 1898. The wife of
Prime Minister Blehr presided and speeches were delivered
by the two chief leaders in the movement in Norway, Miss
Gina Krog and Miss Aasta Hansteen. The latter was still
more relentless and caustic in her hatred of "he-beasts" than
in the days when she had served as Ibsen's model for Lona
Hessel; the tenor of her feelings in the Nineties is indicated
by her reaction to Theosophy, which appealed to her as
eminently just in its doctrine of reincarnation: "Yes," she
snorted to Gina Krog, "the men-folk will be repaid. They
will be born as women—next time!"

It is not surprising that with such a speaker on the program
Ibsen made a few reservations regarding his patronage of the
Woman's Rights League. He disclaimed having written anything with the conscious thought of making propaganda—
he considered himself a poet rather than a social philosopher.
The question of rights for women appeared to him a problem
of humanity in general and his task had been the *description
of humanity*. He closed his remarks:

The task always before my mind has been to advance our country
and give the people a higher standard. To obtain this, two factors
are of importance: it is for the mothers by strenuous and sustained
labor to awaken a conscious feeling of *culture* and *discipline*. This
must be created in men before it will be possible to lift the people
to a higher plane. It is the women who are to solve the social
problem. As mothers they are to do it. And only as such can they

do it. Here lies a great task for woman. My thanks! And success to the Woman's Rights League!

The Norwegian women had prepared an event particularly fitting at a celebration whose aim was to express their gratitude for what Ibsen had given them. The lights in the hall were dimmed and one by one all of Ibsen's female characters passed before the poet, each presenting him a rose. What memories must have been awakened in the dramatist as he beheld fifty years of intense creative activity reincarnated before him! The Vestal Furia,—Lady Inger—Margit of Solhoug—Hjördis the Valkyrie—Svanhild—Margrete, daughter of Skule—Agnes—Solveig—Lona Hessel—little Nora defying the whole world—Mrs. Alving—Petra Stockmann—Hedvig, the wistful adolescent—Rebecca West,— Ellida, the lady from the sea—Hedda Gabler—Hilda Wangel —Rita, mother of Little Eyolf—and finally the two shadows, Ella Rentheim and Gunhild Borkman.

As the long line passed Ibsen to the strains of gentle music the Master Builder knew that, aside from Shakespeare, no artist had ever created such a gallery of living characters.

4

In a recently published Ibsen letter dated Dresden, January 13, 1870, there is a very clear expression of what he felt throughout his creative period as the essential weakness in his character; he lacked the courage necessary in a man of action, and therefore he had become a poet. The letter is written to the Danish historian C. F. V. Rosenberg, who had asked Ibsen for contributions to *Nordisk Tidskrift*, a periodical that gave its enthusiastic support to political Scandinavianism. He says in part:

I thank you heartily for your review of *The League of Youth* which Hegel has sent me, and no less for your kind lines. I am

thinking of coming to Copenhagen this summer; I hope there to
greet you personally and to talk about the many things in which we
are mutually interested. When I think of you all up there at home,
who year in year out stand arrayed in battle, I am ashamed of myself. But I feel at the same time that I am not fit to fight in any
other way than I am doing.

Today we have the Knut festival; this evening I shall remember
all brave warriors in a good glass of punch, and with this I sign
myself,

Yours respectfully,

HENRIK IBSEN.

When the aged Ibsen came to write what he called his
Dramatic Epiloque he was fully conscious of his failure in
not having fought like Dr. Stockmann, as well as of his failure
in not having enjoyed life robustly like one of the old Vikings. He had been an artist-ascetic, too timid to grasp the
good things of life for himself, fearful lest he should fail in
"writing for eternity." Toward the end of his days he felt
keenly what he had missed, as is clearly evidenced by the
dedication he wrote in a copy of *Brand* presented to a one-
year-old child, daughter of Professor A. Arstal in Christiania, on April 28, 1896:

To little Eldrid!
May your life take shape like a poem of beauty
On the great reconciliation of happiness and duty!

Meanwhile the whole world and his compatriots in particular paid tribute after tribute to his greatness. It was
certainly with mixed emotions that he received the demon-
strations in his honor; at the dinner tendered him on his
seventieth birthday he spoke of "the misconception . . . that
there should be a feeling of absolute happiness connected with
that rare fairytale fate which I have had: to gain fame and
name yonder in many lands."

The very climax of Ibsen's fame came in September, 1899,

when there was dedicated the stately National Theater in Christiania, which bears on its façade hewn in stone the three names: Ibsen, Holberg, Björnson; while before it stand bronze statues of the two men who more than four decades previously had been president and vice-president of the struggling little society for the promotion of a national Norwegian theater; Björnson and Ibsen. It was indeed a fine reward for a long and brave fight, a crowning of their careers. But in 1899, in place of the hearty cooperation of youth, there had come between the two old men the sense of their dignity and each felt that he must insist on it by preserving a due distance from the other. During the first of the three dedication performances (devoted to Holberg, lest either rival feel slighted) they sat in special *fauteuils* in the center of the dress circle, separated, however, by a vast garland of red and white roses! The King from his box graciously smiled down on his two most famous subjects. The second night was given over to a national ovation to Henrik Ibsen. He sat alone in the manager's box, saw his beloved Dr. Stockmann fight for truth and freedom, and was cheered by the audience at the close of the acts until he made a pathetic, but vain attempt to escape from so much vociferous applause. Certainly, if ever an artist had honors and rewards from his work that artist was Henrik Ibsen.

All of this was grist to the mill of the dramatist, who was then at work on *When We Dead Awaken,* perhaps the most personal of all his works. In this play he deals at the hand of his own career with the problem of the conflict between art and life; characteristically Ibsen did not write regarding himself with any smug self-satisfaction, but in the spirit in which more than thirty years previously he had delineated some of his own traits in *Peer Gynt:* "In my quiet moments I sound and probe and dissect my own inward parts—and where it hurts most, too." Into his chief character, Professor Rubek, a sculptor of world fame, Ibsen puts so many of his own traits that the artist's speeches concerning his career sound like the poet's own reminiscences. As a matter of fact, Ibsen had been contemplating during the last years an autobiographical work, but he never wrote it, preferring evidently the "Dichtung und Wahrheit" of a symbolical drama.

Most of these autobiographical passages occur in the conversations between Professor Rubek and Irene, his former model. In the first act Irene reproaches Rubek for no longer having had any use for her after he had completed his masterpiece:

IRENE (*nods with a touch of scorn*) : The work of art first—then the human being.
RUBEK: You must judge me as you will; but at that time I was utterly dominated by my great task—and exultantly happy in it.
IRENE: And you achieved your great task.

The conversation sounds like an echo from the ardent years in Rome when Ibsen "felt the exaltation of a Crusader," when he said he was fighting "for the possibility of devoting myself to the task which I believe and know has been laid upon me by God" but when he wrote also "Friends are an expensive luxury." Irene in the second act places her finger on the raw spot in Ibsen's soul (as it were, echoing Björnson's words to Richard Le Gallienne): ". . . you were an artist and an artist only—not a man!" Repeatedly she calls him "poet" using the word as a term of contempt, "because there is something apologetic in the word, my friend. Something that suggests forgiveness of sins—and spreads a cloak over all frailty."

If Ibsen confesses his weaknesses in the person of Professor Rubek, he also endows him with the qualities that were his own strength and greatness. A picturesque comparison

made by the bear-hunter characterizes the Master Builder's
manner of working at his chosen task:

ULFHEIM: . . . We both work in a hard material, madam—both
your husband and I.   He struggles with his marble blocks, I
daresay; and I struggle with tense and quivering bear-sinews.
And we both of us win the fight in the end—subdue and master
our material.   We never rest till we've got the upper hand of
it, though it fight never so hard.
RUBEK (*deep in thought*) : There's a great deal of truth in what
you say.

In the setting in which this last conversation takes place
there is probably also a considerable biographical element,
albeit not actual, but day-dreaming; the aging artist travelling in the company of a young wife.   Miss Emilie Bardach
told me in conversation that in the course of the summer in
Gossensass, 1889, Ibsen had spoken to her of the possibility
of a divorce and of a subsequent union with her, in the course
of which they were to travel widely and see the world.   If
Ibsen—like many an aging married man—dreamed of a
marriage with a young and beautiful girl his dreams were
spun out to an ending characteristic of the soul-searching
realist; Rubek and Maia soon find themselves consumed with
boredom, they run out of material for conversation, and they
represent a little family scene not without its touch of humor.
Ibsen frequently makes the distinction between what the poet
actually experiences and what he lives through mentally; the
first he did not consider very important, but it was his principle never to write anything that he had not mentally lived
through.

In this opening scene of the play in which the elderly
artist has just returned to Norway after having gained world
fame while living in exile there are many more instances of
Ibsen serving as his own model.   The bitterness against his

countrymen, engendered in 1864 when the Norwegians rudely shattered his youthful faith in ideals by failing to keep their pledge to come to Denmark's aid, still lives in the aged poet. In a letter to Georg Brandes of June 3, 1897, he says: "Here all the sounds are closed in every acceptation of the word, —and all the channels of intelligence are blocked." Professor Rubek sees in the purposeless stopping of the train and the "toneless, meaningless" talk of the station guards symbols of the life in Norway; then he pays his fellow citizens the compliment of saying that they have changed "a little, perhaps. And not at all in the direction of amiability." This is quite in the tone of the aged Ibsen as he appeared at the only interview his biographer Gerhard Gran had with him; Gran refrains from telling details, stating only that Ibsen had not lost his poison-fangs.

Another interviewer, Mrs. Alec Tweedie, reports of her visit to Ibsen in Christiania:

Casting our eyes around, we noticed that by the side of the ink-pot on the table on which so many remarkable books have been written, there stood a little tray, and on the tray one of those small carved bears that are so common in Switzerland. Beside it was a little black devil for holding a match, and two or three little cats and rabbits in copper, one of the former of which was playing the violin.

"What are those funny little things?" we queried.

"I never write a single line of any of my dramas, unless that tray and its occupants are before me on the table. I could not write without them. It may seem strange—perhaps it is—but I cannot write without them," he repeated; "but why I use them is my own secret," and he laughed quietly.

Professor Rubek reveals the secret in his conversation with Maia: he sees the whole world as a menagerie, just as Daniel Heire, the mocking rogue of *The League of Youth*, had seen it. He adds at this point another savage thrust at the Nor-

—From *Vikingen,* August 6, 1898.

IBSEN AND THE ENGLISH TOURISTS

Free translation of the verse:

In Kurland they titter and giggle
The English chat all in one breath;
Their staring makes poor Ibsen wriggle,
The old man's embarrassed to death.

wegians, who had paid high prices to see in the theaters their "striking likenesses" behind which lurk animal features: "And it is these double-faced works of art that our excellent plutocrats come and order of me. And pay for in all good faith—and in good round figures too—almost their weight in gold, as the saying goes." Ibsen has a good laugh at the expense of the critics, for which one can hardly blame him when one considers how the critics dealt with him: "All the world knows nothing! understands nothing!"

Professor Rubek has his villa at the Lake of Taunitz, and Ibsen had his dream of using his wealth to build himself one, as he writes Georg Brandes June 3, 1897: "Can you guess what I am dreaming about, and planning, and picturing to myself as something delightful? The making of a home for myself near the Sound, between Copenhagen and Elsinore, on some free open spot whence I can see all the sea-going ships starting on and returning from their long voyages." This is the way in which Ibsen felt when he longed to be away from the Norwegians, from Christiania, and from the applause of the mob. Professor Rubek expresses a similar mood when he tells Maia, "Men's laurels and incense nauseated me, till I could have rushed away in despair and hidden myself in the depths of the woods."

But far more interesting than these and other somewhat external details is the symbol in which Ibsen's Epilogue sums up his entire life's work in a statuary group: *The Resurrection Day*. This is an inspired conception of the life of the courageous prophet who banned so many ghosts and led millions of people to realize themselves in freer, fuller, and nobler life; while literary production so homogeneous in its great variety as was the life-work of Henrik Ibsen can find no better symbol than a unified statuary group on a single base.

The group consists of three parts. The first symbolizes the

great poetic dramas of idealism written in the enthusiasm of
the Crusader. Rubek describes it to Irene who had served
as the model for this figure: "The Resurrection, I thought,
would be most beautifully and exquisitely figured as a young
unsullied woman—with none of our earth-life's experience—
awakening to the light and glory without having put away
from her anything ugly and impure." This was the phase
of the soul-stirring "All or nothing!" and of the battle between the Emperor and the Galilean that was to usher in the
Third Empire of a free and ennobled humanity.

But the artist was young then—with no knowledge of life.
After the poet's youth begun in gladness came the sombre
problem plays up to the time of *The Master Builder*. Rubek
explains how this came about: "I learned worldly wisdom in
the years that followed, Irene. *The Resurrection Day* became
in my mind's eye something more and something—something more complex. The little round plinth on which your
figure stood erect and solitary,—it no longer afforded room
for all the imagery I now wanted to add. . . . I imagined
that which I saw with my eyes round me in the world. I had
to include it—I could not help it, Irene. I expanded the
plinth, made it wide and spacious. And on it I placed a seg-
ment of the curving, bursting earth. And up from the fissures
of the soil there now swarm men and women with dimly suggested animal faces. Women and men—as I knew them in
real life." This is the period of the creation of those haunt-
ingly life-like characters, immortal figures on the world's
stage: Nora, Pastor Manders, Hjalmar Ekdal, Rebecca West,
Hedda Gabler, and the whole long line.

Finally comes the phase of the plays of Ibsen's old age,
of the psychological dramas of self-analysis. "Yes, but let
me tell you, too, how I have placed *myself* in the group,"
continues Rubek: "In front, beside a fountain—as it were
here—sits a man weighed down with guilt, who cannot quite

free himself from the earth-crust. I call him remorse for a forfeited life. He sits there and dips his fingers in the purling stream—to wash them clean—and he is gnawed by the thought that never, never will he succeed. Never in all eternity will he attain to freedom and the new life. He will remain forever prisoned in his hell." Thus the aged Ibsen saw himself and his life-work. Before the bar of his high ideal and his tender conscience his life was a forfeited one; as Solness, the Master Builder, had summed it up: "Nothing really built. Nor anything sacrificed for the chance of building. Nothing, nothing, the whole is nothing." His aim had been so high—the regeneration of mankind—that the great things he had achieved seemed quite futile.

In Ibsen's own judgment his greatest work was *Emperor and Galilean,* and from this point of view must we understand the sculptor's feeling of guilt at having moved the Resurrection figure a little into the background, and at having subdued a little the light that transfigured her face. Ibsen had turned from his idealistic dramas to realism, and critics had not spared him the charge of having commercialized his art. The man beside the purling stream felt a deep sense of guilt also because he had preached ideals and left it to others to fight for them; he had not been able to climb as high as he had built. He had fled from "life" and had been merely a "poet." He had lured people high up on a dizzy mountain top and beguiled them by promising all the glory of the world —but the whole thing turned out to have been an idle trick. The aged Ibsen at times finds himself in a mood of doubting the validity of his own ideals; Rubek speaks at times as another Gregers Werle, whose destiny it was to be the thirteenth at table.

In Irene, the beautiful, ardently devoted young woman, symbolizing the ideal, Rubek might have found the vital combination of the spiritual and physical. There is a tide in the affairs of men—if Rubek had followed his impulses on the completion of the great common task instead of stifling them and dismissing Irene with thanks for the "beautiful episode" his life would have been rich and full. But now, when the dead awaken, they see that they have never really lived.

This great love story of the artist for Irene ends—like *Tristan and Iseult,* like *Romeo and Juliet*—in frustration and death. It is the work in which, probably more than in any other, Ibsen has unlocked his heart and caused us to feel a tragic shudder as we come in contact with his soul, too idealistic and too keenly critical to be anything but melancholy. Critics have pointed out the weaknesses of the piece; it is the work of an old man whose strength is slipping from him. It required three, instead of the usual two years to complete it. "He wrote *When We Dead Awaken,*" says Dr. Elias, "with such labor and such passionate agitation, so spasmodically and so feverishly, that those around him were almost alarmed. Only finish this, he must finish this! He seemed to hear the beating of dark pinions over his head. . . . Ibsen knew, as he was composing this drama, quite definitely that it would be the last, that after this he would write nothing—his relatives are firmly convinced of that. And soon the blow fell."

Ibsen's *Epilogue* was published in December, 1899, and on March 15 of the following year he suffered a stroke; a second one followed in January, 1901. It seems an added touch of tragedy that the poet who many years previously had characterized his life as "one long Passion Week" now had to suffer six years of physical and mental enfeeblement. Ibsen had rounded off his life-work so well, he had thought of death as it came to Brand, to Rosmer, to Hedda Gabler, to Solness, to John Gabriel Borkman, and to Rubek, but in his own case it was long drawn out. His physical suffering is said to have been not very great, but he was afflicted with amnesia, of which he was painfully conscious. At the table where so many great dramas had been written sat the old man painfully and persistently learning and forgetting the alphabet. "Look," he said one day to his son, in a voice full of melancholy. "See what I am doing! I am sitting here, learning to make my letters—my *letters!* I who was once an author!"

Despite the fact that Ibsen could no longer continue at his work he took great interest in what went on about him. A great pleasure that filled his heart with pride came to him when in 1903 his son came to show him his appointment as "Staats-minister," the highest office in Norway under the King. Ibsen's interest in politics continued longer than that in the theater—probably because of the pleasure he took in Sigurd's career. He had become reconciled to his son's course in politics, despite the fact that he had at first quarreled with him violently over his espousal of the cause of Björnson; Ibsen was objective enough to appreciate Sigurd's right to a realization of his own personality.

Ibsen's doctor engaged for him a masseur and attendant, Herr Arnt Dehli, who for five years accompanied him on the daily drives in carriage or sleigh that now took the place of the walks he had enjoyed so much. The poet's attitude toward this daily companion was at first very reserved and silent, but before long he became quite fond of him; Herr Dehli thinks it was because he was absolutely prompt in his engagements and respected the clock-like division Ibsen made of his day. He says that he has never met a pleasanter or wittier person to chat with than Ibsen was on these daily drives, nor a more grateful patient. Often when they met friends Ibsen would ask the coachman to stop. One day, as they overtook an old friend from the "Hollander" days, Professor Ludvig Ludvigsen Daae, Ibsen waved and called to him; when Daae neither heard nor saw after Ibsen's third greeting, he said to Herr Dehli: "He is angry at me because he believes that he is the model for Rektor Kroll. But I had never thought of him." Ibsen enjoyed very much the opportunity to see and to observe people; he remarked repeatedly that it would be impossible for him to live in the country.

On his seventy-fifth birthday Ibsen had the pleasure of seeing his closest friends among the many callers. When Björnson arrived Ibsen, remembering all that this old friend had done for him and forgetting their petty differences, threw his arms about him, exclaiming, "I have always loved you most of all!" Edvard Grieg and Jonas Lie also came to felicitate the aged poet. Grieg was deeply moved and, no doubt feeling that there was something final in his leavetaking, embraced Ibsen as he exclaimed, "You must permit me to do this." When Jonas Lie departed he said, "Thanks, thanks for all you have done for the Norwegian people." Ibsen protested that Lie had done just as much. "No," said the latter, "you know, no one has done what you have done for this country."

Gradually Ibsen's powers waned until even the daily drive became too much for him and he had to restrict his pleasure in observing humanity to sitting every day at the window of his home on the Drammensvei opposite the royal gardens. At last even this became impossible, and confined to his bed, the mighty poet was reduced through hardening of the arteries to such a wreck of his former self that Sigurd Ibsen said, "We do not admit visitors any more to the mausoleum." On May 23, 1906, he died. Characteristically his last audible word is said to have been "Tvertimot" (quite the contrary) which he exclaimed when, as he woke in clear consciousness after a quiet sleep on one of his last days, someone remarked that his condition was improving; to the last he remained the foe of all palliation and a devotee of truth.

Ibsen's funeral became a great public function under the direction of the State Church. Some of his admirers felt offended that his body should be taken to a church when he was no longer able to protest against it, that the Pillars of Society should appear as his mourners, and a Pastor Manders should speak at his grave. Dr. Julius Elias, who knew Ibsen intimately, thinks it very unlikely that such an arrangement would have been offensive to him, because, while he was the most determined revolutionary when it came to the vital rights of the individual and of personality, yet he conformed to conventions in matters that were simply formal. Ibsen considered ridiculous and quixotic the pose of a revolutionary or Bohemian, who insisted on appearing individualistic in everyday externalities. Perhaps he would have smiled could he have seen most officious about his bier his old friends: Stensgaard and all the politicians, Consul Bernick, Mayor Stockmann, Rector Kroll, and the journalists Mortensgaard, Hovstad, and Billing. Yet despite its official character Ibsen's funeral was marked by genuine feeling on the part of a grateful people. Thousands of humble folk walked past his coffin for a last glimpse of Norway's great poet on the day before the funeral, hundreds of students marched in the rain for hours to follow him to his grave, and among the wreaths two at least were not merely official; when Miss Gina Krog said in presenting hers: "In the name of Norwegian women, thanks and honor to Henrik Ibsen" and the arts student Krogstad, "From the students. We bring the thanks of youth."

In the reserved seats in the church sat the King, the ministers, the Storthing, the foreign diplomats, the magistrates of Christiania, professors of the University, representatives of the Academy of Sciences, of the army, women in black, old men in frock coats, theologians with white ruffs, and courtiers in gold lace and orders. In short, it was a gala assembly with Ibsen's friends very little in evidence. But the pastor who spoke was Christopher Brunn, Ibsen's friend in his Roman days and the model for Brand, the only clergyman in

all his plays who enjoys the author's sympathy.   Brunn,
whom Ibsen admired because of his sincerity, had visited
the dramatist frequently during his last years.   At the funeral
he spoke very briefly, thanking Norway's greatest man for
what he had created: "for Brand and Agnes, for Dr. Stockmann, for Strawman and *Ghosts*, and the entire endless row."
He gave thanks for Ibsen's genius which had for its aim, as he
himself had expressed it, to arouse his nation and to lead it to
think great thoughts.   He closed by saying: "I must add one
word more.   We do right in thinking of his wife, the woman
who has followed him in love and deep understanding, in
greatness and in the days of happiness, who guarded him in
the time of infirmity, sickness, and trial with self-denying,
with self-effacing loyalty."

Ibsen's body was laid to rest in *Vor Frelsers Cemetery* in
a round plot before some white birches.   A monument designed by Mrs. Ibsen was later erected: a simple granite shaft
with neither name nor inscription carved upon it, only a
miner's hammer, symbolical of the man who delved deeper
and deeper—

> Hammer blow on hammer blow,
> Till the lamp of life burns low!

In the evening of the day of the funeral, June 1, 1906, a
performance of *Peer Gynt* was given at the *National Theater*.
Here it was, says Dr. Elias, that Ibsen's real funeral sermon
was preached in the words of the priest over the body of the
peasant who in his youth had been afraid to go to war (Act V,
Scene III):

> He was short sighted.   Out beyond the circle
> Of those most near to him he nothing saw.
> To him seemed meaningless as cymbals' tinkling
> Those words that to the heart should ring like steel.
> His race, his fatherland, all things high and shining,

Stood ever, to his vision, veiled in mist.
But he was humble, humble, was this man;
And since that sessions-day his doom oppressed him
As surely as his cheeks were flushed with shame,
And his four fingers hidden in his pocket—
Offender 'gainst his country's laws? Ay, true!
But there is one thing that the law outshineth
Sure as the snow white tent of Glittertind
Has clouds, like higher rows of peaks, above it.
No patriot was he. Both for church and state
A fruitless tree. But there, on the upland ridge
In the small circle where he saw his calling,
There he was great, because he was himself.
His inborn note rang true unto the end.
His days were as a lute with muted strings.
And therefore, peace be with thee, silent warrior
That fought the peasant's little fight, and fell!

It is not ours to search the heart and reins;—
That is no task for dust, but for its ruler;—
Yet dare I freely, firmly, speak my hope:
He scarce stands crippled now before his God!

After the play followed an epilogue spoken by an actress;
then the curtains parted again revealing a larger than life-
size bust of Ibsen in brilliant light. This simple happening,
coming on that particular day, had a tremendous effect on
the audience. The people arose and trembled, for Ibsen was
looking them in the eye once more with those searching eyes
of his that penetrated to the most secret thoughts, and before
which the social lies would not hold water. All felt the man
buried on that day was one

Of those immortal dead who live again
In minds made better by their presence.

At this point it might be well, as Christopher Brunn suggested, to think for a moment of Susannah Ibsen, the faithful
wife who had been the model for Hjoerdis standing by the

side of her hero in the thick of battle, who also in his last days of suffering was called by the poet: "Min söde, kjaere, snille frue" (my sweet, dear, kind wife). She was a woman of distinct personality, but she made it the purpose of her life to further her husband's work in every way, and for this purpose she frequently resigned her own wishes, putting herself in the background. But whenever she could be of service to him she was promptly at hand, serving as his first audience, as a touchstone of great acumen. But more than that, she was his inspiration in many ways; especially for his ideas on the position of women was he indebted to her. The two had read together Camilla Collett and John Stuart Mill, but an even more convincing argument was the individuality and independence that lay in her character, for she was what Nora wished to become—"a human being"; to a large extent she is to be found also in Lona Hessel and Mrs. Alving. About the time when Ibsen first made her acquaintance he wrote in *Lady Inger of Oestraat*: "A woman is the mightiest power in the world, and in her hand it lies to guide a man whither God Almighty would have him go." During the almost fifty years of their life together Ibsen increasingly became the poet who believed in woman, in the power of her love and her ethical mission—in his personal experience and in his message a direct contrast to his enemy, the unhappily married and woman-hating Strindberg. Ibsen had found the power of woman's personality in Susannah Ibsen, to which his lyric poems bear eloquent witness. They had lived a real marriage with faithfulness toward the outside while guarding their individuality in an inner liberty, allowing each to live the life of a free personality. Like her husband, she was repelled by all that was not genuine, and for this reason she declined to be acclaimed by the crowd merely because she happened to be the wife of the famous poet; on the occasion of a serenade on his seventieth birthday Ibsen asked her to step with him to the window, but she insisted that he get the glory for himself.

In her last years she suffered a great deal. She was unable to attend his funeral; she had designed his monument, but she never saw it. In fact, after his death she did not once leave her home, living, as he had done, according to the clock in different rooms of the house, and further honoring his memory by assisting Dr. Julius Elias and Professor Halvdan Koht in the publication of Ibsen's posthumous writings, chiefly sketches for the plays. In 1914 Susannah Ibsen died and was buried by the dramatist's side under a slab on which are engraved Ibsen's lines to her entitled *Thanks.*

Henrik Ibsen has been a brave pioneer and a mighty prophet who has weathered the storms of criticism that swept about his head for the half-century of his literary activity. On the very occasion of his death the Manders and Krolls raised their voices as loudly as ever, as can be seen from the (anonymous) article of the *New York Tribune,* reprinted in a prominent place in the *Literary Digest,* and here quoted in part:

The later years of the nineteenth century were ripe for the unsettling ministrations of men like Nietzsche and Ibsen, men keen on meeting the animal in man halfway, and on throwing a glamor of "naturalness" over its lustful affirmations and its callous rejections of undesired obligations. In other words, Ibsen came to tell thousands just what they wanted to be told. He delivered his "message" with all the more aplomb because he was himself an egotist not only from theory, but from the promptings of his nature. His recently published letters have shown with what sublime selfishness he pursued his own career. He was as cold as a fish and as hard as nails. It is doubtful if he ever felt a passion of tenderness, of gentle, kindly feeling for mankind, and it is certain that he had not one atom of humor. There is something ironical about the fate which promises to overtake him. He wrapped his works in an appalling solemnity, and the world is learning to laugh at his portentous assumptions.

But the facts seem to indicate that it is not Ibsen but such criticism that the world is learning to laugh at. He has realized his aim, the traditional aim of all great poets, to write for eternity, to rear a *monumentum aere perennius*. More than that, not only his plays, but also all modern drama, became his monument, for there is scarcely a dramatist since his day whose work has not been influenced by the Norwegian Master Builder. Above all, the spirit of Ibsen has banished ghosts and admitted fresh air into our lives, the spirit that inspires everyone to realize the strongest and best of which he is capable, to be himself nobly and fearlessly. And, as Richard Dehmel put it in a poem written at the time of Ibsen's death: in the dim future hover many figures who in coming ages will feel impelled to say, "Thanks, Ibsen, thanks!"

CHRONOLOGICAL TABLE

1828. March 20, Ibsen born in Skien.

1844. Leaves Skien for Grimstad to become apothecary apprentice.

1850. Leaves for Christiania to prepare for university.
Catiline.
Conditioned in University entrance examination.
September 26, performance of *The Warrior's Barrow.*

1851. Edits *Andrhimmer* with Botten-Hansen and Vinje.
July 7, police raid—end of Ibsen's political activity.
November 6, appointed theater poet in Bergen.

1852. Visit to Copenhagen and Dresden.

1853. *St. John's Night.*

1855. *Lady Inger of Oestraat.*

1856. *The Feast at Solhoug.*

1857. Returns to Christiania—*The Vikings.*

1858. June 26, marries Susannah Thoresen.

1862. *Love's Comedy.*

1863. *The Pretenders.*

1864. Leaves Norway for Rome.

1866. *Brand.*

1867. *Peer Gynt.*

1868. Settles in Dresden.

1869. Visit to Stockholm and Egypt—*The League of Youth.*

1870. Visits Copenhagen.

1873. *Emperor and Galilean.*

1874. Visits Norway.

1875. Settles in Munich.

1877. *Pillars of Society.*

1878. Returns to Rome.

1879. *A Doll's House.*

1881. *Ghosts.*

1882. *An Enemy of the People.*

1884. *The Wild Duck.*

1885. Visits Norway and Settles in Munich.

1886. *Rosmersholm.*

1888. *The Lady from the Sea.*

1890. *Hedda Gabler.*

1891. Returns to Norway and settles in Christiania.

1892. *The Master Builder.*

1894. *Little Eyolf.*

1896. *John Gabriel Borkman.*

1898. Celebration of Ibsen's seventieth birthday.

1899. Dedication of National Norwegian Theater and Ibsen statue—
When We Dead Awaken.

1906. May 23, Ibsen's death.

BIBLIOGRAPHY

This bibliography lists all important sources with the exception of quotations from and references to Ibsen's plays, which are omitted for reasons of space. These sources are divided into four groups: I. Those referred to by abbreviations adopted according to the system of Otto Heller, *Henrik Ibsen, Plays and Problems*, Houghton Mifflin Company, 1912. II. Those referred to by the name of the author only. III. Translations, referred to by the name of the translator. All those not otherwise accredited are by Lois Miles. IV. Sources infrequently referred to are fully described.

I

CW—The Collected Works of Henrik Ibsen. Copyright Edition. New York, Charles Scribner's Sons, 1923.

SW—Henrik Ibsens Sämmtliche Werke in deutscher Sprache, Durchgesehen und eingeleitet von Georg Brandes, Julius Elias, Paul Schlenther, vom Dichter autorisiert. Berlin, S. Fischer Verlag.

SW^{II}—The continuation (Zweite Reihe) of SW. Nachgelassene Schriften in vier Bänden. Herausgegeben von Julius Elias und Halvdan Koht. Berlin, S. Fischer Verlag.

C—The Correspondence of Henrik Ibsen. The translation edited by Mary Morison. London, Hodder and Stoughton, 1905. Identical with: Letters of Henrik Ibsen. Translated by John Nilsen Laurvik and Mary Morison. New York, Duffield and Co., 1908.

BjC—Björnstjerne Björnson, Brev. Förste Samling: Gro-Tid, Brev fra Aarene, 1857-1870. Utgit av Halvdan Koht, Christiania and Copenhagen, 1912.

SNL—Speeches and New Letters (of) Henrik Ibsen. Translated by Arne Kildal. With an introduction by Lee M. Hollander and a bibliographical appendix. Boston, Richard G. Badger, 1910.

FIW—From Ibsen's Workshop, Notes, Scenarios, and Drafts of Modern Plays. Translated by A. G. Chater. Volume XII of The Collected Works of Henrik Ibsen. Copyright Edition. Edited by William Archer. Scribner's, 1923.

II

Blanc, T., *Henrik Ibsen og Christiania Theater, 1850-1889*, Christiania, 1906.

Brandes, Georg, *Das Ibsenbuch*, Reissner, Dresden, 1923. (Collection of the four essays Brandes wrote on Ibsen—1867, 1882, 1898, and 1906.)

Dietrichson, L., *Svundne Tider*, Christiania, 1906.

Due, Christopher, *Erindringer fra Henrik Ibsens Ungdomsaar*, Copenhagen, 1909.

Gosse, Edmund, *Henrik Ibsen*, Scribner's, 1907.

Gran, Gerhard, *Henrik Ibsen, Liv og Verker*, Christiania, 1918.

Halvorsen, J. B., *Norsk Forfatter-Lexikon, 1814-1880*, Christiania, 1892, Vol. III.

Hoest, Sigurd, *Henrik Ibsen*, Paris, 1924.

Jaeger, Henrik, *Henrik Ibsen*. Translated by W. M. Payne, McClurg, 1901.

Koht, Halvdan, *Henrik Ibsen, eit Diktarliv*, Oslo, 1928, Vol. II, 1929.

Lothar, Rudolph, *Henrik Ibsen*, Leipzig, 1902.

Paulsen, John *Erinnerungen an Henrik Ibsen*, Berlin, 1907. (Translation of *Samliv ved Ibsen*.)

Woerner, Roman, *Henrik Ibsen*, Muenchen, 1902, Vol. II, 1909.

III

Garrett, F. E., *Ibsen: Lyrics and Poems*, Dutton, 1913.

Payne, W. M., in translation of Jaeger's biography, *op. cit.*

Shedd, Percy W., *Oceanides*, Grafton Press, 1902.

Streatfield, R. A., *Ibsen's Lyrical Poems*, London, 1902.

CHAPTER I

P. 1—Ibsen's genealogy: Joh. K. Bergwitz, *Henrik Ibsen i sin Avstamning*, Christiania, 1916; cf. Ibsen's letter to William Archer, C, No. 225, concerning Scotch descent; the computations in 256ths are by G. T. Flom, *Henrik Ibsen*, Scandinavian Studies, Vol. X, p. 67 ff.

P. 2—Magnificent house: Koht, I, p. 20 f.

P. 3—Sketch for *Brand* ("Epic Brand"), Efterladte Skrifter, II, p. 11; German translation: SW[II], II, p. 101 f.

P. 6—Reminiscences: these were written for Jaeger.

P. 7—Building, etc.: Jaeger, p. 29 f.

P. 8—Laughter: Koht, I, p. 26 f.

P. 8—School mates: these two anecdotes are told, Halvorsen, pp. 4 and 5.

P. 10—Eucharist: J. Collin, *Henrik Ibsen*, Heidelberg, 1910, p. 12.

P. 11—Letter to Johan Sverdrup: quoted, Koht, I, p. 33.

P. 12—The photograph Ibsen sent his sister has recently become the property of the Skien Museum.

CHAPTER II

P. 13—Ibsen's life in Grimstad is described in a series of articles in Eidsvold, 1900, Nos. 233, 235, and 238; Bendix Ebbell, *Henrik Ibsen i Grimstad*, Soerlandsheftet, 1925; Hans Hansen, *Skildringer og Oplevelser*, Grimstad (no date). The fullest treatment is in Due. Several anecdotes I also derived from Herr Karl O. Knutsen, Curator of the Ibsen Museum in Grimstad. He also showed me the manuscript of the poems sent by Ibsen to Clara Ebbell, including *The Miner*. See also Botten-Hansen, Paul, *Henrik Ibsen*, Illustreret Nyhedsblad, Christiania, July 19, 1863.

P. 16—For Ibsen's reading: Chr. Collin, *Ibsen als Norweger*, Neue Rundschau, Nov., 1907; Halvdan Koht, *Ibsen as a Norwegian*, The Nineteenth Century, Feb., 1910.

P. 17—Reality of Terje Vigen: Bie, Nicolai, *Har Terje Vigen levet?* Nordisk Tidende, Brooklyn, March 15, 1928; cf. also Dietrichson, I, p. 352.

P. 23—Illegitimate child: Koht I, p. 38 f. This is especially interesting in view of the accusation of Ludovici that Ibsen was sexually subnormal; cf. *Man, an Indictment*, Constable, 1927.

P. 26—The quotations from *Catiline* and Ibsen's *Introduction to the Second Edition of Catiline* are taken from *Henrik Ibsen's Early Plays*, translated by Anders Overbeck, American Scandinavian Foundation, 1921. Other translations: *Memoirs of Spring* by Payne; *Building Plans* by Garrett.

P. 30—For Clara Ebbell, cf. H. Eitrem, *Jugendgedichte Ibsens*, Neue Rundschau, Jan., 1915. (Same in Edda, III, 1915, pp. 68-92.)

CHAPTER III

P. 33—Catiline's death sentence, also for literary plans cf. C, Nos. 1 and 2.

P. 33—Kindness to children: Hoest, p. 25.

P. 34—Essays reprinted: SW, I, p. 284 ff.

P. 35—Walk with Hedvig: Jaeger, p. 44.

P. 36—Heltberg's school: Björnson's poem translated by A. H. Palmer, *Poems and Songs by Björnstjerne Björnson*, American-Scandinavian Foundation; Arne Garborg quoted by Lothar, Chapter II.

P. 39—Ibsen's contributions to Andhrimmer: cf. SW^{II}, I, p. 168 ff. In the notes to these articles a caricature is reprinted which is probably by Ibsen. *Norma* is reprinted SW^{II}, I, p. 21 ff.

P. 41—Letter to Mrs. Schulerud: quoted in appendix to Hoest.

P. 42—Monrad; Norsk Tidskrift for Videnskap og Litteratur, Vol. IV, pp. 310-312.

P. 43—*Catiline* for wrapping paper: Ibsen's humorous account of his days of poverty are in the *Introduction to the Second Edition of Catiline.*

P. 45—Letter to Miss Ebbell: quoted by Eitrem, *Jugendgedichte Ibsens,* Neue Rundschau, Jan., 1915.

CHAPTER IV

P. 47—For life of Ole Bull, cf. *Ole Bull, A Memoir,* Sara C. Bull, Houghton Mifflin Co., 1883. (This book published sixteen years after *Peer Gynt* and four years after *A Doll's House* speaks repeatedly of Björnson, but makes no mention whatsoever of Ibsen.)

P. 49—*Prologue at the Entertainment of the Student Society of Christiania for the Benefit of the Norwegian Theater in Bergen,* Oct. 15, 1851—SW^{II}, I, p. 54.

P. 51—Anecdotes of Bergen days: Paulsen; also the same author's *Mine Erindringer,* Copenhagen, 1900; Peter Blytt, *Minder fra den förste norske scene i Bergen,* Bergen, 1907; cf. also Halvorsen.

P. 53—Stub: Ibsen's reply to Stub is reprinted SW, I, pp. 317-333.

P. 54—Heiberg: Paulsen (chapter "Ibsen und das Heibergsche

Haus"). Also Georg Brandes, *Kindheit und Jugend*, Dresden, 1924, p. 130.

P. 55—Ibsen's impressions of Dresden Gallery: cf. poem *In the Picture Gallery*.

P. 56—*Ibsen's Regiebog:* Can be seen in the Bergen Museum; cf. also William Archer, *Ibsen's Apprenticeship*, Fortnightly Review, Jan., 1904.

P. 57—Henrikke Holst: Paulsen, chapter "Ibsen und Henrikke Holst."

P. 61—Rehearsal of *Lady Inger:* H. Wiers-Jensen, *Erinnerungen an Henrik Ibsen*, Die Zeitschrift, April 12, 1913.

P. 64—Serenaded: Ibsen's *Introduction to the Second Edition of The Feast at Solhoug*, CW, I.

P. 66—King Charles XV: cf. Ibsen's poem, SW^{II}, I, p. 83.

P. 66—Puritanical Atmosphere: cf. *Voyages dans les Mers du Nord à bord de la corvette La Reine Hortense* par Charles Edmond, Paris, 1857.

P. 67—Björnson's criticism: quoted Gran, I, p. 70 ff; cf. Blanc, Chapter IV.

P. 68—Dead Mermaid: John Paulsen, Reisen til Monaco og andre erindringer, Christiania, 1909, chapter "Ibseniana"; also Paulsen, chapter "Ibsen in Bergen"; Georg Brandes, *Kindheit und Jugend*, Dresden, 1924, p. 131 ff.

P. 69—Susannah's character: Dietrichson, I, p. 343; Julius Elias, *Susannah Ibsen*, Berliner Tageblatt, April 15, 1914; same author, *Christianiafahrt*, Neue Rundschau, Dec., 1906.

P. 70—Poetic proposal: translated in C, No. 5.

P. 71—Call on Susannah: Koht, 1, p. 150.

P. 71—*Breve fra Magdalene Thoresen*, Copenhagen, 1919, p. 41.

CHAPTER V

P. 72—Ibsen's relation to Norwegian theater: details can be found in a dissertation, Audhild Lund *Henrik Ibsen og det norske Teater, 1857-1863*, Oslo, 1925.

P. 74—Borgaard affair: SW, I, pp. 396-420; also BjC, No. 10.

P. 75—Meeting with Due: Due, p. 22.

P. 76—Society founding: Gran, I, p. 319, says the initiative came from Ibsen.

P. 77—Gave up painting; personal information from Fräulein Helene Raff, Munich.

P. 77—Antipathy to petty considerations: C, No. 74.

P. 78—Hollanders: Ludvig Daae, *Paul Botten-Hansen*, Vidar, 1888, p. 130 ff.; Fr. Ording, *Henrik Ibsens Vennekreds, Det Laerde Holland*, Oslo, 1927.

P. 78—Björnson: Gerhard Gran, *Björnson und Ibsen*, Vossische Zeitung, Sept. 23, 1913. In Gran's biography is to be found the best treatment of the Björnson-Ibsen relationship. See also a few references to Ibsen (mostly uncomplimentary) in Björnson, *Brytnings-Aar, Brev fra Aarene 1871-1878*, Utgitt av Halvdan Koht, Christiania, 1921.

P. 79—Band of theorists: BjC, No. 111.

P. 79—Letter to Petersen: BjC, No. 10.

P. 81—Foeticide: C, No. 67.

P. 81—Ibsen's letter to Petersen: SNL, Nos. 1 and 2.

P. 81—Ibsen drunk: personal information from Professor Halvdan Koht, whose father was one of the students who had seen Ibsen in the gutter.

P. 82—Criticism of *Love's Comedy:* quoted by Gran, I, p. 153.

P. 83—Anecdote of Carl Lie: Gran, I, p. 97 f.

P. 84—Took the money: Koht, I, p. 259.

P. 85—Host: Randolph Nilson, C, No. 15.

P. 85—Conversation with Due: Due, p. 50.

P. 88—Americanism: C, No. 74.

P. 89—'Twas but a lie then: translated by Payne.

P. 89—Brunn's speech: SW^{II}, II, p. 72 ff.

P. 90—Visit to Berlin: C, Nos. 18 and 22.

CHAPTER VI

P. 91—Soldier mutilating himself: quoted SW^{II}, II, p. 68. This excellent introduction to the first sketch of *Brand* has been drawn upon for other material also: Ibsen's journey to the North, Pastor Lammers, etc.

P. 91—Letter to Björnson: C, No. 44.

P. 92—Ibsen, May 17th speaker: Paulsen, p. 116.

P. 92—Magnus Hejnessön: SW^{II}, IV, p. 217 ff.

P. 92—Through the tunnel: Ibsen's speech in Copenhagen, NLS, p. 61.

P. 93—Danes in Prussian Embassy: C, No. 22.

P. 94—Lorentz Dietrichson: Dietrichson, I, Chapter V, "To Dig-tere."
P. 96—Michelangelo and Bernini: C, No. 17.
P. 99—Thomas Chatterton: Dietrichson, I, p. 339.
P. 102—Ariccia: Paulsen, chapter "Ibsen in Ariccia."
P. 102—Sigurd told: Julius Elias, *Susannah Ibsen,* Berliner Tage-blatt, April 15, 1914.
P. 102—As gray in gray: from first sketch of *Brand,* SW^{II}, II, p. 154.
P. 103—Scorpion: C, No. 74.
P. 104—Co-worker of Kierkegaard: Georg Brandes, *Kindheit und Jugend,* Dresden, 1924, p. 131 ff.

CHAPTER VII

P. 107—Petition to King and Trondhjem Society: C, Nos. 19 and 26; BjC, Nos. 97 and 102.
P. 107—Letter to Björnson: C, No. 24.
P. 108—Ludvig David: C, No. 27.
P. 109—Botten-Hansen: C, No. 33.
P. 110—True story of Arne: Brandes, p. 203.
P. 111—Manderström: Dietrichson, I, p. 342.
P. 112—Bergsoe: all the Ischia anecdotes are taken from: W. Berg-soe, *Henrik Ibsen paa Ischia og "fra piazza del populo,"* Erindringer fra aarene 1863-1869, Copenhagen, 1907.
P. 118—True poetry: cf. Ibsen's spirited letter to Björnson, C, No. 44 and other letters regarding *Peer Gynt.*
P. 119—Björnson guffawed: quoted by Archer, CW, IV, p. XXVII.
P. 119—Don Quixote: Brandes, p. 204.
P. 120—Clemens Petersen's criticism: quoted SW, X, p. 444.
P. 120—Brand no poetry: BjC, No. 110; BjC, No. 111, Björnson writes Ibsen: "Your *Brand* with all its touches of genius (Genialitet) and wonderful power is no poem. You surely feel that yourself."
P. 122—Hearts of millions: BjC, No. 91.
P. 123—Bestow an order: BjC, No. 130.

CHAPTER VIII

P. 124—Earthquake fright: C, No. 43.
P. 124—*As You Like It:* C, No. 74.

P. 124—Bear taught to dance: Ibsen's poem, *Power of Memory* (about 1864).

P. 125—Write a comedy: C, No. 45; BjC, No. 155, Björnson writes: "I am looking forward with great pleasure to *The League of Youth*, because I foresee in it that for which I have been waiting for a long time—your comedy."

P. 125—Friends a luxury: C, No. 64.

P. 126—*The Almighty and Company:* C, No. 49.

P. 126—The good people's own affair: C, No. 46.

P. 126—Performance of *League of Youth*: Blanc, Chapter X.

P. 128—Björnson stabbed in the back (Snigmord): BjC, No. 159.

P. 128—Poem mirror: from Ibsen's poem, *At Port Said*.

P. 128—Unknown handwriting: Diedrichson, I, p. 346 ff.

P. 130—Egypt: cf. Halvorsen, p. 19; "Abydos," SW[II], I, p. 183 ff.

P. 130—*Das neue Reich:* Ibsen's answer is reprinted, SW, I, p. 506 ff. The German poet quoted is Schiller, *Don Karlos*, Act I, Scene 2:
> "Drum soll der Sänger mit dem König gehen,
> Sie beide wohnen auf der Menschheit Höhen."

Ibsen omits the causal, but this cannot exactly be called a misquotation on his part, as the Germans customarily cite: "Es soll der Sänger mit dem König gehen." This letter, like many from Ibsen's pen, is a little masterpiece.

P. 131—Klubien: The letters to Klubien were published Berliner Tageblatt, July 4, 1927; cf. Koht, II, p. 128, for a reproduction of orders which Ibsen scribbled on a page of *Emperor and Galilean* in 1873, evidence showing where his thoughts dwelt.

P. 133—Brandes' criticism: Brandes, pp. 55-67; description of Ibsen, pp. 69-71 and 218-219; Brandes' poem is quoted in his *Kindheit und Jugend, op. cit.;* The English translation (Duffield) omits the lines to Ibsen. The entire poem is quoted in *Henrik Ibsen Festskrift*, Bergen, 1898, p. 20 ff.

P. 135—Terje Vigen: Garrett's translation.

P. 136—His academic training: Paulsen, p. 126.

P. 136—Marie Thoresen: Paulsen, chapter "Ibsen und Marie Thoresen"; translation of poem by Shedd.

P. 137—Traveling Norwegians: August Koren, *Besuch bei Ibsen in Dresden*, Dresdener Neueste Nachrichten, March 20, 1928.

P. 139—Jensen: C, No. 83.

P. 140—Dietrichson's visit: Dietrichson, I, p. 353 ff.

P. 142—Edmund Gosse: C, Nos. 93 and 102.

P. 144—Avoid mental strain: SW^{II}, IV, p. 226 ff.

P. 145—My countrymen: Translation by Gosse.

P. 145—When ten years ago: C, No. 182.

P. 146—Speech to Norwegian students: SW, I, p. 520, and notes; Blanc, p. 32 f.; Paulsen, p. 162 f., discusses effect of procession on Ibsen.

CHAPTER IX

P. 149—Aasta Hansteen: Gran, II, p. 24 f.; also personal information from Miss Daisy Heitmann, Oslo.

P. 150—Americanism: C, No. 74.

P. 151—Took Germany by storm: SW, VI, Introduction by Paul Schlenther.

P. 152—Gentleman of affairs: Gosse, p. 135.

P. 153—Catholic priest: Koht, II, p. 128.

P. 153—Grieg: C, No. 111; Nina (Mrs. Edvard) Grieg, *The Music of Peer Gynt*, The Music Student, Jan., 1916; Blanc, pp. 23-28.

P. 153—Ibsen in Munich: Dietrichson, I, pp. 356-361; also various chapters in Paulsen.

P. 155—Prodigal son: personal information from Herr Konsul Stousland (Ibsen's nephew) and his brother, Captain John Ibsen Stousland.

P. 155—Uncle Christian Paus: C, No. 134.

P. 156—Subjection of Women: Brandes, p. 114 ff.; the quotation is from J. S. Mill, *The Subjection of Women*, Lippincott, 1869, p. 6.

P. 157—She is illogical: C, No. 74.

P. 157—And yet she might have met me: FIW, p. 80 f.

P. 158—Anonymous letter; Paulsen, p. 150.

P. 158—Selma: Brandes, p. 204 ff.

P. 159—Brand's Daughters: C, No. 71; Koht, II, p. 165 ff.; Brandes, p. 204 f.

P. 161—You would hardly believe what bargains: SW, X, p. 479 f.

P. 161—Scandinavian Club: SW^{II}, I, p. 211 ff.; SW^{II}, I, p. 179 ff.; for Ibsen at the ball, cf. *Ibsen als Mensch*, Der Türmer, Aug., 1916.

P. 164—Extinguished the lighthouses: Brandes, p. 116.

P. 164—Barbaric violence: C, Nos. 142 and 143.

P. 164—Frau Ramlo as Nora: John Paulsen, *Mine Erindringer*, Copenhagen, 1900, chapter on *A Doll's House.*

P. 166—Nora went alone: personal information from Frau Dr. Julius Elias.

P. 166—*Women's rights:* from *Die Stimme der Wahrheit* (Detroit) quoted in *Robert Reitzel*, A. E. Zucker, Americana Germanica Press, 1917, p. 35.

P. 167—Continuation of *A Doll's House:* quoted Gran, II, p. 85.

P. 168—Carl Ploug: quoted Gran, II, p. 111.

P. 168—Amico: John Paulson, *Nye Erindringer*, Copenhagen, 1901 (Siste möde med Ibsen); Paulsen, p. 59 ff. (Ein Streit um Orden.)

P. 169—New England girl: Madame L. Hegermann-Lindencrone, *Sunny Side of Diplomatic Life*, Harper's, 1914, p. 100 f.; C, No. 150.

P. 169—Color of wall paper: Paulsen, p. 14 ff.

P. 170—Enfeeblement of judgment: C, No. 158.

P. 170—First sketch of *A Doll's House:* FIW, pp. 109 and 112.

P. 171—Move a few boundary posts: SW[II], I, p. 205.

P. 173—Assassination of Alexander II: Paulsen, p. 138 ff.

P. 174—Black band of theologians: SW, X, p. 487.

P. 174—Criticism of *Ghosts:* William Archer, *Mausoleum of Ibsen*, Fortnightly Review, July, 1893; Brandes, p. 143.

P. 175—Björnson refused to call: Paulsen, p. 183 ff.

P. 175—American publication: Björstjerne Björnson, *Norway's Constitutional Struggle*, Scribner's, 1881, Vol. XXI, pp. 603-611.

P. 176—Youthful modern: Felix Philippi, *Mein Verkehr mit Ibsen*, Neue Freie Presse, Oct. 27, 1902.

P. 177—Sophocles: Brandes, p. 121.

P. 177—English dramatic critic: William Archer, *Ibsen as I Knew Him*, Monthly Review, June, 1906.

P. 178—Anonymous poachers and highwaymen: C, No. 163.

P. 179—Harold Thaulow: SW[II], IV, p. 310 ff.

P. 180—Dietrichson: C, No. 141.

P. 181—Zola: Erik Lie, Jonas Lies Oplevelser, Christiania, 1908, p. 258.

P. 181—He and Dr. Stockmann: C, No. 165.

P. 181—It was when a party: William M. Payne, *Björnstjerne Björnson*, McClurg, 1910, p. 42.

BIBLIOGRAPHY 301

P. 182—Banner of the ideal: Paulsen, p. 180.
P. 182—When the days of the sirocco: Paulsen, p. 166 ff.
P. 185—Put on *Ghosts:* Blanc, p. 47.

CHAPTER X

P. 187—Ibsen is terribly radical: letter by Dr. Undset quoted Gran, II, p. 143 ff.
P. 188—4000 Kroner: Blanc, p. 49 f.
P. 188—State Securities: C, No. 167, and other letters of the time.
P. 188—Exiled critic of Norway: Brandes, pp. 97 and 121.
P. 188—Member of Storthing: Hagbard Berner, C, No. 151.
P. 189—To live is to war with fiends: translation, C, No. 148.
P. 189—Magnus Bagge: SW¹¹, IV, p. 318.
P. 190—As one critic puts it: Woerner, II, p. 163.
P. 191—Energetic individualization: C, No. 180.
P. 191—For the last four months: C, No. 181.
P. 192—William Archer's question: William Archer, *Ibsen as I Knew Him,* Monthly Review, June, 1906; the carpenter Engstrand anecdote was told me by Frau Dr. Julius Elias.
P. 193—Ibsen sewing on buttons: Paulsen, p. 28 ff.
P. 193—Heirlooms: for a reproduction of the frontispiece of Harrison's *History of London,* cf. Koht, II, p. 239.
P. 193—Dodo: C, No. 171.
P. 194—Three drafts: quoted, Gran, II, p. 166; cf. also Paul Lindau, *Nur Erinnerungen,* Stuttgart, 1917, Vol. II, p. 383 ff.
P. 195—Entice young dramatists into new paths: C, No. 181.
P. 195—A new literary era: quoted, Hermann J. Weigand, *The Modern Ibsen,* Holt, 1925, p. 100.
P. 195—Kielland: SW, X, p. 502; SW¹¹, IV, p. 324.
P. 196—Trondhjem labor union: SNL, p. 53 f.; SW, I, p. 668 f.
P. 197—Snoilsky: Dietrichson, I, p. 369 f.; Edmund Gosse, *Portraits and Sketches,* Scribner's, 1912, p. 239 ff.; Brandes, p. 209 f.; SW¹¹, IV, p. 320.
P. 198—Visit to Bergen: Paulsen, chapter "Ibsen und Henrikke Holst."
P. 200—Quarrel with Dietrichson: SW, X, p. 500 and C, Nos. 188 and 189; SW¹¹, IV, p. 323; Gran, II, pp. 188-204; Dietrichson I, end of Chapter V, speaks of their quick reconciliation.
P. 201—Hans Jaeger: Gran, II, p. 186.

P. 205—Students debating club: C, No. 197.
P. 205—A friend from sunny Vienna: Felix Philippi, *Mein Verkehr mit Ibsen,* Neue Freie Presse, Oct. 27, 1902.
P. 206—Munich life: Conrad's account, Lothar, p. 121 ff.; Julius Elias, *Henrik Ibsen und die Andern,* Vossische Zeitung, Dec. 25, 1921.
P. 210—*From Skien to Rome:* SW, X, pp. XIV and XV; C, No. 147 and 163.
P. 211—A little vignette: Gotthilf Weisstein, *Meininger Erinnerungen,* Berlin, 1906; a more amiable Ibsen is presented in Paul Lindau, *Nur Erinnerungen,* Stuttgart, 1917, Vol. II, pp. 368-385.
P. 211—Speech at Göteburg and remarks on the sea: SW^{II}, I, p. 224.
P. 213—The sea hath joined together: Koht, II, p. 283 f., tells how Ibsen and Henrikke Holst in Bergen strung their rings on a key-ring and tossed them out into the sea.
P. 214—Soirée-Billeder: translated in I. C. Gröndal and O. Raknes, *Chapters in Norwegian Literature,* Christiania, 1923.
P. 215—Romanticizing everything: Georg Brandes, *Kindheit und Jugend,* Dresden, 1924, pp. 131 ff.
P. 216—Scandinavian divorce laws: a good popular presentation of the subject can be found in Stephen Ewing, *The Mockery of American Divorce,* Harper's, July, 1928; cf. also Johan Thorsten Sellin, *Swedish Marriage and Divorce Laws,* University of Pennsylvania dissertation, 1922, etc.
P. 217—Freeing the minds of men and women: Koht, II, p. 286, tells that while *The Lady from the Sea* when acted in the eighties and nineties had always failed, it found a much more enthusiastic audience when revived in 1928 because of the psychoanalytical problems since made popular by Freud.
P. 217—March 20, 1888: Conrad's account quoted in Lothar, p. 121 ff.
P. 218—Christian Hostrup: C, Nos. 202 and 204; Olaf Holm, *Christus eller Ibsen,* Christiania, 1903; a Catholic priest, P. Expeditus Schmidt, at present prior of the Franciscan monastery at Fuessen, Upper Bavaria, has proved himself a very sympathetic critic of Ibsen.
P. 219—Ludvig Daae: C, No. 207.
P. 219—Schulerud: Paulsen, p. 182.

BIBLIOGRAPHY 303

P. 219—Norwegian composer: Brandes, p. 208. Mr. Juul Dieserud informs me that the composer was Johan Svendson who was living in Copenhagen estranged from his wife, unable to get a divorce, while the latter was very jealous of his mistress.

P. 220—Björn Björnson: story told me by Herr S. Fischer.

P. 220—Barber story: Paulsen, p. 92; Ole Bull story, Paulsen, p. 6.

P. 221—Inwardly quite free: Helene Raff, *Persönliches von Henrik Ibsen*, Unterhaltungsbeilage zur täglichen Rundschau, July 26, 1906; on Mrs. Ibsen as a reader, cf. Hermann Bang, *Erinnerungen an Henrik Ibsen*, Neue Rundschau, Dec., 1906.

P. 222—*Thanks:* Gannett's translation for stanzas 1, 2, and 4; Shedd's for stanzas 3 and 5.

P. 222—The inhabitants of Skien: Gosse, p. 3.

P. 223—The Pauses: personal information from Captain John Ibsen Stousland.

P. 223—Gossensass: Helene Raff, *Ibsen in Gossensass*, Die Jugend, 1906, No. 24; Heinrich Kana, *Ibsen in Gossensass*, Die Gegenwart, Oct. 5, 1889; Emilie Bardach, *Meine Freundschaft mit Ibsen*, Neue Freie Presse, March 31, 1907; Ibsen's letters to Emilie Bardach are reprinted in Georg Brandes, *Henrik Ibsen*, Berlin, 1907 (in series "Die Litteratur"); parts of Emilie Bardach's diary are reprinted in Basil King, *Ibsen and Emilie Bardach*, Century Magazine, Oct. and Nov., 1923; Katharina Dilthey, *Eine Erinnerung an Henrik Ibsen*, Westermanns Monatshefte, Dec., 1922.

P. 224—Sketches for *White Horses:* FIW, p. 265 ff.

P. 226—The gist of her confessions: Julius Elias, *Christianiafahrt*, Neue Rundschau, Dec., 1906.

P. 227—Letters to Helene Raff: SNL, Nos. XX and XXI. She has informed me that the date of No. XX should be Oct. 29, 1889, and that a dash follows the words "And I—."

P. 228—That Billy Goat; Paulsen, p. 66.

P. 232—Critics have pointed out: Otto Heller, *Henrik Ibsen, Plays and Problems*, Houghton Mifflin Co., 1912, p. 261, and Hermann J. Weigand, *The Modern Ibsen*, Holt, 1925, pp. 267-273.

P. 232—Julius Hoffory: Brandes, p. 205 f. I found a copy of Hoffory's testament among the papers of Dr. Julius Elias; it seems to show that Brandes exaggerates a bit. Ibsen's letter to Dr. Elias, C, No. 218.

CHAPTER XI

P. 235—Conrad: Quoted in Lothar, p. 121 ff.
P. 236—Ibsen in Vienna: Leo Feld, *Eine Begegnung mit Henrik Ibsen*, Berliner Boersenzeitung, Dec. 24, 1922; Ibsen's speech: SW, I, p. 528.
P. 237—Dialog with Marx: Julius Elias, *Henrik Ibsen und die Andern*, Vossische Zeitung, Dec. 25, 1921.
P. 240—Knut Hamsun: Personal information from an eye witness, Juul Dieserud, Library of Congress.
P. 241—Rare fairy-tale fate: Ibsen's speech on his seventieth birthday, SNL, p. 58 ff.
P. 241—I will build me a cloud castle: translated by Garrett.
P. 242—The minstrel has neither house nor home: translated by William H. Eller, *Ibsen in Germany*, Badger, 1918, p. 113.
P. 243—Even the poet can only express: Brandes, p. 96 f.
P. 243—Letter to Georg Brandes: quoted Brandes, p. 212.
P. 244—Edvard Brandes: C, 234; MSS. dedicated: "To Princess Hildur" exhibited in Oslo University Library at the Ibsen Centenary, March 20, 1928.
P. 244—Dearest Miss Raff: SNL, No. XXI.
P. 246—I have been several times: *Breve fra Magdalene Thoresen, 1855-1901*, Copenhagen, 1919, from letter dated May 26, 1894.
P. 246—They dwelt, these two: translation is from FIW, p. 507, with slight changes to conform to Ibsen's first version, SW, I, p. 169.
P. 247—Ibsen wishes to possess me: Basil King, *Ibsen and Emilie Bardach*, Century Magazine, Oct. and Nov., 1923.
P. 248—"New" Norwegian girl: Gran, II, p. 292 f.
P. 249—Sense cannot be discovered: Saturday Review, July 8, 1893.
P. 250—Has it come?   The Norwegian critic, Dr. Just Bing, told me that he had made this experiment.
P. 250—Le Gallienne: Richard Le Gallienne, *The Romantic Nineties*, Doubleday Page, 1925, pp. 67-79.
P. 253—A Christiania gentleman: story told by Hoest, p. 23.
P. 254—Unmasking of pretentious personalities: Brandes, p. 220.
P. 255—This happened with Alfred Allmers: I follow the excellent analysis of this character in Hermann J. Weigand, *The Modern Ibsen*, Holt, 1925, p. 310 ff.
P. 257—Kreutzer Sonata: Gosse, p. 197 and p. 223.

P. 259—For a charming tale of Ibsen's Christiania days, cf. Vilhelm Krag, *Dengang Vi Var Tyve Aar*, Oslo, 1927, pp. 175 ff.

P. 259—Hermann Bang: *Erinnerungen an Henrik Ibsen,* Neue Rundschau, Dec., 1906.

P. 260—An army officer: SW^{II}, IV, p. 350 f.

P. 261—Article in Andhrimmer: SW, I, p. 313.

P. 262—Christopher Due: Due, p. 53.

P. 263—Foldal, SW^{II}, IV, p. 351.

P. 265—Quadrupled prices: Blanc, p. 66 f.

P. 266—A volume issued: *Henrik Ibsen Festskrift*, Bergen, 1898.

P. 266—A world grateful to Ibsen, Gosse, p. 200 ff.; a good description of the birthday festivities is found in the notes to Ibsen's speeches at the time, SW, I, p. 529-536 and 670-674. For a humorous picture of the Copenhagen festivities: Peter Nansen, *Portraetter*, Copenhagen, 1918, p. 106 ff.

P. 271—Recently published letter: translated in Living Age, May 28, 1921, from Morgenbladet, Oslo, Dec. 3, 1920.

P. 272—To little Eldrid: SW^{II}, I, p. 145.

P. 273—Dedication of National Theater: Gosse, p. 202 f.

P. 273—In my quiet moments: C, No. 44.

P. 274—Exaltation of a crusader: C, No. 23.

P. 275—Experience and live through mentally: speech to students, Sept. 10, 1874, SNL, p. 48 f., and C, No. 69: "Oplevede-gennemlevede."

P. 276—Poison fangs: Gran, II, p. 332.

P. 276—Casting our eyes around: Mrs. Alec Tweedie, *A Winter Jaunt in Norway*, London, 1894, p. 253.

P. 279—Greatest work *Emperor and Galilean:* W. H. Scofield, *Personal Impression of Björnson and Ibsen,* Atlantic Monthly, April, 1898; also Herr Arnt Dehli, *Ibsen Privat*, Aftenposten, March 14, 1828.

P. 280—Weaknesses of the piece: most fully treated in Hermann J. Weigand, *The Modern Ibsen*, Holt, 1925, pp. 378-398.

P. 280—Last days and funeral: Julius Elias, *Christianiafahrt*, Neue Rundschau, Dec., 1906, and *Ibsen und die Konvention,* Der Tag, Berlin, June 22, 1906; Alfred Kerr, *Ibsen-Dämmerung*, and *Ibsens Grabfahrt*, Der Tag, Berlin, June 2 and 6, 1906; Gran, II, p. 342; Dagbladet, June 1, 1906; Aftenposten, June 1, 1906; Herr Arnt Dehli, *Ibsen Privat*, Aftenposten, March 14, 1928.

P. 285—Susannah Ibsen: Julius Elias, *Susannah Ibsen*, Berliner
Tageblatt, April 15, 1914; Bergliot Ibsen, *Henrik Ibsens Hustru*, Aftenposten, March 20, 1928; for Mrs. Ibsen in a stern
mood, cf. Peter Nansen, *Portraetter*, Copenhagen, 1918, p.
102 ff.

P. 288—Richard Dehmel's poem: Neue Rundschau, July, 1906.

INDEX OF NAMES

INDEX OF IBSEN'S WORKS

312   INDEX OF IBSEN'S WORKS